FREE online study and revision support available at **www.oup.com/lawrevision**

Take your learning further with:

- Multiple-choice questions with instant feedback
- Interactive glossaries and flashcards of key cases
- Tips, tricks and audio advice
- Annotated outline answers
- Diagnostic tests show you where to concentrate
- Extra questions, key facts checklists, and topic overviews

unique features

New to this edition

- Newly ordered chapters, moving court structure closer to the start of the text and providing a brief introduction to the various sources of law.
- New section on tribunals and other courts such as the Coroners' Court and Court of Protection.
- New section on how to read and cite EU law, to complement the section on reading and citing English law.
- Discussions on aspects of the Queen's Speech in January 2020 relevant to this text.
- Updated to have regard to the routes of qualification as a practising lawyer, taking account of the new Solicitors Qualifying Examination (SQE), solicitor apprenticeships, and the new structure for the vocational study for barristers, replacing the Bar Professional Training Course (BPTC).
- Updated figures, tables, 'Revision tips', and 'Looking for extra marks?'
- Discussion of further devolution to the National Assembly of Wales via the Wales Act 2017.
- Discussion of the introduction of video recording of sentencing in the Crown Court as a result of the Crown Court (Recording and Broadcasting) Order 2020.
- Discussion of the UK's decision to leave the EU ('Brexit') and the interventions of the Supreme Court in this regard (*R (Miller) v The Prime Minister* [2019] UKSC 41).
- Discussion of English Votes for English Laws (EVEL).
- Clearer exposition on the nature of Privy Council judgments in relation to domestic courts following *Willers v Joyce* [2016] UKSC 44.

English Legal System

Concentrate

Mark Thomas

Senior Lecturer in Law
Nottingham Trent University

Claire McGourlay

Professor of Law
The University of Manchester

Great Clarendon Street, Oxford, OX2 6DP,
United Kingdom

Oxford University Press is a department of the University of Oxford.
It furthers the University's objective of excellence in research, scholarship,
and education by publishing worldwide. Oxford is a registered trade mark of
Oxford University Press in the UK and in certain other countries

© Oxford University Press 2020

The moral rights of the authors have been asserted

First edition 2017

Impression: 1

All rights reserved. No part of this publication may be reproduced, stored in
a retrieval system, or transmitted, in any form or by any means, without the
prior permission in writing of Oxford University Press, or as expressly permitted
by law, by licence or under terms agreed with the appropriate reprographics
rights organization. Enquiries concerning reproduction outside the scope of the
above should be sent to the Rights Department, Oxford University Press, at the
address above

You must not circulate this work in any other form
and you must impose this same condition on any acquirer

Public sector information reproduced under Open Government Licence v3.0
(http://www.nationalarchives.gov.uk/doc/open-government-licence/open-government-licence.htm)

Published in the United States of America by Oxford University Press
198 Madison Avenue, New York, NY 10016, United States of America

British Library Cataloguing in Publication Data
Data available

Library of Congress Control Number: 2020935591

ISBN 978–0–19–885502–6

Printed in Great Britain by
Bell & Bain Ltd., Glasgow

Links to third party websites are provided by Oxford in good faith and
for information only. Oxford disclaims any responsibility for the materials
contained in any third party website referenced in this work.

Contents

Table of Cases

Table of Legislation

UK Statutes

UK Bills

UK Secondary Legislation

UK Codes

EU and International Legislation, Agreements, and Conventions

United States

#1 Introduction to the English Legal System

Key facts

- The study of the English legal system (ELS) involves the study of the legal system of both England and Wales. Scotland and Northern Ireland are subject to a separate, yet connected legal system.
- The word 'law' is hard to define, but generally is known as a system of rules created and enforced by the state and recognized to be laws by the citizens of the state.
- The ELS must be considered in its socio-political context and a distinction must be made between 'theory' and 'practice'.

Chapter overview

Dynamism of the English legal system

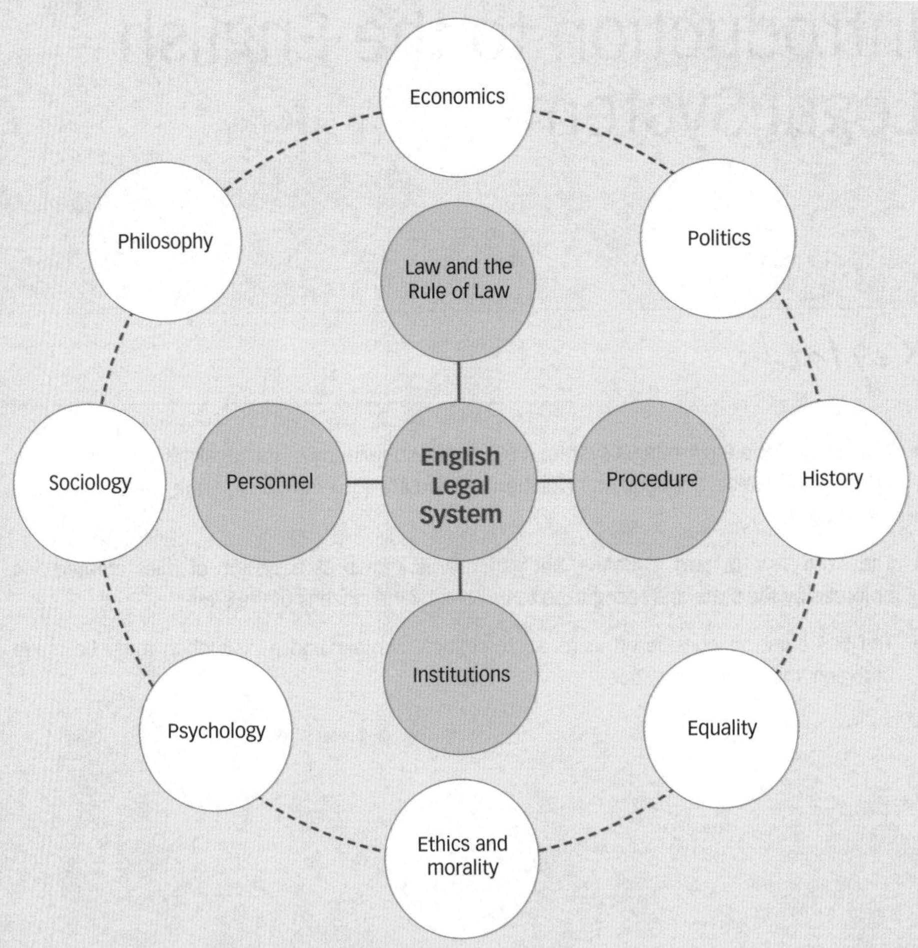

Introduction to the study of the English legal system

The knowledge that you will gain from studying this subject will prepare you for the challenges ahead of you throughout the rest of your degree. This text is not designed to teach you 'how' to study the English legal system (ELS); for that you will have to seek out another book, for example James Holland and Julian Webb, *Learning Legal Rules* (10th edn, Oxford University Press 2019). Rather, this text is designed to give you an insight into the operation of the ELS.

In this text you will learn of the core elements of the ELS, from the institutions of the legal system, including **Parliament** and the courts, through to the personnel of the legal system, namely legal and lay professionals. Although entitled the *English Legal System*, this text will also consider European and international law and the effect they have on our domestic system.

The study of the ELS is often overlooked by students, with the occasional eye roll at the mention of 'learning' the ELS. Indeed, many students who have studied law at A-level often baulk at the idea of 'doing it all again'. Don't be fooled, however. There is much in the ELS that students do not know; they think they know it all until questioned as to how precedent operates or how **solicitors** can appear in the **appellate courts**, for example.

This text provides a detailed yet concise account of the core principles you need to be aware of when studying the ELS. We recommend that you use this text alongside an up-to-date textbook on the ELS, many of which are published by Oxford University Press.

"Glanville Williams, in his text *Learning the Law* (12th edn, Sweet & Maxwell 2002), stated:"

> Law is the cement of society and also an essential medium of change. Knowledge of law increases one's understanding of public affairs. Its study promotes accuracy of expression, facility in argument and skill in interpreting the written word, as well as some understanding of social values.

The English legal system

As a starting point it is worth emphasizing that our ELS can helpfully be divided into three distinct elements. Ironically, those are:

- English;
- legal; and
- system.

It is not as simple as it first appears, however, and each of these elements will now be considered in greater detail.

'English'

For the purposes of this text we are concerned with English law.

England

England is a constituent element of the 'United Kingdom of Great Britain and Northern Ireland' alongside Wales, Scotland, and Northern Ireland. So why is it that you are studying the 'English' legal system and not the 'United Kingdom' legal system?

The answer boils down to a single word that many of you may be familiar with: devolution. We shall be considering this term in greater detail later; however, in brief, the UK is divided into the above four constituent 'countries'. These four countries are subjected to the laws of the United Kingdom; however, each individual constituent has devolved powers (i.e. powers given to them from another body; similar in concept to delegated powers) allowing them to legislate in particular areas. Where a conflict between laws of the UK and laws of the constituent country arises, the UK law takes precedence.

As a cross-border comparison, observe the United States of America (USA), which has a 'federal' law covering all 50 states of the USA, such as the **US Constitution (1787)**, and 'state law', which grants certain devolved powers for each individual state, for example the death penalty (which is lawful in 32 states). Likewise, in the USA, where a conflict arises between federal and state law, federal law takes priority as a result of the 'Supremacy Clause' (**US Constitution (1787), Article IV**).

Wales

Wales, as a result of the **Laws in Wales Acts 1535 and 1542**, does not have a separate legal system but rather is an 'annex' to English law. This means that the laws of England apply equally to Wales. As a result, therefore, it is technically incorrect to speak of the laws of England. Rather, we should speak of the laws of England and Wales. Created by the **Government of Wales Act 1998**, and amended by the **Government of Wales Act 2006**, the National Assembly acts as the devolved government for Wales. Following the **Wales Act 2017**, Wales now operates under a 'reserved powers' model. This model, the same adopted by Scotland, defines the powers under the control of Westminster, with everything else assumed to be within the power of the Welsh Assembly. The former model adopted by Wales, the 'conferred powers' model, operated on the alternate basis (i.e. that the powers of the Assembly were defined, with everything else being assumed to fall within the powers of Westminster).

Scotland

The **Act of Union** in 1707 (composed of two Acts: the **Union with Scotland Act 1706** passed by the Parliament of England and the **Union with England Act 1707** passed by the Parliament of Scotland) joined England and Scotland together to form the United Kingdom of Great Britain. The Act had the effect of dissolving the Parliaments of both England and Scotland in order to create a single Parliament of the United Kingdom (the same Parliament that stands today).

Unlike Wales, however, Scotland holds its own legal system distinct to that of the ELS, known as Scots law. What this means is that Scotland is responsible for the creation and implementation of law in its own country. This is done through the Scottish Parliament, as established by the **Scotland Act 1998**. This does not mean that an Act of the UK Parliament does not apply to Scotland; but rather, that there is no assumption that such a law applies to Scotland. This is part of the reserved powers model indicated in relation to our discussion of Wales. Scotland adopted this model in the **Scotland Act 1998**.

Northern Ireland

The final constituent of the UK is Northern Ireland, which came to join the UK in 1920 after the **Government of Ireland Act 1920** split the country in two. The partition came about largely because of religious reasons and some tension remains in today's UK regarding the unification of Ireland as a distinct country. Like Scotland, Northern Ireland retained its separate legal status, ensuring that it may pass its own form of **legislation** alongside that of the UK Parliament. The Northern Ireland Assembly was established as a result of the Belfast Agreement on 10 April 1998, which was subsequently given legal force through the **Northern Ireland Act 1998**. Power is shared in Northern Ireland between the Democratic Unionist Party and Sinn Fein; the two parties forming the Northern Ireland Assembly, based in Stormont.

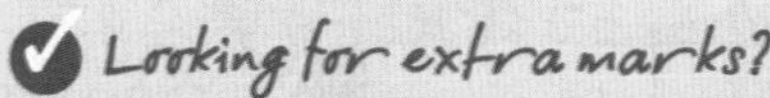

Demonstrate that you are aware of the difficulties faced by the Northern Ireland Assembly. In January 2017, the DUP/Sinn Fein-led power-sharing coalition collapsed due to rows over a green energy scheme. As a result of this, Northern Ireland had no devolved government; the Northern Ireland Assembly being suspended. On 11 January 2020, the DUP and Sinn Fein re-entered devolved government after both parties supported a deal to restore the political institution in Stormont.

The United Kingdom and 'extent'

As stated earlier, the laws of England and Wales are distinct from those of Scotland and Northern Ireland; however, this does not mean that the UK cannot pass laws that affect either of these two distinct jurisdictions. When Parliament passes an **Act of Parliament** (see Chapter 3), it must declare the 'extent' to which the Act of Parliament applies.

If the Act is silent as to its extent, then it is presumed the Act will only apply in England and Wales. However, if the Act states that it extends, or a particular provision extends, to Scotland or Northern Ireland, then they must obey and follow that law. This is what is known as parliamentary supremacy (see Chapter 3) and unless Scotland or Northern Ireland achieve independence, they will remain subject to the laws of the UK when expressly prescribed to them.

Devolution and independence

The effect of devolution (i.e. the decentralization of power) from the UK to Scotland, Wales, and Northern Ireland does not affect this supremacy. It has been argued for some time that devolution of power has not gone far enough in allowing Scotland or Northern Ireland to govern themselves. Figures 1.1–1.3 provide an overview of the history of devolution in Scotland, Wales, and Northern Ireland.

In 2014, Scotland held a referendum with the question asked: 'Should Scotland be an independent country?' The turnout was high, with over 3,500,000 votes being cast (the residents of England, Wales, and Northern Ireland were not entitled to vote). With a majority of 55.3 per cent (2,001,926 votes), the 'No' campaign won the referendum, resulting in Scotland's continued unification with England, Wales, and Northern Ireland. Although calls for a border poll (similar to a referendum) have been made in the Assembly post-**Brexit**, there is, as of yet, no serious talk of an independence referendum for Northern Ireland or Wales. For more detail, see Colin Faragher, *Public Law Concentrate* (6th edn, Oxford University Press 2019).

Figure 1.1 Devolution—Scotland

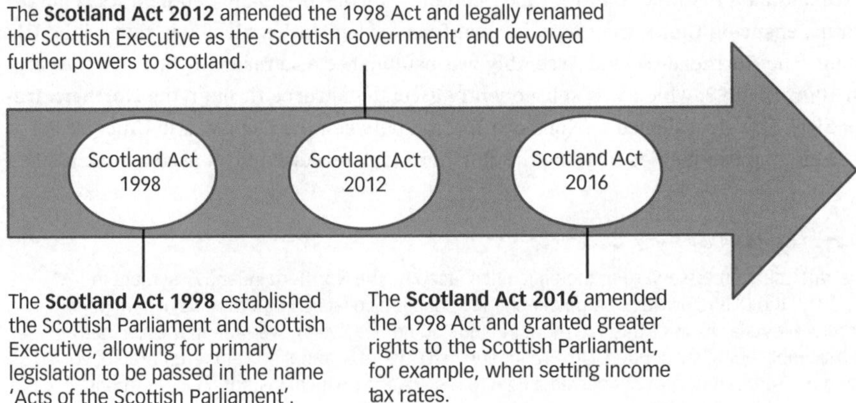

Figure 1.2 Devolution—Wales

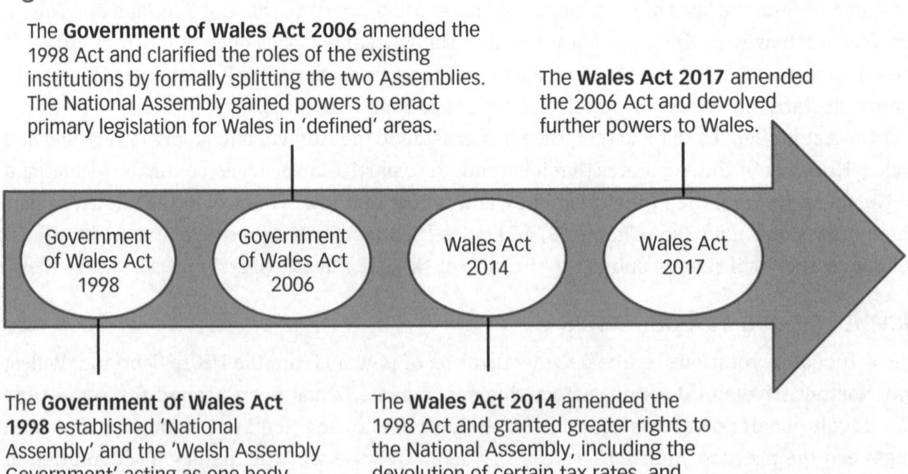

Figure 1.3 Devolution—Northern Ireland

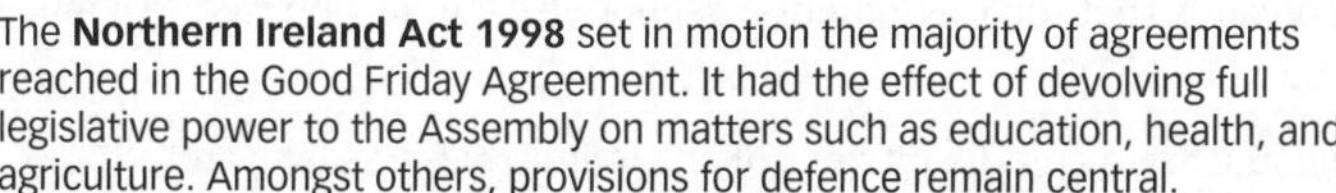

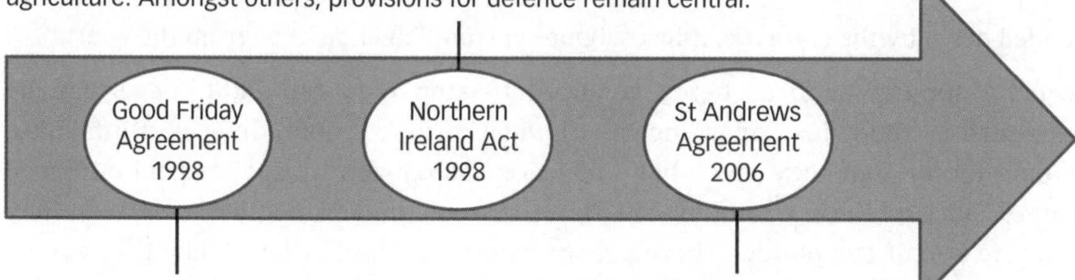

The **Good Friday Agreement 1998** created the Northern Ireland Assembly, designed to bring together nationalist and unionist, in an effort to govern Northern Ireland.

The **St Andrews Agreement 2006** was a collection of major talks between the UK Government and the Government of Northern Ireland. It resulted in the restoration of the Northern Ireland Assembly and the formation of a new Northern Ireland Executive.

Looking for extra marks?

It is essential that throughout your studies you are as up to date as possible on events that may affect English law. Be sure to keep an eye on the possibility of a second Scottish Referendum (especially after the UK's decision to leave the EU, known as Brexit). When writing an essay-style answer, try to include comments by such persons as Nicola Sturgeon (First Minister for Scotland), who commented that a second referendum was 'on the table' as a result of Brexit. On 28 March 2017, the Scottish Parliament voted (by 69 to 59 votes) in favour of a call for a second independence referendum. However, the then Prime Minister, Theresa May, stated that it was 'not the time' for another referendum; focus should be on negotiating the UK's departure from the EU. In December 2019, following the election victory of the Conservative Party, Nicola Sturgeon made a new request for an independence referendum. On 15 January 2020, Nicola Sturgeon wrote a letter to the Prime Minister, Boris Johnson, requesting a new independent vote. The Prime Minister refused this request and it appears that he will continue to refuse to allow a further referendum.

'Legal'

What is law?

Some of the most common definitions of law include:

- a statement of rules created and recognized by the state;
- a body of rules that govern citizens of the state in relationship with other citizens and with the state;
- a set of rules founded on principles of justice and morality.

What we understand law to mean are all three of the above bulleted statements in combination with each other. We consider that the fundamental aspect of a law, as opposed to a mere rule or guideline, is that it is:

(i) recognized as law, i.e. the state and the citizens of the state treat it as law; and

(ii) handed down by the state (i.e. it has originated from Parliament or from the courts).

Laws can be simple—such as being required to stop at a red light. Laws can be complex—such as the rules governing the division of assets upon divorce. Both share the common factor that they are a body of rules recognized by society and enforced by the state. Both of these examples are those that are understood by society as they feature in the eye of the public. There are, of course, certain areas of law that you no doubt go through life without even considering. For example, did you ever consider that when you board a system of public transport, such as a bus, by stating your required destination and paying your fee, you are entering into a legal contract with the bus company? There is an offer, acceptance, consideration, and an intention to enter into legal relations.

Take another example. Have you ever seen a sign stating, 'Trespassers will be prosecuted'? Interestingly, this is an inaccurate statement of law, as generally trespass is not a criminal wrong, but rather, a civil wrong. Therefore, trespassers cannot be 'prosecuted' as such, but they can be 'sued' by the owner of the private property on which they are trespassing. Obviously, should an individual steal, cause injury, or damage property whilst trespassing, they may be subject to prosecution (for burglary—**s9 Theft Act 1968**); however, the simple act of trespassing without consent is not a criminal offence for which one may be subject to prosecution. There are exceptions to this general rule, of course, such as trespass on a railway line, but this only goes to demonstrate the potentially complex nature of law as a subject.

What these examples hopefully show is that the law surrounds us; it guides us and directs how certain activities are conducted.

Revision tip

These examples are hopefully useful to you; however, your knowledge will improve if you can go out and find your own examples of law affecting daily life. By finding your own examples, your knowledge of the law will deepen and your practical application of the law will strengthen. We shall give you a few to consider for yourself:

- signs that exclude liability for harm to persons or damage to property;
- the legal consequence of a 'zebra crossing' on drivers—must they stop?
- a supermarket sign offering goods at a price different to that stated on the packaging;
- the legality of a pub serving a pint of Carling® lager in a Fosters® glass.

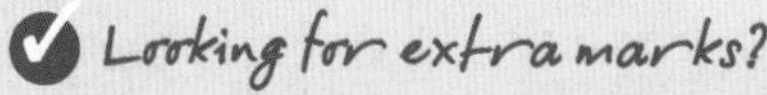

There are numerous theories that revolve around the idea of 'law', including concepts of positivism and natural law; however, these concepts are outside the scope of this work. Nevertheless, it may assist your understanding of what you think the law is by considering these theories. We have given you two examples.

POSITIVISM:

- **John Austin** (a nineteenth-century English jurist) described law as 'A rule laid down for the guidance of an intelligent being by an intelligent being having power over him.' He also defined it as 'A body of rules fixed and enforced by a sovereign political authority.'

MARXISM:

- **Karl Marx (1848)** described law as a 'tool of oppression used by capitalists to control the proletariat'.

A moral law?

As stated earlier, law can be described as 'A set of rules founded on principles of justice and morality'. Does that mean, therefore, that all laws are morally correct? There are many reasons why all laws cannot be morally correct. Here are two:

- Morality is subjective and what amounts to morally correct and incorrect conduct is a matter personal to the individual.
- Morality governs the idea of behaviour that is 'right' and 'wrong'. Who, however, decides what is right and wrong morally? Is it not the case that this group/society will change with the passage of time, meaning that morality will change also?

Let us give you a few examples:

- Until the introduction of the **Sexual Offences Act 1967**, homosexual activities between two consenting individuals over the age of 21 were unlawful.
- Abortion, where medically certified, has been legal since the **Abortion Act 1967**; however, it is still regarded by much of the population as morally wrong.
- There is no requirement for a man to stop and assist another who is dying in the street. In the terms of the law, there is no 'Good Samaritan' law. Morally, however, there may be a duty to act.

Whether law and morality should coincide and interact is outside the scope of this text; however, it is still useful to understand how morals may affect the operation or function of the law. For more information on law and morality, see the infamous debates between Lord Devlin and Professor H.L.A. Hart (the Hart v Devlin debates: Patrick Devlin, *The Enforcement of Morals* (Oxford University Press 1965) and H.L.A. Hart, *Law, Liberty and Morality* (Oxford University Press 1963) and *The Morality of the Criminal Law* (Oxford University Press 1964)).

Legal personalities

When we speak of the operation of the law, we must bear in mind that law only has effect on so-called 'legal personalities'. Only legal persons may sue or be sued or have criminal offences committed against them or by them. Legal persons may come in two forms:

- a natural person, i.e. a human being; and
- an artificial person, i.e. a company.

To give an example, take the criminal offence of murder. According to Sir Edward Coke CJ, murder is 'the unlawful killing of a human being, under the Queen's Peace, with malice aforethought, express or implied' [modified to reflect modern terminology]. A question that has come before the courts on a number of occasions is whether a foetus is a 'human being' in the eyes of the law. According to ***R v Enoch* (1833)**, in order to be classed as a human being, a child must have 'an existence independent of its mother' and must be 'wholly expelled' from the mother's body (***R v Poulton* (1832)**). Therefore, a 'child in waiting' (yet to be born) does not have the same rights as a child in being.

This can be contrasted with the position where a baby has been injured whilst in the womb and dies once it has been born. According to the court in ***AG's Ref (No. 3 of 1994)* (1997)**, this will amount to murder, so long as the **defendant** has the requisite intention, as the child is considered a person in being (a living person) once born, regardless of how short that life may turn out to be.

You may say that this means that criminals cannot be liable in such situations. Indeed, a foetus is not considered a person in being and thus no criminal offence can be committed against it. However, the mother remains a person in being and thus has a number of rights. For example, should a defendant stab his pregnant girlfriend in the stomach, causing an abortion, this may amount to an offence under the **Offences Against the Person Act 1861**.

The point is that only legal personalities have obligations under the law and benefit from use of the law in times of need. For a more detailed discussion on legal personalities, particularly artificial persons, see Lee Roach, *Company Law Concentrate* (5th edn, Oxford University Press 2018).

Rule of Law

The **Rule of Law** is a fundamental concept in most modern societies. It prescribes a collection of characteristics that must be secured for the functioning of a civilized state. A useful definition comes from John Finnis, *Natural Law and Natural Rights* (Clarendon Press 1980), who defines the Rule of Law as 'the name commonly given to the state of affairs in which a legal system is legally in good shape'.

The Rule of Law is too complex and broad a subject to be considered in any detail in this text. We advise seeking a constitutional law textbook which will explain the term with authority in much greater detail. You may wish to consult Lord Bingham's text, *The Rule of Law* (Penguin 2011).

Revision tip

The Rule of Law is an established concept in England and Wales and requires capital letters for both 'Rule' and 'Law'. Making this mistake in an examination under timed conditions may be forgiven by examiners; however, this mistake should be avoidable in an assessed piece of coursework.

According to Lord Bingham (2011), the 'core concept' of the Rule of Law is that 'all persons and authorities within the state, whether public or private, should be bound by and entitled to the benefit of laws publicly and prospectively promulgated and publicly administered in the courts.' This statement can be divided into eight core characteristics, or, as Lord Bingham cites, 'sub-rules'.

You might think at this stage that the Rule of Law is merely a fanciful concept that one can only hope the law lives up to. Or, as Lord Bingham notes, you may throw your hands into the air and 'accept that the Rule of Law is too uncertain and subjective an expression to be meaningful'.

Although it remains true that the Rule of Law is an ideal legal system that should be looked up to, it has made its way into the operation of our English legal system. The main source of this statement is the **Constitutional Reform Act (CRA) 2005**, which provides in **s1** that 'This Act does not adversely affect—(a) the existing constitutional principle of the Rule of Law, or (b) the Lord Chancellor's existing constitutional role in relation to that principle.' This constitutional role is found in **s6A Promissory Oaths Act 1868** (as amended by **s17 CRA 2005**) as requiring the Lord Chancellor, upon taking office, to swear an oath to 'respect the Rule of Law'.

The Rule of Law is now present in statutory form and thus must be adhered to by the courts. It no longer remains a fanciful ideal to aspire to, but rather is a legal obligation on the part of the courts, as led by the Lord Chancellor.

Table 1.1 describes the 'core characteristics' of the Rule of Law as stated by Lord Bingham.

A valuable summation of the Rule of Law was provided by Lord Denning in ***Gouriet v Union of Post Office Workers and Others* (1977)**, where he stated, 'Be you ever so high, the law is above you.'

Table 1.1 Characteristics of the Rule of Law

Characteristic	Explanation
Accessibility	The law must be accessible and so far as possible intelligible, clear, and predictable.
Law, not discretion	Questions of legal right and liability should ordinarily be resolved by application of the law and not the exercise of discretion.
Equality	Laws of the land should apply equally to all, save to the extent that objective differences justify differentiation.

Characteristic	Explanation
Human rights	The law must afford adequate protection of fundamental human rights.
Resolution of disputes	Means must be provided for resolving, without prohibitive cost or inordinate delay, bona fide disputes which the parties themselves are unable to resolve.
Reasonable use of ministerial power	Ministers and public officers must exercise the powers conferred on them reasonably, in good faith, for the purpose for which the powers were conferred, and without exceeding the limits of such powers.
Fair procedures	The adjudicative procedures provided by the state should be fair.
International obligations	The state must comply with its obligations in international law.

Functions of law

The functions of law, also known as the purposes of law, are full and varied. Some commentators rank certain functions above others, whilst other commentators argue that the functions act in conjunction to provide for a consistent and clear approach. Some of the main functions of the law can be listed as:

- protection of individual rights and liberties;
- maintenance of public order;
- the conferral of obligations;
- the regulation of economic activities; and
- the regulation of human behaviour and relationships.

Looking for extra marks?

When you discuss the 'functions' of law, be sure to provide examples to accompany the statement.

For example, if you are discussing the regulation of economic activities, you could discuss the creation of regulatory bodies such as the Financial Services Authority (FSA), which was responsible for ensuring banks and other organizations follow set standards of activity in order to protect consumers from 'bad deals'. (Note: as a result of the **Financial Services Act 2012**, the FSA was disbanded and in its place the Prudential Regulation Authority (PRA) and the Financial Conduct Authority (FCA) were created.)

Classification of law

As will be explained in greater detail throughout different chapters in this text, law may be classified into various different types of law. These types of law will determine how a particular area of law is governed, the procedure adopted within that type of law, and the personnel involved in that type of law. Table 1.2 details the three broad classifications of law.

Table 1.2 Classifying laws

Public vs private law (*see Chapter 2 for more information*)	
Public These are matters between the state and the individual (i.e. the citizen of the state). They cover such matters as **criminal law** and constitutional law.	**Private** These are matters between two individuals with minimal involvement from the state. They cover such matters as personal injury (tort generally) and breach of contract, and many others.
Criminal vs civil law (*see Chapter 2 for more information*)	
Criminal These are matters (generally) between two or more individuals with the involvement of the state in bringing a 'prosecution' on behalf of the Crown (i.e. the **Monarch**) where a criminal offence has been committed. Criminal offences range from offences against the person and property, to offences against the state.	**Civil** These are generally matters involving two or more individuals with no involvement from the state concerning a civil wrong. The civil wrong may be a breach of contract or liability arising out of the tort of trespass. There are, of course, civil matters that can involve the state, including such cases as judicial review.
Substantive vs procedural law	
Substantive This concerns the actual law itself. For example, the offence of murder is a matter of substantive law. The substantive law informs us that to be guilty of murder there has to be an 'unlawful killing'. The substantive law will operate within the framework of the procedural law.	**Procedural** This concerns the practical application and operation of the substantive law; for example, the powers of the police in arresting a suspect accused of murder or the admissibility of witness testimony to support a defence of loss of self-control.

'System'

A system can best be described as the manner by which the law operates. There are numerous different legal systems across the globe and each concern the administration/operation of the laws of the land. England and Wales operate under a '**common law**' system. The phrase 'common law' is, however, used in a number of different contexts and can be confusing from the outset. Table 1.3 details the varying types of system that you will come across throughout your degree and distinguishes the different uses of 'common law'.

Table 1.3 Classifying legal systems

Common law vs civil law (*see Chapter 4 for more information*)	
Common law A system of rules determined by binding **judicial precedent**. Common law systems exist alongside legislation and are used to interpret the legislation accordingly. The UK (not just England and Wales) is a common law system.	**Civil law** A system of rules that does not involve the use of binding judicial precedent. Civil systems rely upon established 'codes' to act as their law. France and Germany are **civil law** systems (also known as 'continental' systems).
Common law vs equity (*see Chapter 4 for more information*)	
Common law Decisions of the common law are based upon the law as it stands. Even if a decision appears harsh, the common law operates to follow the letter of the law.	**Equity** **Equity** attempts to reduce the harshness of the operation of the common law, with equality and fairness being the determinative factors in decision making. The UK operates a unified system of common law and equity (following the the **Judicature Acts of 1873–75**).
Adversarial system vs inquisitorial system	
Adversarial This system is based on an apparent 'contest' between the two or more opposing sides, with an independent **judge** acting as an umpire. The judge's role is to ensure that both sides follow procedural rules and should not undertake an investigation of the case him or herself. Adversarial systems allow for the parties to call, examine, and challenge witnesses. A key element is the principle of orality, namely that evidence should be presented by way of live oral testimony. The United Kingdom and the majority of common law systems operate under an adversarial system.	**Inquisitorial** This system is based more upon an investigation conducted by an independent judge, who will ask questions of witnesses in the hope of finding the truth. The roles of **counsel** and the judge are essentially reversed in that counsel will act as umpire, ensuring that the judge follows the correct procedural rules. The majority of civil law systems, including France and Germany, operate an inquisitorial approach.

Other legal systems

This text is concerned with the English legal system; therefore, if you wish to consider other legal systems, please consult an appropriate textbook, many of which may be examined on the Oxford University Press website under 'Systems of Law'.

However, it is important to understand how other systems of law affect our own English system of law. Specifically, our current membership in the **European Union (EU)** and our signatory status in the **European Convention on Human Rights (ECHR)** are considered in Chapter 5 of this text.

Dynamism

The ELS must be considered contextually. What this means is that you must maintain a practical and real-world approach to the study of the ELS. This is what we mean by 'dynamism'. Refer back to the chapter overview diagram.

Inner circle

You will see that the inner circles form the core elements that make up the ELS. The ELS is composed of four essential elements, highlighted in bold below. How each element will be considered throughout this text is detailed beneath each element:

- **Law**:
  - legislation; **case law**; **EU law**.
- **Procedure**:
  - criminal; civil; funding the ELS.
- **Institutions**:
  - courts; officers of the law.
- **Personnel**:
  - legal professionals; **judiciary**; laypersons.

Outer circle

The outer circle is what *we* refer to as the 'dynamism' of the ELS. Essentially, the ELS operates in a legal–political and legal–sociological context. This dynamism is reflective of the purpose of law and explains why and how the law operates in a certain context. We call this exercise 'joining up the dots' and it requires you to make the subtle distinction between 'theory' and 'practice'. Understanding this dynamism will stand you in good stead throughout your degree when you are required to take a contextual approach to your other modules of study.

Table 1.4 will help explain this dynamism further. The following example further illustrates dynamism within the ELS.

As a result of the decisions of ***Lawrence*** **(1972)** and ***Gomez*** **(1993)**, it has been argued that the definition of 'appropriation' in the law of theft has been so 'overextended' that any interaction with property now amounts to an appropriation. This has led David Ormerod and Karl Laird, *Smith, Hogan, & Ormerod's Criminal Law* (15th edn, Oxford University Press 2018) to write that 'any acts which would normally be regarded as merely "preparatory acts" now amount to an appropriation'. What this means is that if D touches a bottle of wine in a supermarket and they have the dishonest intention to permanently deprive the store of that wine, they are liable for the offence of theft. They need not leave the store or attempt to conceal

Dynamism

Table 1.4 Example of ELS dynamism

Example	Dynamism
Parliament creates law.	Legal—Parliament is the supreme law-making body.
Parliament is made up of MPs who are elected into power.	Political—MPs will vote in favour of laws that they agree with or feel they may benefit from. Re-election may affect the manner in which an MP acts.
Parliament relies upon expert opinion to inform it of the effects a law may have on society.	Sociological—looking at how certain policies will affect individuals may have a great effect on whether the policy is implemented.
Parliament must consider how it will fund this law.	Economic—funding will determine whether it is feasible for the law to be implemented. It may result in the law being implemented in stages, or in particular areas first.
Parliament must ensure the law applies equally to all.	Equality—as a result of our membership in the EU, the UK must ensure, subject to a number of exceptions, that all laws are equal to individuals of different ages, genders etc. Despite the UK's future removal from the EU, the principle of equality will continue to apply.

the wine. Simply touching the product with such dishonest intent is sufficient for an offence. That is the law in theory. In practice, the police are unlikely to arrest an individual and the **Crown Prosecution Service (CPS)** is even more unlikely to prosecute an individual who has entered a store with the intention to steal, but had neither left the store nor attempted to leave the store with the wine (this is because there would be little to no evidence to prove that D committed the offence).

Legally, therefore, an individual is liable for theft upon simply touching an item with dishonest intent. In practice, however, the individual is unlikely to be prosecuted for the theft.

Looking for extra marks?

This advice applies to all legal subjects that you may study. Ensure that you remain practical in your thinking throughout your degree. Consider the economic affects a particular law may have or has had when critiquing its implementation. Consider the objections made to the introduction of a new law by those directly affected by it, for example in the area of employment. Consider whether there is any evidence to suggest a particular piece of law was introduced for reasons personal to an individual.

How am I assessed?

The manner of assessment will depend entirely on your individual institution. Many institutions assess students' knowledge of ELS through a traditional unseen examination. An unseen examination may include both essay-style questions and problem-style questions.

Students may also be assessed by way of assessed coursework requiring the student to research a particular area of the ELS and write an answer accordingly.

Topic	**Adversarial v inquisitorial systems**
Academic	Michael Zander
Viewpoint	Argues that the inquisitorial system guarantees that 'all relevant witnesses are heard' as opposed to the adversarial system, for which the calling of witnesses is determined by the parties and thus if a witness's evidence is not helpful, they will not be called to testify.
Source	Michael Zander, *Cases and Materials on the English Legal System* (10th edn, Cambridge University Press 2007) 375
Topic	**The Rule of Law**
Academic	Albert Dicey
Viewpoint	Defines the Rule of Law as containing three components: **(i)** that no man should be punished or penalized for an act unless that act is contrary to established law; **(ii)** that no man is above the law and all men are subject to the same law and administration of law; **(iii)** general principles of the constitution result from the operation of judicial decisions from the courts. There need not be a codified constitution.
Source	Albert Dicey, *Introduction to the Study of the Law of the Constitution* (Springer 1985)

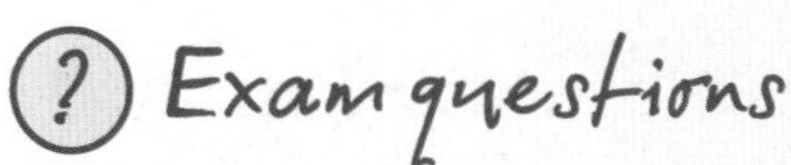

Essay question 1

'Law and morality cannot mix. The law is the law and to consider morals would undermine the law as we know it.'

Critically consider this statement.

Exam questions

****

Essay question 2

'The law is a dynamic and contemporary subject. It cannot survive without its context.'

Critically discuss this statement.

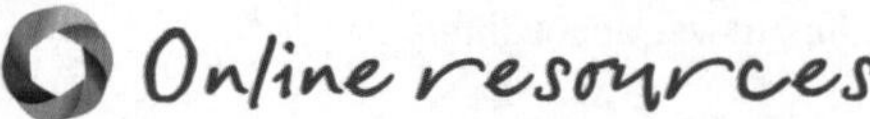

For outline answers to these essay questions, as well as multiple-choice questions, please visit the online resources.

#2

Introduction to Sources of Law and Court Structure

Key facts

- The courts of England and Wales can be divided into numerous different classifications.
- The necessity for such classification can be questioned.
- The courts follow a structured hierarchy, with cases being heard only in certain courts.
- The UK is a signatory state to the European Union (EU) and the European Convention on Human Rights (ECHR). It thus must act in accordance with those institutions.

Chapter overview

Sources of law in England and Wales

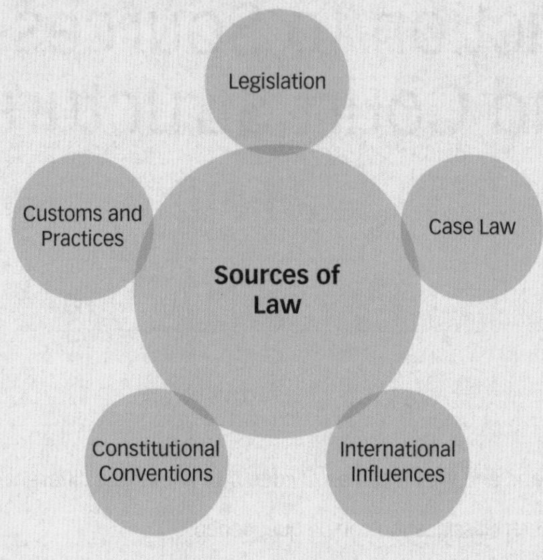

You will see from the contents page of this book that this chapter, along with Chapters 3, 4, and 5, deal with the 'sources' of English law. This chapter introduces you to the various sources of law, their respective positions, and worth in the English legal system. The chapter then introduces you to the court structure of England and Wales—this is a necessary read before you consider the principles of precedent in Chapter 4.

Sources of law: an introduction

During the course of your studies, you will be faced with a vast number of sources which you will need to read, understand, apply, and analyse. It is first necessary to make an initial distinction between the different sources of law (see Table 2.1). The distinction to be made is between 'primary sources' and 'secondary sources'.

Whilst you will come into contact with both sources of law during your time in study, the remaining part of this section of the chapter focuses on primary sources of law and their influencers. For more information on how best to use secondary sources, see Stacie Strong, *How to Write Law Essays and Exams* (5th edn, Oxford University Press 2018). Before we

Table 2.1 Sources of law

Primary sources of law	Secondary sources of law
Primary sources are the pre-eminent forms of legal information. Primary sources include legislation (Chapter 3) and case law (Chapter 4). These sources are 'primary' in nature, given that they are a statement of law passed down by a legal institution (whether that be Parliament passing an Act of Parliament, or the **Court of Appeal** handing down a judgment in a case). Primary sources are respected for their legal status and binding nature in law.	Secondary sources are best characterized as sources which supplement primary sources of law. They include such things as journal articles, textbooks, and reports. Secondary sources are a vital part of your studies, given that they are often intended to assist with your understanding of the primary sources (e.g. a journal article which critically analyses the state of case law in a particular area of law). Whilst these secondary sources are not statements of law, they can be exceptionally persuasive in a legal argument.

proceed to introduce you to legislation and case law, it is first necessary to introduce you to the concept of a 'constitution' and the respective 'lawmakers' in the UK.

Constitution

The first question is: 'What is a "constitution"?' A constitution is best described as a system of governance; a set of statements detailing the role, powers, duties, structure, and responsibility of the state and its citizens. Jonathan Law, *A Dictionary of Law* (9th edn, Oxford University Press 2018) defines a constitution as: 'The rules and practices that determine the composition and functions of the organs of central and local government in a state and regulate the relationship between the individual and the state'.

It is often said that the UK does not have a 'written constitution'. Indeed, this statement is correct to an extent. In comparison to the USA, for example, which has had a written (or 'codified') constitution since 1787, the UK does not have a single written document laying down the fundamental rights and responsibilities for their citizens and the operation of the state. However, it is incorrect to say that the UK has an entirely unwritten constitution; rather, it is better to express that the UK has a *largely* unwritten constitution. The UK's constitution consists largely of legislation (contained in various different **statute** books; not one single document) and case law. In addition, the UK's system of governance features concepts known as 'customs' and 'constitutional conventions'. Customs indicate practices that are followed to such an extent that they are treated as law, whilst constitutional conventions are sets of non-legally binding rules and principles which are treated as though they were binding due to their historical backing. We discuss these in more detail in Chapter 3.

Looking for extra marks?

Consider the respective advantages and disadvantages of a written constitution. By way of advantage, a codified constitution provides simple access, which should be easy to understand and comprehend. An aggrieved individual will be able to point to the constitution in respect of rights which they →

→ allege have been infringed. On the other hand, a codified constitution is a rigid construct and is generally inflexible; should any changes need to be made to a constitution, this would often require a special procedure to be adopted (unlike a change in UK legislation, which requires no special procedure to change).

Lawmakers

Before we go on to consider these varying sources of law, it is important to establish who the makers of the law are. The UK is built on a tripartite system involving three branches of the government. These branches are:

- the **executive**;
- the **legislature**;
- the **judiciary**.

Looking for extra marks?

In considering the tripartite system of lawmakers, give thought to the notion of 'separation of powers'. This concept, notably explained by the political philosopher Baron de Montesquieu, is a fundamental aspect of UK governance in that the three branches of government are separate, preventing any one institution from becoming too powerful. This system can be compared with the United States, which adopts a 'fusion of powers' model. See Colin Faragher, *Public Law Concentrate* (6th edn, Oxford University Press 2019).

Table 2.2 explains these branches in further detail and their role in the law-making process.

Table 2.2 Lawmakers of the UK

Branch of government	Description	Role
Executive	The executive is made up of senior members of the political party currently in power. The executive is headed by the Prime Minister.	To implement the law
Legislature	The legislature is another word for 'Parliament' and includes the **House of Commons**, the **House of Lords**, and the Monarch.	To make the law
Judiciary	The judiciary is the courts system in England and Wales, including both senior and first instance courts.	To interpret and apply the law (see Chapter 4 as to whether the judiciary has overstepped its role)

Influences on lawmakers

It must be appreciated that certain events, bodies, and pressures may have a strong influence on the lawmakers. The most prevalent examples of influences on the lawmakers can be seen in three entities:

- the Law Commission;
- the media; and
- public pressure groups.

The Law Commission, established by the **Law Commissions Act (LCA) 1965**, is an independent, permanent, and full-time body responsible for keeping 'under review all the law' (**s3 LCA 1965**). The Law Commission consists of a Chairman, and four Law Commissioners, each specializing in a particular area of law (e.g. criminal law). The Law Commission may conduct an investigation into an area of law by recommendation of the government (through the Lord Chancellor) or of its own accord. The Law Commission's success has varied over the years. Examples of such achievements include the introduction of the **Occupiers' Liability Act 1984**, the **Land Registration Act 2002**, and the **Fraud Act 2006**. Figure 2.1 details the general approach taken by the Law Commission.

The media represents (and often influences) public opinion to the extent that such opinion may in itself influence the law. A classic example is that of the double jeopardy rule abolished by the **Criminal Justice Act (CJA) 2003** in cases where there is new compelling evidence which

Figure 2.1 Approach of the Law Commission

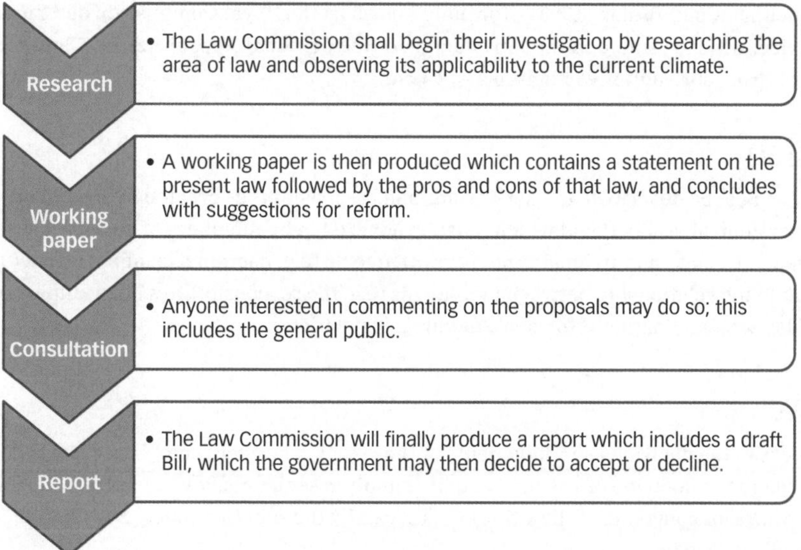

indicates that an acquitted person is, in fact, guilty. This rule was abolished as a result of significant pressure from the media in a campaign after the suspects in the Stephen Lawrence murder trial were acquitted despite substantial evidence against them. The media influenced the government to undertake an inquiry led by Sir William Macpherson. This inquiry in itself led to a Law Commission Report which recommended the law of double jeopardy be changed.

Pressure groups are groups of individuals who share a common interest, idea, or campaign. There are many different forms of pressure group, including the likes of 'section groups' and 'cause groups'. Pressure groups work in many different ways, including lobbying of MPs, signing of petitions, publicity campaigns, and organized marches. Pressure groups rely significantly on the media to get their message across and often work in unison to achieve a certain goal.

Some well-known pressure groups include the likes of:

- Fathers4Justice (campaigning for fathers' rights to have access to their children);
- Amnesty International (campaigning for human rights); and
- Greenpeace (campaigning for environmental issues).

Other law reform bodies include the Criminal Law Revision Committee (CLRC), which existed between 1957 and 1987 and the Law Reform Committee, which contributes to law reform in civil matters. In addition, special commissions or committees may be created to review a specific area of law. These commissions are often chaired by a presiding or retired judge (the commission being named after that judge). Some examples of these temporary commissions include:

- the Philips Commission (1981)—formally known as the Royal Commission on Police Procedure, which resulted in the introduction of the **Police and Criminal Evidence Act (PACE) 1984**.
- the Runciman Commission (1993)—formally known as the Royal Commission on Criminal Justice, which resulted in the introduction of the **Criminal Appeal Act 1995** and the **Criminal Procedure and Investigations Act 1996**.

Legislation

Legislation can best be described as a set of rules and responsibilities created by the government (whether central or local) and which must be adhered to by members of society. These rules may indicate what an individual is not permitted to do (e.g. commit a criminal offence), or may regulate the relationship between individuals (e.g. the responsibilities of an employer to their employee). See Chapter 3 for more detail on legislation.

Case law

Case law refers to the decisions and judgments of the courts. The operation of case law is determined through the doctrine of precedent; quite simply, a senior court will bind an inferior court (i.e. the inferior court must follow the law as stated by the superior court). See Chapter 4 for more detail on case law.

International influences

UK law is also dictated and influenced based upon the UK's membership or position in relation to a number of international sources of law. For instance, between 1972 and 2020 the UK was a member of the European Union (EU). The EU dictates substantive law, procedure, and rules that are to be followed by Member States (e.g. the EU states law regarding worker rights in employment which must be followed by Member States). The UK is in the process of leaving the EU which will mean that it will no longer be bound by EU law; however, this does not mean that EU law will not still be influential. In addition, the UK is a signatory of the **European Convention on Human Rights (ECHR)**; an international treaty protecting certain fundamental rights (e.g. the right to life, freedom of expression etc.). See Chapter 5 for more detail on the EU, the ECHR, and other international influences.

Hierarchy of the courts

As detailed in Chapter 4, understanding court hierarchy is essential to the concept of judicial precedent. Precedent dictates which courts must follow the decision of the appeal court in question.

A useful layout of such a hierarchy is detailed in Figure 2.2.

Figure 2.2 Court hierarchy

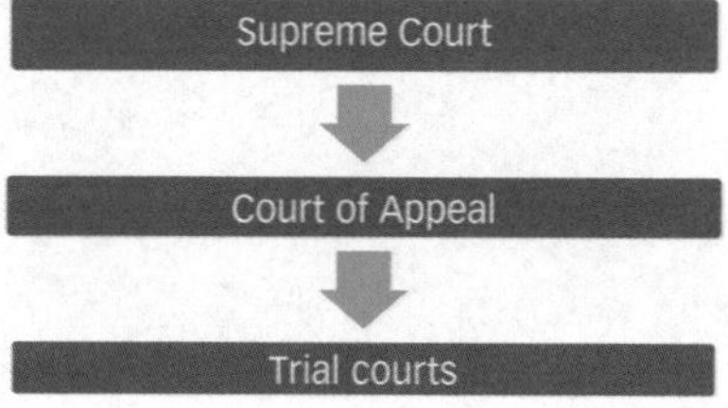

Classification of the courts

Courts may be classified in three different ways:

- criminal and civil courts;
- trial and appellate courts; and
- superior and inferior courts.

Criminal and civil courts

In England and Wales, there is often thought to be a stark divide between criminal and civil courts. Table 2.3 demonstrates the different type of courts and the work they generally undertake.

As Table 2.3 shows, however, the jurisdiction of some courts is not limited to one area of law, but rather is approachable for both substantive areas of law. The obvious examples are the **Supreme Court** and the Court of Appeal, with both courts hearing appeals in criminal and civil matters. However, dual jurisdiction is also present in the lower courts. For example, the **magistrates' court** may deal with civil law matters such as licensing, betting and gaming, civil debts etc. Likewise, the **High Court of Justice** is largely a civil court but it also has a limited criminal jurisdiction on such matters as appeals from the magistrates' court on points of law (appeal by way of case stated).

It is as a result of this dual jurisdiction exercised by some courts that Steve Wilson et al., *The English Legal System* (4th edn, Oxford University Press 2020) comment that it is 'not possible to classify courts as criminal or civil courts', while Gillespie remarks that such classification is 'impracticable' (Gillespie and Weare (2019), see 'Key debates' below). Despite this, we shall consider the general differences between criminal and civil courts.

Table 2.3 Criminal and civil courts

Criminal matters	Civil matters
Magistrates' court	Magistrates' court
Youth Court	**County Court**
Crown Court	High Court
High Court	Family Court
Court of Appeal (Criminal Division)	Court of Appeal (Civil Division)
Supreme Court	

Looking for extra marks?

When citing a secondary source, for example Gillespie, ensure that you 'critically engage' with that source. Do not simply cite what the source says, engage with it. This means:

(i) stating whether you agree or disagree with the source;

(ii) stating the extent to which you agree or disagree with the source;

(iii) explaining your reasoning for holding that view; and

(iv) if you disagree with a source, stating why your argument is stronger/better and, if you can, providing authority to substantiate your point.

Critical engagement is a key skill that one must adopt when studying law and will assist you in reaching your highest potential.

The role of the courts

As you would expect, criminal courts deal with individuals who have 'allegedly' committed a criminal offence and it is the role of the arbiters of fact to determine the guilt or innocence of a defendant based on the evidence presented before them. If convicted, it is then for the arbiter of law to determine the appropriate punishment in line with statutory guidelines.

Civil courts, on the other hand, deal primarily with the resolution of private disputes between individuals. Such disputes can include matters of contract law, personal injury, and family law. At the conclusion of a civil matter, the trial judge will then award appropriate remedies to the successful party. Monetary damages, often known as 'compensation', are the most common remedy.

Revision tip

One important point to note is that a particular circumstance may give rise to proceedings in both the criminal and civil courts. For example, should Mark be driving his car recklessly and knock Claire down whilst she was walking in the street, this could lead to a criminal charge being brought against Mark under the **Road Traffic Act 1988**, whilst at the same time a claim in the civil courts may be brought for negligence. Evidence that Mark was convicted in the criminal proceedings can subsequently be used against him in the civil proceedings (**s11 Civil Evidence Act 1968**).

Public vs private law

Given the relationship between the state and the individual in criminal matters, it is often appropriate to refer to criminal law as an element of '**public law**'. One may question this statement on the grounds that, 'Well, surely criminal offences against the person or property are not matters of public law.' All criminal matters are an element of public law due to the vertical relationship between the state and the individual. The state brings the case against the defendant, not the victim. You may assume then that civil law, as the counterpart to criminal law, is solely to do with '**private law**'. This is an accurate statement with regard to actions in contract law and tort law; however, other civil matters which concern a relationship between the state and the individual, such as child proceedings brought by the local authority, are deemed to be matters of public law. Likewise, although disputes over taxation often fall within the remit of the criminal law, such disputes are generally civil law matters between the individual and the state, thus amounting to a public law matter.

Procedures of the criminal and civil courts

In criminal courts, the case (known as a 'charge') is brought against the defendant generally by the Crown Prosecution Service (CPS); however, all persons have the right to bring criminal proceedings against an individual. This power is preserved by **s6(1) Prosecution of Offences Act 1985** and is what certain bodies, such as the RSPCA use to bring private prosecutions for particular actions. Where the charge is brought by the CPS, any such charge is on behalf of the Crown (known as 'Regina'), i.e. the monarch-in-law.

The 'golden rule' in criminal proceedings is that the burden of proving guilt in a criminal trial is on the prosecution (***Woolmington v DPP* (1935)**). They must prove the guilt of a defendant 'beyond a reasonable doubt', or as the Court of Appeal held in ***R v Majid* (2009)**, so that the arbiters of fact are 'sure'. This golden rule is subject to exceptions, the most notable being the defence of insanity, where the burden of proof is reversed and the defence bears the burden to prove insanity in accordance with ***M'Naghten's Case* (1843)**. As opposed to the prosecution, who must prove such matters beyond a reasonable doubt, the defence bears the lower standard of the 'balance of probabilities' (see below for the definition of this term).

***Woolmington v DPP* [1935] AC 462 (HL)**

FACTS: The defendant, Woolmington, stole a double-barrelled shotgun and cartridges from his employer and shot and killed his wife, Violet.

HELD: Throughout the web of the English Criminal Law one golden thread is always to be seen that it is the duty of the prosecution to prove the prisoner's guilt subject to . . . the defence of insanity and subject also to any statutory exception. If, at the end of and on the whole of the case, there is a reasonable doubt, created by the evidence given by either the prosecution or the prisoner . . . the prosecution has not made out the case and the prisoner is entitled to an acquittal. No matter what the charge or where the trial, the principle that the prosecution must prove the guilt of the prisoner is part of the common law of England and no attempt to whittle it down can be entertained.

(Viscount Sankey)

In the civil courts, however, the individual who brings the claim against the defendant is known as the claimant. Prior to the **Civil Procedure Rules (CPR) 1998**, the claimant was known as the plaintiff. If you read any case law before 1998, then references will be made to the plaintiff; however, the correct language used today is claimant.

Generally, in civil proceedings, the claimant will be suing the defendant or applying for an order against the defendant. Both proceedings are brought in accordance with the **CPR 1998**.

In civil proceedings, the burden of proof remains on the claimant. This is in accordance with the Latin maxim '*ei incumbit probatio qui dicit*' ('He who asserts must prove'). The civil standard of proof is on the balance of probabilities, which has been interpreted by Denning J in ***Miller v Minister of Pensions* (1947)** as 'more probable than not'. Table 2.4 provides an overview of the differences between the two courts.

Trial and appellate courts

A case, whether it be a criminal or a civil case, will always commence in a **court of first instance** (also known as a court of original jurisdiction). The court of first instance is synonymous with a court of trial. Such courts are concerned with undertaking a fact-finding exercise and reaching a decision on the facts presented before it. The decisions reached by the trial courts may, and often are, challenged on appeal. For example, convictions in the Crown Court may result in an appeal to the Court of Appeal which, if successful, quashes any such conviction and replaces it with an acquittal. Likewise, in civil law, where a decision is plainly wrong in law, this too can be challenged and the decision corrected.

Table 2.4 Comparison between criminal and civil courts

Comparator	Criminal courts	Civil courts
Name of parties	Prosecution Defendant	Claimant Defendant
Burden of proof	Generally on the prosecution	On the claimant
Standard of proof	When the burden is on the prosecution: 'Beyond a reasonable doubt' When the burden is on the defendant: 'Balance of probabilities'	'Balance of probabilities'

Such challenges take place in the appellate courts, which are concerned with questions of law, as opposed to questions of fact. As with the hurdles that are faced when one attempts to categorize the courts by division of criminal and civil law, one also faces challenges in attempting to categorize by jurisdiction. This is because, unlike the magistrates' court, which maintains only original jurisdiction, other courts, such as the Crown Court and the High Court of Justice exercise both original and appellate jurisdiction. For example, the Crown Court holds original jurisdiction in hearing cases on indictment or either-way offences and appellate jurisdiction in hearing appeals, in the form of a full retrial, from the magistrates' court. Likewise, the County Court has a sort of internal appellate jurisdiction in that appeals from decisions of district judges in the County Court would remain in that Court, but would be heard by a circuit judge. It is perhaps better, therefore, to express that it is circuit judges that have appellate jurisdiction, as opposed to the County Court itself. See Chapter 7 for more on criminal procedure and Chapter 8 for civil procedure.

Gillespie and Weare (2019) concludes that as a result of this, categorization by jurisdiction 'does not assist either'.

Table 2.5 demonstrates which courts act as trial courts and which act with appellate jurisdiction. Also, refer back to the diagram featured in the chapter overview.

Superior and inferior courts

Finally, the courts can also be divided into 'superior courts' and 'inferior courts'.

Superior courts

The starting point is **s1(1) Senior Courts Act (SCA) 1981**, which provides:

> The Senior Courts of England and Wales shall consist of the Court of Appeal, the High Court of Justice and the Crown Court, each having such jurisdiction as is conferred on it by or under this or any other Act.

Prior to the creation of the Supreme Court by the **Constitutional Reform Act (CRA) 2005**, the Senior Courts were known as 'The Supreme Court'. This renaming, which was an obvious

Table 2.5 Trial courts and appellate courts

Court	Trial court	Appellate court
County Court	✓	✓
High Court of Justice	✓	✓
Family Court	✓	✓
Magistrates' court	✓	✗
Youth Court	✓	✗
Crown Court	✓	✓
Court of Appeal	✗	✓
Supreme Court	✗	✓

necessity, was brought about by **s59(1) CRA 2005**. There are other courts that have been declared as 'superior' by statute.

Two key examples are:

- the Supreme Court (**s40(1) CRA 2005**); and
- the Employment Appeal Tribunal (**s20(3) Employment Tribunals Act (ETA) 1996**).

Does this mean that the superior courts are those established by statute? Interestingly, the House of Lords acted as a superior court without legislative recognition, and perhaps the true understanding of the superior courts can be found in Goff LJ's judgment in ***ex parte Muldoon and Others* (1983)**, where his Lordship stated:

> It is necessary to look at the relevant functions of the tribunal in question including its constitution, jurisdiction and powers and its relationship with the High Court in order to decide whether the tribunal should properly be regarded as inferior . . .

Following Goff LJ's statement, then, a superior court is one:

- with unlimited jurisdiction; and
- that is not subject to supervision by the High Court of Justice.

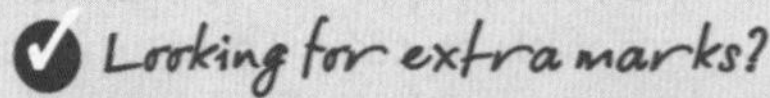

The above statement is not 100 per cent accurate. You can demonstrate your knowledge to an examiner by making clear that certain courts, such as the Crown Court, are senior courts and yet →

→ remain subject to the supervision of the High Court of Justice (e.g. appeals originating from the magistrates' court and proceeding to the Crown Court may be appealed further to the High Court). It may be the case, therefore, that this is not the most appropriate way to categorize senior courts.

Inferior courts

The inferior courts include the magistrates' court and the County Court and are those which are limited in their jurisdiction and powers, and are subject to review by a superior court. With no statutory statement that a court is 'superior', one could assume that a lack of express statement implies the court is, in fact, 'inferior'. By no means should the word 'inferior' cast an opinion that the court is 'subordinate' or 'less worthy of recognition', especially given that the majority of cases are determined by the inferior courts, often without a successful appeal.

Revision tip

Remember to always ask 'Why?' The best **lawyers** are those that live in continuous doubt and always wonder why something is so. You should hopefully be asking yourself: 'Why is there a need to classify the courts?' Once you have considered arguments for and against your question, you can use authority to substantiate any argument that you make, ultimately leading to higher marks than a person who simply accepts the law as it is.

The courts of England and Wales

Now we shall consider in greater detail the specific courts within England and Wales. Figure 2.3 provides you with an overview of the court structure to get a feel of the hierarchy of the courts and the stages that a case may proceed through the system.

The old 'higher courts' of the Middle Ages were reorganized into the modern court structure we know today by the **Judicature Acts of 1873 and 1875**, which created the High Court of Justice and the Court of Appeal.

Civil cases

There are several civil courts which hold civil jurisdiction; they are the County Court, the magistrates' court the High Court of Justice, and the Family Court. Below we shall also consider tribunals, which form an important aspect of the civil justice system but sit outside the ordinary court structure.

County Court

As a result of **s17 Crime and Courts Act 2013**, there is now one single County Court. Prior to this Act, like the magistrates' court, there were a number of county courts (173 to be exact) but no single entity. Now, like the Crown Court, County Court business is dealt with in one of the many County Court centres. Most County Court centres are assigned at least one circuit judge and one district judge. These numbers may vary, however.

Figure 2.3 Court structure

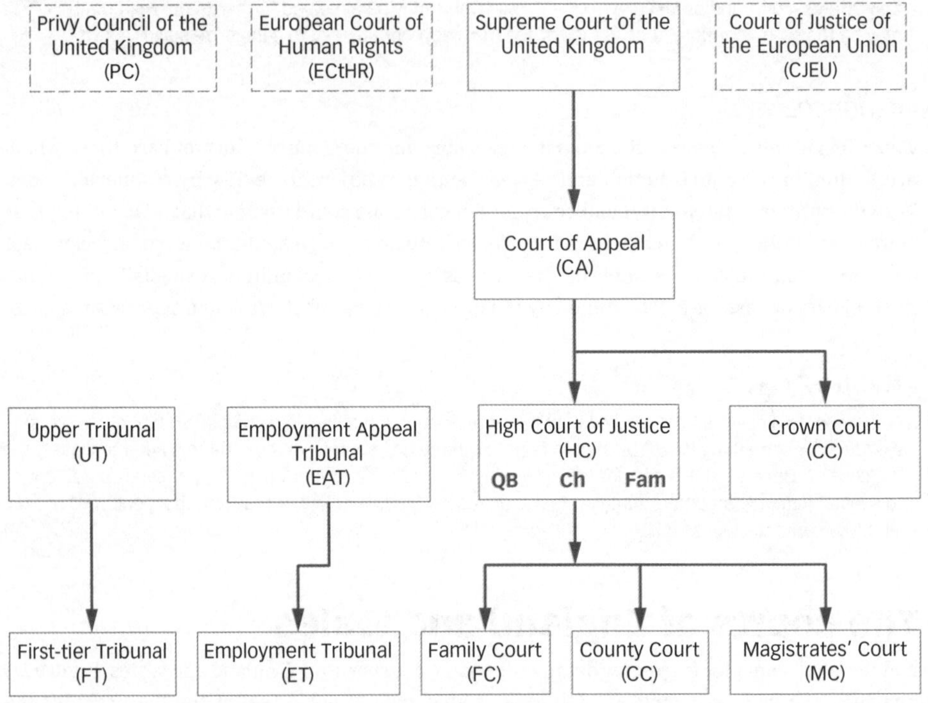

Generally, cases worth over £15,000 or involving greater importance or complexity will be heard by a circuit judge. Cases worth less than £15,000 or involving less complexity or importance will generally be heard by a district judge. **Section 17** also established the County Court as a court of record.

Magistrates' court

Whilst the majority of the work of the magistrates' court is concerned with criminal matters (see below under 'Criminal cases'), the magistrates' court does hold limited jurisdiction in civil matters. In particular, specially trained magistrates sit as a 'family panel' in the Family Proceedings Courts dealing with both public and private family law work. In addition, the magistrates' courts hold jurisdiction over civil matters such as non-payment of council tax and licensing appeals from decisions of local authorities.

Family Court

Section 17 Crime and Courts Act 2013 also had the effect of introducing a new court, known as the Family Court. Prior to this, family law matters were divided between the jurisdiction of the county courts and the magistrates' courts. As a result of **s17**, however, all family law matters, with a small number of exceptions, must be commenced in the Family Court. Family law is divided into public and private family law (see Table 2.6).

Table 2.6 Types of family law

Type of law	Work undertaken
Public	These are cases brought by local authorities or an authorized person (the National Society for Prevention of Cruelty to Children, NSPCC) in relation to care orders, supervision orders, and emergency protection orders.
Private	These are cases brought by private individuals. These cases generally concern divorce or separation and child arrangement orders (CAOs). These cases may also include circumstances of adoption and domestic violence.

High Court of Justice

The High Court of Justice, more commonly known simply as the High Court, is a single court that sits in the Royal Courts of Justice alongside the Court of Appeal (though, do note that the High Court has a number of 'District Registries' which sit in various parts of England and Wales). The High Court acts in both a trial and appellate capacity; this section focuses on the trial capacity of the court, whilst the next section, 'Divisional Courts of the High Court', focuses on the appellate capacity. In its travelling capacity, the High Court was once known as the Assize Court. The Assize Court was abolished upon the creation of the Crown Court in 1972.

The High Court is composed of three 'divisions' which deal with certain types of work. These divisions are:

- Queen's Bench Division (QBD): deals with all 'common law' cases relating to contract and tort, except those specifically allocated to the Chancery Division. The QBD consists of a specialist court, called the Administrative Court, which largely deals with judicial review proceedings. The Administrative Court itself features a specialist court, namely the Planning Court, which deals with any planning matters (e.g. planning permission for building sites). The head of the QBD is the **Lord Chief Justice**, who is assisted by the President of the QBD.
- Chancery Division (Ch): deals with specialist civil work involving companies, intellectual property, disputes relating to trust property, and probate. Although the work may be wide and varied, it is focused on business and property disputes. The head of the Chancery Division is the Chancellor of the High Court ('the Chancellor') and cases in the Division are heard by a single specialist judge.
- Family Division (Fam): created by the **Administration of Justice Act 1970**, the Family Division deals with appeals from the Family Court and has exclusive original jurisdiction in certain family matters, such as wardship (i.e. giving custody of a child to the state). The head of the Family Division is the President of the Family Division.

Interestingly, the QBD and the Chancery Division operate a dual role for certain 'specialist courts' which cover a multitude of different courts designed for certain commercial disputes. On 13 March 2017, it was announced that these specialist courts would become one single entity known as the 'Business and Property Courts of England and Wales'. This change brought together a number of different courts under one heading. This is designed to allow for greater flexibility and ease of access for international disputes. The Business and Property Courts sit in the Rolls Building in the Royal Court of Justice. However, these courts also sit in numerous locations across the country to ensure that there is sufficient access to the courts. By way of example, the Admiralty Court also sits in Birmingham, Bristol, Leeds, Liverpool, Manchester, and Newcastle. Table 2.7 details the courts which feature under this heading.

The civil system, similar to the criminal system, is designed to be as efficient as possible. To be so efficient, civil claims are divided into different 'tracks'. Where a claim will be heard

Table 2.7 Business and property courts

Court	Division	Work they undertake
Commercial Court	QBD	Deals with national and international business disputes, including insurance, banking, arbitration, and other commercial matters
Admiralty Court	QBD	Deals with matters relating to shipping and maritime disputes, including such matters as collision of ships and damage to cargo
Technology and Construction Court	QBD	Deals with national and international construction, engineering, and technology disputes; also deals with computer litigation, environmental issues, and nuisance claims
Business List	Ch	Deals with business-related matters, such as banking and financial services, claims against directors, and partnership disputes
Insolvency and Companies List	Ch	Deals with corporate and personal insolvency and pure company work (in the specialist Companies Court)
Financial List	QBD/Ch	Deals with financial disputes over £50 million or equivalent, or which require particular market expertise, or raise issues of general market importance
Competition List	Ch	Deals with competition claims under the EU and national competition rules, e.g. market abuse by restricting or distorting competition

Court	Division	Work they undertake
Intellectual Property List	Ch	Deals with all disputes involving intellectual property. Work is divided into **(i)** the Patents Court, which deals with patent and registered design disputes; and **(ii)** the Intellectual Property and Enterprise Court (IPEC), which deals with all other IP disputes, such as copyright and trade-mark infringement.
Property, Trusts and Probate List	Ch	Deals with such matters as landlord and tenant disputes, administration of estates, and probate claims

will depend on the track. **Rule 26.1(2) CPR 1998** sets out that there are three tracks: **small-claims track**; **fast-track**; and **multi-track**. Table 2.8 sets out the different tracks in greater detail.

A second important point to note, which shall be expanded upon later in this text, is that in general the County Court and the High Court of Justice have concurrent jurisdiction. This means that the claimant has the choice as to where proceedings are commenced (**Practice Direction 7A.1 (PD7A.1) CPR 1998**).

However, **r7.1 CPR 1998** states that there are certain restrictions on where proceedings can be started. We shall address these when dealing with the County Court and High Court of Justice individually. Civil courts will be dealt with in more detail in Chapter 8.

Table 2.8 Civil claim tracks and their courts

Type of claim and court	Qualifications	Examples
Small-claims track County Court	Less than £10,000; and Claims for pain, suffering, and loss of amenity (PSLA) are not more than £1,000	Personal injury cases valued at £4,000 for loss of earnings and other losses plus a claim for £800 for damages for PSLA
Fast-track County Court	Between £10,000 and £25,000; and Lasts not longer than one day; and Does not require more than one expert per party	Personal injury cases valued between £10,000 and £25,000 Personal injury cases valued under £10,000 but damages for PSLA exceed £1,000
Multi-track County Court or High Court of Justice (if over £50,000 for personal injury cases or otherwise over £100,000)	Over £25,000; or Under £25,000 BUT requires longer than one day or more than one expert per party	Personal injury case valued at £32,000 Breach of contract case valued at £18,000, but requiring at least three days' hearing

Divisional Courts of the High Court

The name of this court is rather confusing given that the High Court is divided into three divisions (as discussed above). The Divisional Courts, however, are the appellate courts of the High Court. Each of the Divisions listed above have the capacity to act as a court of appeal from the courts and tribunals below them. By **s66(3) Senior Courts Act 1981**, a Divisional Court must sit with no less than two High Court judges, but will generally sit as a bench of three. Table 2.9 details the types of appeals faced by the Divisional Courts:

Table 2.9 Appeals to the Divisional Courts

Divisional Court	Examples of types of appeal
Queen's Bench Divisional Court	Judicial review cases of decisions made by inferior courts and tribunals. The majority of cases are dealt with by the specialist Administrative Court.
Chancery Divisional Court	Decisions of masters in courts below, income tax cases from the Commissioners of Inland Revenue, and bankruptcy claims/insolvency decisions from the County Court
Family Divisional Court	Appeals from the Family Court and family cases which are considered to be complex or of importance

Criminal cases

The two main criminal courts are:

- the **magistrates' court** (and the Youth Court); and
- the **Crown Court**.

Revision tip

Ensure you correctly spell magistrates' court. The apostrophe follows the 's'. It makes little sense to lose marks on such simple spelling mistakes. Please also note that magistrates' court is spelled with a lower case 'm' and 'c', whereas the Crown Court is spelled with an upper case 'C' and 'C'. This is because there is only one Crown Court but multiple magistrates' courts.

Before we proceed into our discussion on the two different courts, it will first be useful to discuss the categories of offences which determine whether an offence will be tried in the magistrates' court or the Crown Court.

In general, the classification of an offence will be prescribed by the statute creating it, normally by way of the description of the nature of the penalty on conviction. The three types of offences are as follows:

- **Summary-only offences**: these are the least serious of the three offences and are triable only in the magistrates' court. Created by statute, all **summary offences** can be identified by statement of the maximum penalty, which may range from a custodial to a community sentence, which may be imposed upon conviction for an offence (e.g. driving whilst intoxicated through drink or drugs is a summary-only offence contrary to **s4(1) Road Traffic Act 1988**).
- **Either-way offences**: these are offences which, dependent on the particular facts of the case, may or may not be serious. Such offence may be identified in two ways. First, **sch 1 Magistrates' Courts Act (MCA) 1980** lists the offences that are **triable either way**. Secondly, the statute that creates the offence will specify two penalties, one upon conviction summarily and the other upon conviction on indictment (e.g. theft is a triable either-way offence contrary to **s1 Theft Act 1968**).
- **Indictable-only offences**: these are the most serious of the three offences and are triable only in the Crown Court. A helpful starting point is **sch 1(a) Interpretation Act 1978**, which provides that 'indictable offence' means an offence which is 'triable on indictment, whether it is exclusively so triable or triable either way'. It is important to note at this stage that all common law offences are indictable, for example murder.

Revision tip

Pay close attention to the wording of **sch 1(a)**! It provides that an indictable offence includes both an indictable-only offence and an either-way offence. Therefore, if you ever see reference to an 'indictable' offence (not an 'indictable-only' offence), be aware that it includes offences triable either-way. By way of example, a 'citizen's arrest' may be effected under **s24A(1) Police and Criminal Evidence Act 1984** where another person is (amongst other circumstances) in the act of committing an 'indictable' offence. This means that the power of citizen's arrest is available for both either-way and indictable-only offences, but not summary-only offences. A fine but vital distinction.

Table 2.10 details the types of criminal offences in England and Wales.

Table 2.10 Types of offences

Type of offence	Court in which it will be heard	Examples and sentence
Summary-only	Magistrates' court	*Common assault*—six months maximum
Either-way	Magistrates' court or Crown Court	*Assault occasioning actual bodily harm (ABH)*—six months (Mags) or five years (Crown) maximum *Theft*—six months (Mags) or seven years (Crown) maximum
Indictable-only	Crown Court	*Murder*—life maximum *Rape*—life maximum

Magistrates' court

In England and Wales, there are around 330 magistrates' courts which deal, roughly, with 99 per cent of all criminal cases. The magistrates' courts deal with all summary-only offences and the vast majority of either-way offences. The magistrates' court may consist of lay magistrates or a district judge. Lay magistrates sit as a bench of at least two—but normally three—in criminal matters (one chair and two 'wingers'), whilst a district judge will sit alone. Magistrates are arbiters of both fact and law, by which we mean that they must make decisions on any points of law raised and make a factual finding. They are assisted in their task by a legal adviser (also known as a legal clerk), who may advise the lay bench on any points of law. All criminal cases, regardless of their classification, will start in the magistrates' court. The process of hearing the case is dependent on the classification of offence (see Chapter 7 for more detail):

- summary-only: everything is heard in the magistrates' court;
- either-way: the magistrates will conduct a 'mode-of-trial' hearing to determine whether the offence will stay in the magistrates' court or will be sent to the Crown Court;
- indictable-only: whilst the magistrates will determine matters such as bail, the case will be automatically sent for trial in the Crown Court (**s51 Crime and Disorder Act (CDA) 1998**).

Youth Court

The Youth Court deals with criminal cases involving juveniles (i.e. those persons between the ages of 10 and 17, inclusive). As soon as an individual reaches the age of 18, they will be tried in the ordinary adult courts. Magistrates hold jurisdiction to sit in the Youth Court and must sit as a mixed bench of three. In addition, magistrates who sit in the Youth Court must have special training. The procedure in the Youth Court is less formal and only authorized persons may attend (attendance of the media is restricted).

All criminal cases (regardless of whether they are summary or indictable) involving juveniles must be dealt with in the Youth Court; however, there are a number of notable exceptions:

- Charges involving homicide, firearms, or violent offences must be sent to the Crown Court (**s51A CDA 1998**).
- Charges involving 'specified offences', such as rape and manslaughter, and where the court considers the youth to be a 'dangerous offender' must be sent to the Crown Court (**s51A(2) CDA 1998**).
- Charges involving 'serious offences', i.e. those that are punishable by life imprisonment or imprisonment for 10 years or more, and where the offence charged might attract a lengthy sentence, must be sent to the Crown Court (**s51A(2) CDA 1998**).

There are other exceptions to this rule, for which you are advised to consult a criminal procedure text.

Crown Court

Created by the **Courts Act 1971**, the Crown Court deals with the more serious criminal offences which will be heard by a judge and **jury**. Unlike the magistrates' courts, the Crown Court is a single entity which sits in 77 court centres across England and Wales. For example, the Old Bailey (or more formally, the Central Criminal Court) is just another Crown Court centre which sits in the City of London. In addition to its original jurisdiction over serious criminal matters, the Crown Court also hears appeals from the magistrates' court. These appeals are dealt with in more detail in Chapter 7.

There are three different types of Crown Court centre, based on the type of work that they deal with. These are:

- first-tier centres: these centres are visited by High Court judges for criminal work in the Crown Court and civil work in the High Court;
- second-tier centres: these centres are visited by High Court judges for criminal work in the Crown Court only;
- third-tier centres: these centres are not normally visited by High Court judges and handle criminal work in the Crown Court only.

Further to this, offences that are to be tried in the Crown Court are divided into three classes of seriousness. These classes determine the type of judge which will sit in the case:

- Class 1 offences: the most serious criminal offences, including treason and murder; generally heard by a High Court judge.
- Class 2 offences: very serious offences, including rape; generally heard by a circuit judge, under the authority of the Presiding Judge.
- Class 3 offences: includes all other offences not covered by Class 1 or 2 including burglary, grievous bodily harm, and robbery; generally tried by a circuit judge or recorder.

Criminal courts shall be dealt with in more detail in Chapter 7.

Divisional Court

The Divisional Court of the High Court of Justice holds a limited criminal jurisdiction. In particular, criminal appeals in summary cases may proceed to the Divisional Court. The process is rather confusing so it may be helpful to refer to Figure 2.4, which demonstrates the appeal process.

From decisions of the magistrates' court, any party to the proceedings may appeal to the Divisional Court by way of 'case stated' (**s111 Magistrates' Courts Act 1980**). In addition, should a case be appealed first to the Crown Court from the magistrates' court for a rehearing, it may then be subsequently appealed to the Divisional Court by way of case stated (**s28 Senior Courts Act 1981**).

Figure 2.4 Appeals to the Divisional Court

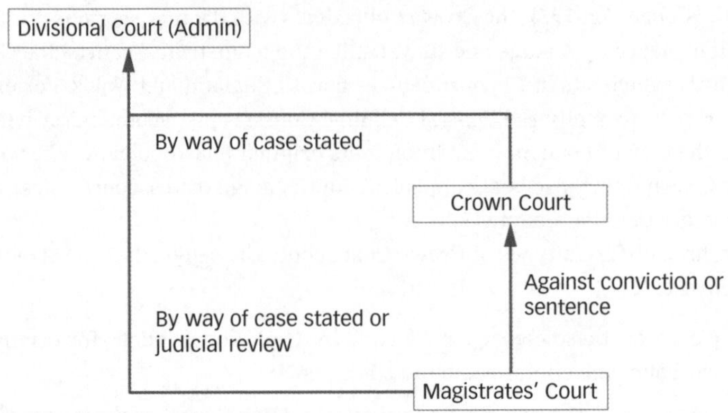

The Administrative Court of the Queen's Bench Division will hear these criminal appeals in the capacity of a Divisional Court. Any further appeals then proceed to the Supreme Court, leapfrogging the Court of Appeal (**s1(2) Administration of Justice Act 1960**).

Appellate courts

This section deals with the two main appeal courts in England and Wales, the Court of Appeal and the Supreme Court. For a discussion of the appellate jurisdiction of the Divisional Court and the Crown Court, see 'Criminal cases' above.

Court of Appeal

Based in the Royal Courts of Justice, the Court of Appeal is the highest of the 'senior courts'. Formerly divided into the Court of Appeal (CA) and the Court of Criminal Appeal (CCA), the Court became a single entity split into two divisions—the Civil Division and the Criminal Division—in 1966, following the **Criminal Appeal Act 1966**.

The CA is comprised of Lord and Lady Justices of Appeal, abbreviated to 'LJ'. The head of the Civil Division is the **Master of the Rolls** and the head of the Criminal Division is the Lord Chief Justice.

Court of Appeal (Civil Division)

Appeals from the County Court and the High Court are governed by **Part 52 Civil Procedure Rules (CPR) 1998** and **Practice Direction 52**. An appeal can be heard by a single judge (**s54(2) SCA 1981**) but ordinarily the Court will sit with at least two judges (normally three).

The test for allowing an appeal in civil proceedings is provided by **r52.21(3) CPR 1998**, which states that:

The appeal court will allow an appeal where the decision of the lower court was:

(a) wrong (meaning that the court below (i) erred in law; or (ii) erred in fact; or (iii) erred (to the appropriate extent) in the exercise of its discretion); or
(b) unjust because of a serious procedural or other irregularity in the proceedings in the lower court.

Court of Appeal (Criminal Division)

The Criminal Division mainly deals with appeals from the Crown Court against conviction or sentence. The Court may also hear appeals from the **Attorney General**, known as 'references' under **s36 Criminal Justice Act (CJA) 1972** and **s36 CJA 1988**. The **1972 Act** concerns appeals on points of law, meaning that an acquittal in the lower courts will not be affected by the decision of the Court of Appeal. The **1988 Act**, however, is concerned with appeals against 'unduly lenient sentences'. The CA also hears cases referred to them by the Criminal Cases Review Commission (CCRC) under **s9 Criminal Appeal Act (CAA) 1995**.

The Criminal Division ordinarily sits in panels of three. When determining an appeal against conviction, the Court must sit in an uneven number of no less than three judges (**s55(2) SCA 1981**). When determining an appeal against sentence, the Court may sit as a panel of two (**s55(4) SCA 1981**). In the event of a stalemate, where the judges are divided, the matter must be relisted and heard before a new bench of not less than three judges (**s55(5) SCA 1981**).

The test for allowing an appeal in criminal proceedings is provided for by **s2(1) CAA 1968**, which provides that:

> Subject to the provisions of this Act, the Court of Appeal—
> (a) shall allow an appeal against conviction if they think that the conviction is unsafe; and
> (b) shall dismiss such an appeal in any other case.

Looking for extra marks?

Consider whether the test of 'unsafe' is sufficient to ensure that there are no miscarriages of justice in England and Wales. The common problem that arises is that the Court of Appeal will find that evidence was improperly admitted or procedure was not correctly followed; however, often it concludes that such wrongs do not make the conviction unsafe, i.e. the arbiters of fact would have still reached the same conclusion, regardless.

Supreme Court

The Supreme Court, formerly the Judicial/Appellate Committee of the House of Lords, was created on 1 October 2009 by **s23 Constitutional Reform Act (CRA) 2005**. The change was made as a statement of the separation of powers between the House of Lords in its legislative capacity and the Appellate Committee of the House of Lords in its judicial capacity. This was made clear by Lord Phillips during a speech opening the Supreme Court.

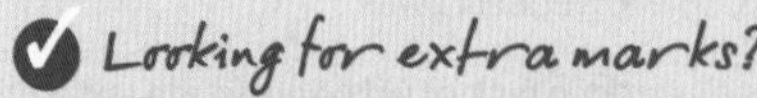

Often questions are asked as to the function of the Supreme Court as the highest court in the land. In answering this question, it is important to question why the Supreme Court was created in the first place. It is even more important for you to state your own opinion as to whether such creation was the correct decision on the part of the legislature and whether the Court has fulfilled its function as a result of its creation.

Table 2.11 Legislative routes of appeal to the Supreme Court

Area of law	Court appealing from	Legislation
Criminal	Court of Appeal	**s33(2) Criminal Appeal Act (CAA) 1968**
	High Court	**s1(1)(a); s1(2) Administration of Justice Act (AJA) 1960**
Civil	Court of Appeal	**s1(1) Administration of Justice (Appeals) Act (AJAA) 1934**
	High Court ('Leapfrog')	**ss12–15 Administration of Justice Act (AJA) 1969**

The Supreme Court acts as the final court of appeal for all civil cases and criminal cases from England, Wales, and Northern Ireland. In civil matters, the Supreme Court also hears appeals from Scotland; however, in criminal matters, the highest court in the land in Scotland is the High Court of Justiciary and criminal appeals will never be heard from Scotland in the UK Supreme Court.

The Supreme Court will only hear cases which have been designated as a 'matter of general public importance' and they consider that such a case ought to be heard by the Court.

Looking for extra marks?

In recent times, the Supreme Court has been criticized for 'overstepping the mark' in light of the decisions it has reached involving constitutional matters. Particularly, following the decision of the Supreme Court in 2019 that Parliament was unlawfully prorogued (see Chapter 3), there have been numerous calls to take action in relation to the highest court of the land. Some commentators have contended that the Court be abolished (see comments of Martin Howe QC on www.lawyersforbritain.org) or for the justices of the Court to be elected to their posts. Consider the following three decisions and assess where you stand on this matter: has the Court overstepped the mark?

- ***R (Miller) v The Prime Minister*** **(2019)**—Supreme Court rules that Parliament was unlawfully prorogued (see Chapter 3 for more details). ➔

- R (Privacy International) v Investigatory Powers Tribunal (2019)—Supreme Court rules that the Investigatory Powers Tribunal (IPT) is subject to judicial review by the High Court, despite an express legislative statement to the contrary in the **Regulation of Investigatory Powers Act 2000, s67(8)**.
- *R (UNISON) v Lord Chancellor* (2017)—Supreme Court rules that a Fees Order introduced to Employment Tribunal hearing and appeals by the Lord Chancellor was unlawful (see below under 'Employment Tribunal' for more details).

The legislative routes to the Supreme Court vary according to the court and the area of law. Table 2.11 sets out the routes of appeal to the Supreme Court.

The Supreme Court consists of 12 judges, known as **'Justices of the Supreme Court'** (**s23(6) CRA 2005**). They are led by a President and a Deputy President. Substantive appeals are generally heard by five justices, although it can sit in larger panels, so long as there is an odd number of justices (**s42(1)(a) CRA 2005**).

Looking for extra marks?

Look up and remember the names of the key judicial officers at the present moment. Key names to research include the holder of the office of the Lord Chief Justice, the President and Deputy President of the Supreme Court, and the Master of the Rolls. This is a simple and easy way to demonstrate to the examiner that you are aware of the key personnel in the legal system and the power they hold.

The Supreme Court website has published the criteria used to determine whether the Court will sit in panels of more than five. They are:

- if the court is being asked to depart, or may decide to depart from, a previous decision;
- a case of high constitutional importance (11 justices sat in the ***R (Miller) v The Prime Minister* (2019)**);
- a case of great public importance;
- a case where a conflict that arises between decisions in the House of Lords, Judicial Committee of the Privy Council, and/or the Supreme Court has to be reconciled;
- a case raising an important point in relation to the ECHR.

European and international courts

Privy Council of the United Kingdom

Governed by the **Judicial Committee Act 1833**, the Privy Council (formally known as the Judicial Committee of the Privy Council) hears appeals from 23 Commonwealth countries and four independent republics, which formed part of the former colonial empire. The Court is composed of the same justices that appear in the Supreme Court. Given this composition, the Privy Council sits in the same building as the Supreme Court. The Privy Council does not have any appellate capacity within the English legal system. The impact of Privy Council judgments on domestic courts is considered in Chapter 4.

Court of Justice of the European Union

Based in Luxembourg, the **Court of Justice of the European Union** (**CJEU**, formerly known, but still referred to, as the European Court of Justice (ECJ)) has jurisdiction to make rulings interpreting EU law. The CJEU is composed of one judge from each of the Member States, together with a number of Advocates General who advise on law only.

The CJEU's role under the **Treaty on the Functioning of the European Union (TFEU)** is 'to ensure that in the interpretation and application of the Treaties the law is observed'. **Article 267 TFEU** states that the CJEU has jurisdiction to give rulings on interpretation of the TFEU and the acts of EU institutions. English courts can make an 'Article 267 reference' to the CJEU on matters of EU law. See Chapter 5 for more information on the CJEU and other EU institutions.

European Court of Human Rights

The **European Court of Human Rights (ECtHR)**, which sits in Strasbourg, has jurisdiction over all cases involving the interpretation or application of the ECHR. Such rights can be enforced in our own law as a result of the **Human Rights Act (HRA) 1998**, which transposed the Convention into domestic law.

Tribunals and other courts

Tribunals

Tribunals can best be described as adjudicative bodies which apply laws and rules to a case in order to resolve disputes between individuals and the state. Originally established by Parliament on an ad hoc basis to enable individuals to challenge decisions of state officials which were outside the formal court system, tribunals are now an established and unified element of the civil justice system. By way of the **Tribunals, Courts and Enforcement Act (TCEA) 2007**, a simplified two-tiered statutory framework of tribunals was created. These were:

- First-tier Tribunal; and
- Upper Tribunal.

Revision tip

It is technically incorrect to say that tribunals are not a part of the justice system. Indeed they are, but they are outside the formal court structure.

These two tribunals are organized into '**chambers**', each headed by a chamber president. The First-tier Tribunal acts as a court of first instance and consists of seven chambers, such as the Social Entitlement chamber, the Tax chamber, and the Property chamber. The Upper Tribunal acts as the appellate tribunal (on a point of law) and consists of four chambers: the Administrative Appeals chamber, Tax and Chancery chamber, Immigration and Asylum chamber, and Lands chamber. If, however, an individual wishes to appeal from the Upper Tribunal, they must do so in the civil courts, specifically the Court of Appeal and Supreme Court.

Looking for extra marks?

In ***Gilchrist v Revenue and Customs Commissioners*** **(2014)**, the Tax and Chancery chamber ruled that the Upper Tribunal is not bound by decisions of the High Court. Richards J declared that upon enactment of the **TCEA 2007**, the Upper Tribunal became a court of superior record and was not to be bound by decisions of the High Court. Use this knowledge to indicate the sheer importance and weight afforded to the tribunal system by the **TCEA 2007**.

Cases in the tribunals are heard by tribunal judges who are led by the Senior President of Tribunals. In broad terms, there are two types of tribunals:

- those which resolve disputes between the individual and the state, for example the Asylum Support Tribunal; and
- those which regulate disputes between private parties, for example the Employment Tribunal.

For a full list of tribunals in England and Wales, see www.judiciary.gov.uk.

Employment Tribunal

Despite the unification in the **TCEA 2007**, the Employment Tribunal (ET) remains outside of the unified tribunal structure. Employment Tribunals are governed by the **Employment Tribunals Act 1996**, which identifies the jurisdiction, membership, and procedure of the ETs. The ETs, as the name suggests, deal with disputes involving workers and their labour rights. Such disputes often involve contentious terms of employment, dismissal claims, and redundancy payments. Discrimination claims are also within the jurisdiction of the ETs by way of the **Equality Act 2010**; matters such as sex discrimination and gender pay have been particularly newsworthy in recent years. For example, on 10 January 2020 Samira Ahmed, a television presenter, won a claim for sex discrimination in the Employment Tribunal on account of the pay gap between herself and her male counterparts (***Ahmed v BBC (2020)***).

Appeals are made to the Employment Appeal Tribunal (EAT) on a point of law, and further appeals to the Court of Appeal and Supreme Court. As an alternative to the tribunal structure, a judicial mediation scheme is available to bring the parties together before an employment judge for a mediation case management discussion. The judge remains neutral and seeks to assist the parties to resolve the dispute between themselves. The Advisory, Conciliation and

Arbitration Service (ACAS) also offers a voluntary arbitration process in relation to unfair dismissal claims as an alternative to the tribunals.

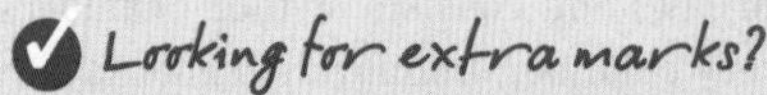

Tribunal fees have been a controversial matter since the introduction of the **Employment Tribunals and the Employment Appeal Tribunal Fees Order 2013** ('the Fees Order'). Prior to that Order, a claimant could bring proceedings in an ET and appeal to the EAT without paying any fee. In ***R (UNISON) v Lord Chancellor*** **(2017)**, UNISON brought a judicial review claim on the ground that the Fees Order unlawfully prevents or restricts access to justice. Whilst the lower courts dismissed the claim of UNISON, the Supreme Court unanimously allowed the appeal, ruling that the Fees Order was unlawful and quashed the Order on the basis that that there was a 'real risk that persons will effectively be prevented from having access to justice', and that the degree of intrusion was 'greater than is justified by the objectives which the measure is intended to serve'. This case arguably demonstrates an increasing willingness on the part of the Supreme Court to intervene in constitutional matters.

Coroners' Court

The Coroners' Court is not part of the unified court structure administered by HM Courts and Tribunals Service. Instead, as of May 2019, there are 88 separate Coroner Areas in England and Wales, each with their own jurisdiction, and funded by their local authorities. It is for these reasons that Coroners' Courts are often referred to as 'territorial', in the sense that it is the location of the dead body which dictates which coroner has jurisdiction in any particular case. Despite this territorial nature, the coroner system is headed by a Chief Coroner, a role created by the **Coroners and Justice Act (CorJA) 2009**. Under **s1 CorJA 2009**, the Coroners' Court has a duty to conduct an investigation into a person's death if the coroner has reason to suspect that:

(a) the deceased died a violent or unnatural death;
(b) the cause of death is unknown; or
(c) the deceased died while in custody or otherwise in state detention.

As part of an investigation, a coroner must undertake an 'inquest' (**s6 CorJA 2009**). The general rule under **s7(1)** is that a jury is not required for an inquest. However, by **s7(2)**, an inquest into a death must be held with a jury if the senior coroner has reason to suspect that the deceased died while in custody or otherwise in state detention, and that either the death was a violent or unnatural one, or the cause of death is unknown, or that the death resulted from an act or omission of a police officer, or a member of a service police force, in the purported execution of the officer's or member's duty as such, or that the death was caused by a notifiable accident, poisoning, or disease. In addition, by **s7(3)** an inquest may be held with a jury if the senior coroner considers that there is sufficient reason for doing so.

Court of Protection

The Court of Protection is a specialist court, established under the **Mental Capacity Act (MCA) 2005**. The Court is a supreme court of record and is treated in the same vein as the

High Court in terms of authority. The role of the Court of Protection is to make specific decisions, or appoint other people to make decisions (known as 'deputies') on behalf of individuals who lack the capacity to do so themselves under the **MCA 2005**. Such decisions include property matters and matters of health and welfare. The Central Registry sits at Archway in North London, as well as a number of regional courts across England and Wales. Cases are heard by district, circuit, and High Court judges. Hearings are normally in private, but certain hearings may allow for media attendance.

Online courts and the future

Technology and the world around us continue to modernize. Despite this so-called 'digital boom', the English courts have been slow to accept the changes, with a continuing unwillingness to change their procedures. Many spectators continue to baulk at the sight of stacks upon stacks of lever-arch files bound in pink tape, bulging at the sides.

Despite popular belief, in both the criminal and civil setting there has been a remarkable (and often reluctant) increase in the use of technology over the years. At the start of 2016, the government announced a system of 'digital by default' whereby both the civil and criminal courts would become 'paperless'. The government commented that it was committed to investing £675 million in modernizing the legal system by going digital, a number that shocked many in the legal profession. This investment would appear futile, however, given the closure of court buildings left, right, and centre across the UK. As a result, the government had little choice but to consider new ways of dealing with individuals and their legal issues.

In the criminal context, the then **Director of Public Prosecutions (DPP)**, Alison Saunders, appeared content with the idea of 'e-bundles' to reduce the use of paper and to speed up criminal trials.

Likewise in civil cases, and as a result of the final report of the Civil Courts Structure Review (published in July 2016) by Briggs LJ, the proposal of an 'Online Court', allowing for disputes to be resolved by the courts in an online and interactive fashion, appears to be an element of our not-so-distant legal future (expected April 2020).

The use of information and communication technology (ICT) in **alternative dispute resolution (ADR)** has developed radically in recent years. Online dispute resolution (ODR), also known as internet dispute resolution (iDR) or electronic ADR (eADR), allows for disputes and disagreements to be resolved in an online setting. Techniques such as e-negotiation, e-mediation, and e-arbitration are commonly employed to resolve matters across a range of issues, such as sale of goods and personal injury. In the private sector, these techniques have been successfully operated for a number of years by such corporations as eBay, Cybersettle, and Modria, to name a few. eBay, in particular, handles over 60 million disputes each and every year using their own ODR with an e-negotiation focused approach.

In his Final Report, Briggs LJ observes that it remains 'practically inevitable' for the future to involve the creation of a single online portal for the issue and conduct of all court proceedings. Such creation would be a sign of moving with the times, but whether such a move is at the cost of justice to those involved is a matter yet to be seen. There remains a number of 'sticking points' that have been raised by those in practice that any pilot stage will need to bear in mind. For example, there is a need to ensure that costs are still awarded to allow legal professionals to remain involved in their client's or potential client's affairs and to have computers available in court buildings in order to allow those without access to technology a chance to have access to justice.

Key debates

Topic	Creation of the Supreme Court
Academic	Kate Malleson
Viewpoint	Argues that the introduction of the Supreme Court is of an 'evolutionary nature' as opposed to a revolution and recounts that such a constitutional change is likely to 'be marked by continuity rather than radical change'.
Source	Kate Malleson, 'The Evolving Role of the Supreme Court' [2011] PL 724, 771

Topic	Use of the County Court
Academic	John Baldwin
Viewpoint	Argues that litigants who used the County Court system were 'generally satisfied' due to the informal and layman nature of the court's operations.
Source	John Baldwin, 'Litigants' Experiences of Adjudication in the County Courts' (1999) 18 Civil Quarterly Review 12, 14

Topic	Classification of courts
Academic	Alisdair Gillespie and Siobhan Weare
Viewpoint	Argues that 'In practice it is rarely necessary to classify the courts and instead a distinction is drawn between the types of justice. Some would argue that there are three types of justice systems: criminal, civil, and family, but in reality, the distinction is between two: civil and criminal. Accordingly, it can be said that the need for classification, at least in practice, is perhaps questionable.'
Source	Alisdair Gillespie and Siobhan Weare, *The English Legal System* (7th edn, Oxford University Press 2019) 195

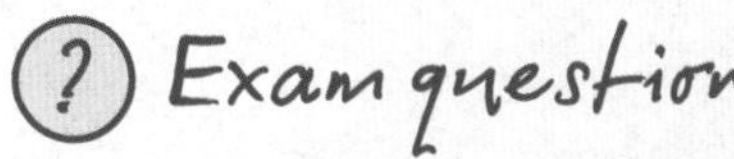

Essay question

'The classification of courts in England and Wales is a pointless exercise. We have criminal courts and civil courts and that is the end of the matter.'

Critically discuss this statement with reference to the court structure, classification, and functions of the court.

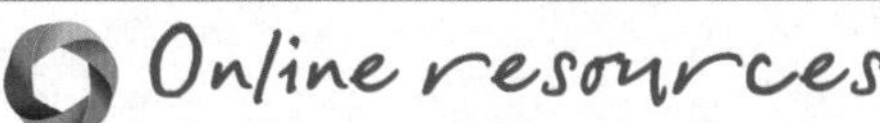

For an outline answer to this essay question, as well as multiple-choice questions and interactive key cases, please visit the online resources.

#3

Sources of Law I: Domestic Legislation

Key facts

- Legislation is the most authoritative source of law and for the most part cannot be challenged by the courts. The courts do, however, have the power to interpret legislation that is unclear or ambiguous.
- Legislation can be divided into **primary** and **secondary legislation**. Primary sources of legislation are known as Acts of Parliament whilst secondary legislation can consist of **statutory instruments** and byelaws, for example.
- Domestic legislation is created by Parliament, which consists of the House of Commons, the House of Lords, and the Monarch. A bypass procedure exists where the House of Commons can pass legislation without approval of the House of Lords.
- The **European Communities Act 1972** and the **Human Rights Act 1998** have had a significant impact on domestic legislation since their introduction. The effect of these sources of law may be questioned in light of Brexit.

Chapter overview

Legislation in England and Wales

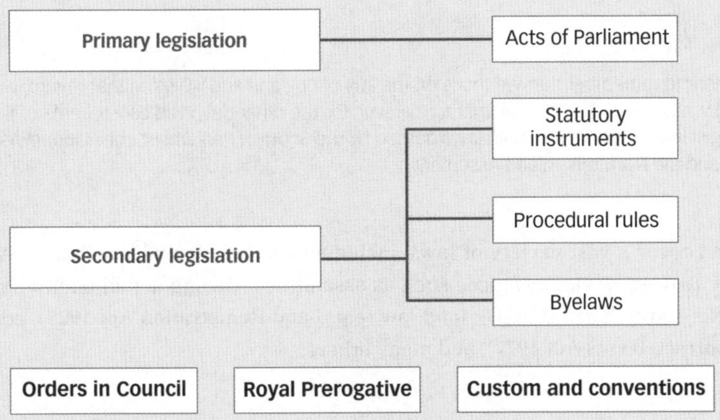

Pre-eminence of legislation

Although England and Wales can be described as a common law system, the majority of laws in the jurisdiction are now covered by legislation passed by Parliament. Traditionally, the common law, i.e. case law, was the most important source of law, given that almost all laws were found in previous judgments. There are now few laws that are contained in the common law, the most prominent being the offence of murder, which remains a common law offence. Despite its former dominance, case law has for centuries been, and remains, subordinate to legislation. Where there is a conflict between the common law and statute, the latter prevails. This is as a result of the principle of parliamentary supremacy (see later in this chapter).

Domestic legislation is helpfully divided into:

- primary legislation; and
- secondary legislation.

There are certain sources of law that fall outside the definition of 'legislation'. These are customs and conventions which, although of no legal force, are to be observed in the UK. It thus makes sense to deal with them in this chapter. Prerogative power held by the Monarch shall also be considered. The remainder of this chapter will focus on the various types of legislation and the inherent interpretation required for these forms of legislation.

Primary legislation

Primary legislation takes the form of 'Acts of Parliament', commonly referred to as 'statutes'. The word 'primary' is used to designate the significance of the law as the highest form of UK law.

Revision tip

It is important to remember that we focus on the law of England and Wales; in that regard, we are concerned with Acts of the UK Parliament. However, for the other devolved constituents of the UK, primary legislation refers to the main laws passed by the Scottish Parliament, the National Assembly for Wales, and the Northern Ireland Assembly.

Statutes can cover a vast variety of laws, including criminal law (e.g. **Offences Against the Person Act 1861**—covering offences such as assault occasioning actual bodily harm (ABH) and grievous bodily harm (GBH)), land law (e.g. **Land Registration Act 1925**), contract law (**Unfair Contract Terms Act 1977**), and many others.

Revision tip

Acts of Parliament and statutes are synonymous and are interchangeable; however, do not mix statutes and legislation. Legislation is a much broader term and can include both statutes and other forms of 'secondary' legislation, for example, statutory instruments.

Although statutes are 'typical' in the sense that they contain a title, introductory text etc., statutes are not standardized, as they can come in many lengths. For example, the **Theft Act 1978** contains a mere seven sections, whilst the **Companies Act 2006** contains an overwhelming 1,300 sections.

Statutes that remain either in force or partially in force, dating back to 1801, are available on www.legislation.gov.uk for free.

Revision tip

Do not rely too much upon the government's website: www.legislation.gov.uk. It has been known to be out of date for many different pieces of legislation. You may wish to consult other legal search engines which are available to you as a law student.

Types of legislation

Primary legislation can come in many different forms and may come about in many different ways. Table 3.1 details the most important distinctions.

Table 3.1 Forms of primary legislation

Public vs private vs hybrid legislation		
Public These are **Bills** introduced to Parliament by Members of Parliament (MPs) and concern matters affecting the public as a whole. Most government Bills are public Bills. • **European Communities Act 1972**.	**Private** These are Bills submitted to Parliament by a person or body who requires parliamentary authority to carry out a certain activity or work. This form of legislation is used less often due to the use of statutory instruments. • **Transport for London Act 2016**.	**Hybrid** As the name suggests, these are a mix of public and private Bills. Can be best described as a public Bill that affects a private individual. • **High Speed Rail (London - West Midlands) Act 2017**.

Consolidating vs codifying legislation	
Consolidating Consolidation is best described as when a single statute re-enacts the law as it was contained in numerous different statutes. There is a presumption that such re-enactment does not materially change earlier legislation, but rather brings together the legislation in a 'more convenient, lucid and economical form' (***Farrell v Alexander* (1977)** (Lord Simon)). • **Equality Act 2010**, which consolidated Acts such as the **Equal Pay Act 1970**, the **Sex Discrimination Act 1975**, and the **Race Relations Act 1965**.	**Codifying** Codification is best described as when a single statute places the law, formerly found in the common law, onto a statutory footing. Codification can also take a much broader exercise in codifying law that was previously both statute and common law based. As opposed to consolidating legislation, codifying legislation *may* change the law as it previously stood. • **Sexual Offences Act 2003**, which combined the previous legislation and the common law into one statute. The definition of consent was previously one of common law basis, but is now contained in **s74 2003 Act**.

UK vs devolved legislation *(See Chapter 1 for more detail)*	
UK There is a presumption that all primary forms of legislation will apply solely to England and Wales unless the statute is express as to its application in Scotland or Northern Ireland also.	**Devolved** As a result of the **Government of Wales Act 1998**, the **Scotland Act 1998**, and the **Northern Ireland Act 1998**, each jurisdiction within the UK has a limited power to pass legislation exclusive to its own jurisdiction. The limited competency of each jurisdiction includes legislating on such matters as health and education.

Parliamentary supremacy

Parliamentary supremacy, also known as **parliamentary sovereignty**, is a term used to describe Parliament as the supreme law-making body in the UK. As a result of the **Bill of Rights 1689**, power to create laws was removed from the Monarch acting alone and now is firmly within the remit of a full Parliament.

Albert Dicey in *Introduction to the Study of the Law of the Constitution* (Blackwells 1885) stated that:

> The Principle of Parliamentary Sovereignty means neither more nor less than this: namely, that Parliament . . . has, under the English constitution the right to make or unmake any law whatever; and further that no person or body is recognised by the law . . . as having the right to override or set aside the legislation of Parliament.

Table 3.2 explains what Dicey meant in his conception.

Whether Dicey's conception remains accurate is hotly debated, given the UK's present membership in the European Union (EU) and the European Convention on Human Rights (ECHR). For a more in-depth discussion of Dicey and the concept of parliamentary sovereignty, see Colin Faragher, *Public Law Concentrate* (6th edn, Oxford University Press 2019).

Table 3.2 Dicey's conception

Principle	Explanation
Positive limb	Parliament can create, amend, or remove any piece of legislation it desires.
Negative limb	Parliament cannot be questioned by any individual or body, most specifically the courts.
Continuing sovereignty	Parliament is not bound by its predecessors and cannot bind its successors.

Looking for extra marks?

Parliamentary sovereignty is a matter you will no doubt be assessed on during your Constitutional Law module. However, it is still essential that you understand the importance of parliamentary supremacy when answering questions on legislation. More specifically, although Parliament is supreme, the courts have the power and ability to interpret legislation. One should question the extent to which the courts can and should intervene in the interpretation of legislation.

Effect of the EU on parliamentary sovereignty

As a result of the introduction of the **European Communities Act (ECA) 1972**, the UK formally joined the EU and became subject to the laws of the EU. In particular, **s2(1) ECA 1972** requires all laws of the UK to be subject to EU law. Parliament would appear, therefore, no longer supreme when the matter before it is one of EU law. For more on this, and the UK's withdrawal from the EU, see Chapter 5.

Effect of the Human Rights Act on parliamentary sovereignty

Upon enacting the **Human Rights Act (HRA) 1998**, the UK government transposed the ECHR into our domestic law. According to **s3 HRA 1998**, both primary and subordinate legislation 'so far as it is possible to do so' must be read and given effect to in a way which is compatible with Convention rights. Further, **s19** requires a government minister to declare before a Parliamentary Bill is given its second reading that it is compatible with the **HRA**.

Compared with EU law, which has a great effect on our parliamentary supremacy, the **HRA** does not appear to have such a great effect. This is because the courts do not have the power to strike down legislation (except secondary legislation), but simply have the power to declare legislation 'incompatible'. For more on this, see Chapter 5.

Judicial review

Dicey's conception is particularly called into question in relation to judicial review proceedings. Whilst primary legislation is not subject to judicial review and cannot be challenged, secondary legislation is, and can be effectively challenged by the courts.

Judicial review has been described by Hilaire Barnett, in *Constitutional and Administrative Law* (11th edn, Routledge 2015), as representing 'the means by which the courts control the exercise of governmental power'. The most common challenge to delegated legislation is on the grounds that the legislation is *ultra vires*. *Ultra vires* can be defined as 'acting beyond and exceeding legal powers' (***ex parte Leech* (1993)**). Often, this is where the delegated body has then sub-delegated their role to another individual or body. Unless such sub-delegation is permitted by the parent Act, this action will be considered *ultra vires*. For a more in-depth discussion of judicial review, see Colin Faragher's *Public Law Concentrate*.

The general principle that Acts of Parliament cannot be challenged by the courts was provided in ***British Railways Board v Pickin* (1974)**. As a result of the ***ex parte Factortame (No. 2)* (1991)** judgment, however, there remains one exception to this rule, namely, where a statute is inconsistent with EU law. ***Factortame (No. 2)*** will be discussed in greater detail in Chapter 5.

Legislative process

Before a piece of law becomes an 'Act of Parliament', it must first go through a specific and detailed legislative procedure (see Figure 3.1). The legislative programme of Parliament will be set out in the Queen's Speech at the opening of Parliament. Prior to receiving **royal assent**,

Primary legislation

Figure 3.1 Legislative procedure

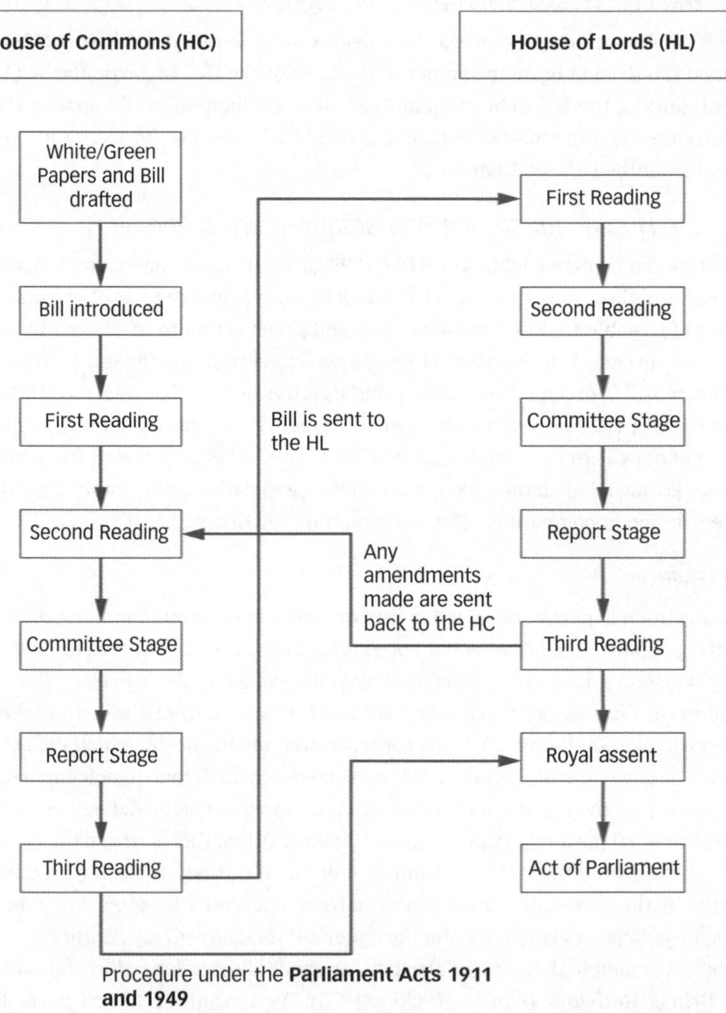

such laws (i.e. draft Acts) are known as 'Bills'. The life of any Bill that has proceeded or is proceeding through Parliament can be found at www.parliament.uk/business/bills-and-legislation.

The introduction of Bills into Parliament can be divided into government Bills and private members' Bills:

- **government Bills**: these are introduced by the government as part of their legislative programme. They are introduced by the relevant minister for that Bill; for example in 2018 the Justice Secretary introduced the Civil Liability Bill, which aimed to lower car insurance premiums. If the government has a majority in Parliament, these Bills will be passed with relative ease.

- **private members' Bills**: these are non-governmental Bills introduced by individual MPs (specifically a backbench MP). The time for this kind of Bill is rather restricted; the majority of which do not become law unless they have the backing of the government. One example of a successful private members' Bill is the **Abortion Act 1967**, which was introduced by backbench MP, David Steel. The Bill had the support of the government and became law.

Below is a brief overview of the stages in the life of a Bill before it becomes an Act of Parliament.

White and Green Papers and drafting the Bill

Before a Bill is introduced into Parliament, it may be preceded by a White Paper or a Green Paper. The differences between the two types of Papers are detailed in Table 3.3.

Table 3.3 White and Green Papers

Description	White Paper	Green Paper
Definition	Policy documents produced by the government that set out their proposals for future legislation. Often accompanied by a draft Bill annexed to the Paper	Consultation documents produced by the government that set out proposals for discussion without any guarantee of legislative action or consideration of the legislative detail
Aim	To provide a basis for further consultation and discussion with interested or affected groups	To allow feedback on the government's policy or legislative proposals to be given by people in and outside of Parliament

The Bill will then be drafted by the parliamentary draughtsman (or more modernly 'draftsman'), officially known as Parliamentary Counsel. According to the Office of the Parliamentary Counsel, their role is to 'work closely with departments to translate policy into clear, effective and readable law'. The government department responsible for the Bill will work closely with the draughtsman.

Introduction of the Bill

Figure 3.1 details the procedure for legislation as though the Bill was introduced in the House of Commons. This is because most Bills begin their life in the House of Commons. Please note, however, that a government Bill can be introduced into either the House of Commons or the House of Lords. On the occasion that the Bill begins in the House of Lords, simply switch the headings in Figure 3.1.

You can tell where a Bill was first introduced by the letters that follow the Bill's name, i.e. (HC) and (HL). There are a few exceptions to the general rule that Bills may start in either House; these exceptions are detailed in Figure 3.2.

Figure 3.2 Where to introduce Bills

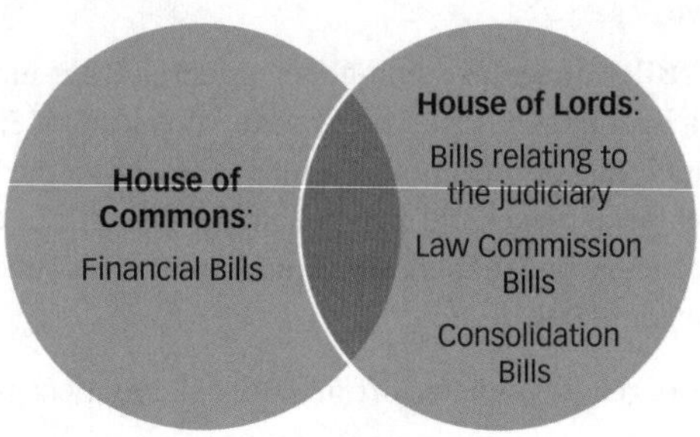

First Reading

The First Reading is simply a formality. The title of the Bill is read by the Clerk of the House, a date is fixed for the Second Reading, and the Bill is ordered to be printed. There is no debate of the content of the Bill at this stage (the purpose of the First Reading is to merely note the existence of the Bill). Conventionally, the Second Reading does not normally take place before two weekends have passed.

Second Reading

The Second Reading involves the main debate on the principles of the Bill. The responsible minister opens the Reading and sets out the policy objectives of the Bill, before the debate which then ensues. A vote is generally taken on the Bill at the end of the Reading as to whether the Bill ought to proceed. If so, the Bill will then move to a Standing Committee.

Committee Stage

Once a Bill has passed through the Second Reading, it will then proceed to the Standing Committee. The Committee is not responsible for considering the desirability of the Bill in principle, as that has already been approved by the House during the Second Reading. Their role is to examine the provisions of the Bill, in particular its wording, and comment on their workability. Votes are taken on each clause in the Bill and any amendments moved upon.

> **Looking for extra marks?**
>
> Examiners like detail. It shows that you understand the concept and that you are comfortable with the area of law. When discussing the legislative procedure a Bill may take, you could discuss the composition of a committee. The Committee is composed of not less than 16 and not more than 50 members chosen by the 'Committee of Selection'. The members are chosen according to their particular interest or expertise in the subject matter of the Bill. The Chair of each Standing Committee is selected by the Speaker of the House of Commons from a panel of chairmen. Each committee will be given a name in accordance with the Bill. For example, if a Bill is entitled the Musical Theatre Bill, the committee will be named the Musical Theatre Committee.

Report Stage (also known as 'Consideration in the Commons')

Once the Committee has agreed a draft Bill, including any amendments made, it returns it to the House in the form of a report. Only amendments made are tabled for discussion (if there are no amendments, this is merely a formality stage). The government may reject the changes made at Committee stage and may make further changes. The amended Bill will be reprinted and voted upon by the House.

Third Reading

This is the final vote on the Bill. The Bill may be debated (albeit briefly) one final time during the Third Reading. No amendments are made at this stage; it being a general formality before the Bill is formally handed over to the other House. Once the Third Reading is complete, the Bill is then fastened with a green ribbon and taken to the House of Lords by the Clerk of the House of Commons with a message requesting the Lords to agree with its content.

House of Lords

The Bill is then sent to the second House for its consideration (for our purposes, given that we started in the House of Commons, this second House is the House of Lords). The procedure in the House of Lords mirrors that of the House of Commons and can be described as virtually identical. As with the House of Commons, the Bill will begin with a First Reading and is followed with a debate in the Second Reading. The Bill will then proceed to the Committee stage. Please note that unlike the House of Commons, the Committee stage is generally one involving the whole House. The House will then debate the matter one final time during the Third Reading. At the end of the Third Reading there is a formal motion 'that this Bill do now pass'. If the Bill began in the Commons, it is sent back after Third Reading for consideration of the Lords' amendments, or, if there have been no amendments in the Lords, is sent to the Monarch for royal assent.

Looking for extra marks?

There have been numerous calls over the years for the abolition of the House of Lords, replacing it with a second elected House (akin to the Senate in the USA). Recently, in January 2020, Rebecca Long-Bailey, the Shadow Business Secretary, as part of her campaign to be voted in as the Labour Leader, announced that she would abolish the House of Lords. Such abolishment has been called due to the fact that the House of Lords is an entirely unelected body, the peers who sit in the House remain there until their death, there is a lack of representation for certain ethnic groups, and a gender imbalance. What do you think? Do you think the House of Lords should be abolished? If so, what should it be replaced with?

Consideration of amendments

If amendments are made, the Bill must then return to the House it began in for consideration of the proposed amendments. This process is best described as the 'ping pong' stage, with both Houses attempting to resolve any differences they may have on a particular Bill. It is at this stage that the majority of amendments to the Bill are made. In practice, the House of Lords generally accepts the second proposal from the House of Commons and the Bill proceeds to royal assent; however, if there is a stalemate on a particular clause or the Bill overall, there are three possible consequences of such a stalemate:

1. The Bill dies—this means that the Bill has been rejected by the House of Lords and the House of Commons does not attempt to 'save' the Bill. An example of this is the Fraud (Trials without a Jury) Bill, rejected on 20 March 2007.
2. The parliamentary session expires—this means that the time allowance granted to that Bill has ended. This means that the Bill must die or be started up again in the next parliamentary session; for example, the Prisons and Courts Bill, which was abandoned in 2017 as a result of the call for a general election.
3. The House of Commons proceeds without approval of the House of Lords via the **Parliament Acts 1911 and 1949**.

Looking for extra marks?

Although the first two of these consequences are self-explanatory, don't simply leave your answer with a full stop after 'the Bill dies'. Take your answer that one step further. What does it mean for a Bill to die? Can the Bill be revamped? What exactly does it mean for a parliamentary session to expire? Answers to these questions will provide the greater level of detail required for those top marks.

English Votes for English Laws (EVEL)

On 22 October 2015, the House of Commons approved changes to the Standing Orders to introduce a new legislative procedure for enacting Bills that apply only to English law, or English and Welsh law. This procedure is known as 'English votes for English laws' (EVEL). This process affects all government Bills, with a number of exceptions, such as consolidation Bills and private members' Bills. This change was justified in response to the so-called, 'West Lothian Question': the situation where English MPs were unable to vote on matters which have been devolved from Westminster, but Scottish, Welsh, and Northern Ireland MPs were still able to vote on matters relating only to England. The process for EVEL can be demonstrated through Figure 3.3.

Parliament Acts 1911 and 1949

These Acts provide a process by which the House of Commons can bypass the approval of the House of Lords and present a Bill to the Monarch for royal assent. The **1911 Act** provided that the House of Lords may only delay a money Bill for one month and that after this has elapsed the Bill may receive royal assent without the authority of the House of Lords (**s1**), and where a Bill had failed to gain parliamentary support in at least two successive parliamentary sessions (years) and then after its rejection for the third time, the Bill could receive royal assent without the approval of the House of Lords (**s2**).

Figure 3.3 The EVEL process

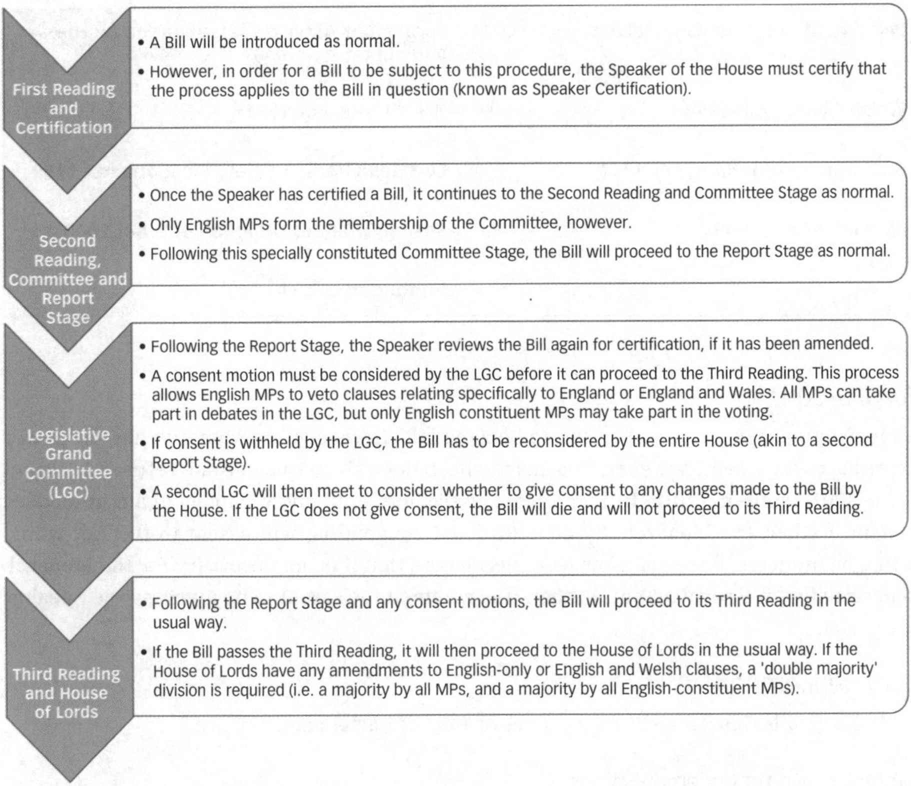

First Reading and Certification

- A Bill will be introduced as normal.
- However, in order for a Bill to be subject to this procedure, the Speaker of the House must certify that the process applies to the Bill in question (known as Speaker Certification).

Second Reading, Committee and Report Stage

- Once the Speaker has certified a Bill, it continues to the Second Reading and Committee Stage as normal.
- Only English MPs form the membership of the Committee, however.
- Following this specially constituted Committee Stage, the Bill will proceed to the Report Stage as normal.

Legislative Grand Committee (LGC)

- Following the Report Stage, the Speaker reviews the Bill again for certification, if it has been amended.
- A consent motion must be considered by the LGC before it can proceed to the Third Reading. This process allows English MPs to veto clauses relating specifically to England or England and Wales. All MPs can take part in debates in the LGC, but only English constituent MPs may take part in the voting.
- If consent is withheld by the LGC, the Bill has to be reconsidered by the entire House (akin to a second Report Stage).
- A second LGC will then meet to consider whether to give consent to any changes made to the Bill by the House. If the LGC does not give consent, the Bill will die and will not proceed to its Third Reading.

Third Reading and House of Lords

- Following the Report Stage and any consent motions, the Bill will proceed to its Third Reading in the usual way.
- If the Bill passes the Third Reading, it will then proceed to the House of Lords in the usual way. If the House of Lords have any amendments to English-only or English and Welsh clauses, a 'double majority' division is required (i.e. a majority by all MPs, and a majority by all English-constituent MPs).

The **1949 Act** amended the **1911 Act** to the extent that the threshold in **s2** was reduced to one year from two. This means that a Bill, since 1949, must simply fail after it has been entered in two consecutive Parliaments and would now be passed, without House of Lords approval, after the second, rather than third, defeat.

The **1911** and **1949 Acts** apply generally to all Bills before Parliament except for:

- Bills which intend to prolong the length of a Parliament beyond five years;
- private Bills;
- Bills sent to the Lords less than a month before the end of the parliamentary session; and
- Bills which are introduced in the Lords.

For a discussion on the validity of the **Parliament Act 1949** and the decision of the House of Lords in ***Jackson v HM Attorney General* (2005)**, see Colin Faragher's *Public Law Concentrate*.

Table 3.4 details the use of the Parliament Acts throughout their existence.

Table 3.4 Use of the Parliament Acts 1911 and 1949

Parliament Act 1911 (Original Act)	Parliament Act 1911 (as amended by the Parliament Act 1949)
Welsh Church Act 1914	War Crimes Act 1991
Government of Ireland Act 1914	European Parliamentary Elections Act 1999
Parliament Act 1949	Sexual Offences (Amendment) Act 2000
–	Hunting Act 2004

Royal assent

All legislation requires royal assent to become law. In theory, the Monarch has the power to refuse royal assent; however, this has not been done since Queen Anne refused to assent to the **1707 Scottish Militia Bill**, and looks extremely unlikely to happen again in modern Britain. Rather, the Monarch, by constitutional convention, will assent to the Act whilst acting on ministerial advice. However, please note that it is not necessary for the Monarch to personally give royal assent. Rather, it is common for assent to be given by the Speaker of the House.

Commencement

Table 3.5 details the commencement dates of Acts of Parliament.

Table 3.5 Commencement dates

Statutory provision	Commencement
No express provision	Deemed to come into force on the day (which includes the whole day) that it receives royal assent (***Tomlinson v Bullock* (1879)**)
Specified date	Deemed to come into force on a date specified within the Act itself
'With effect from a date to be appointed'	Deemed as 'not yet in force' until the Act, or a particular section of the Act, has been enacted via a statutory instrument

Criticism exists for use of 'appointed date' sections in an Act; there is often difficulty in identifying whether a particular section is in force or not. There are numerous examples of statutes that come into force later, often much later, than the date upon which royal assent was given. There are also sections that have never been brought into force or only partially so. For example:

- **Youth Justice and Criminal Evidence Act 1999, s28**—royal assent was given in July 1999; **s28**, in particular, is still not fully in force;
- **Human Rights Act 1998**—royal assent was given in November 1998 but only came into force via statutory instrument in October 2000.

Layout of a statute

All Acts of Parliament, and the majority of statutory instruments, take the same format and layout. The list below demonstrates the standard layout of an Act of Parliament. We shall use the **Sale of Goods Act (SGA) 1979** as an example throughout:

1. **Royal Coat of Arms**: all statutes must receive royal assent. Thus, when any legislation is passed the Royal Coat of Arms is affixed to the statute to act as a seal for the legislation.
2. **Short title**: most statutes will be referred to by their short title; however, there must be an express statutory provision stating what the short title is. In the **SGA 1979**, the short title is contained within the final section of the Act (**s69(1)**).
3. **Chapter number/citation**: modern statutes are governed by the **Parliament Numbering and Citation Act 1962**, which provides that each statute will be cited according to the number enacted during that parliamentary session (i.e. statutes are numbered chronologically within the year they are enacted; numbering re-starting each year). The **SGA 1979 (C.54)**—this means that the **SGA** was the 54th statute to be created in the year 1979 (the 'C' stands for 'Chapter').
4. **Long title**: this serves as a description of the Act of Parliament and is contained towards the start of the Act. The long title for the **SGA 1979** is 'An Act to consolidate the law relating to the sale of goods'.
5. **Date of royal assent**: the date of royal assent shall be affixed to each copy of the Act. Royal assent was given to the **SGA 1979** on 6 December 1979.
6. **Enacting 'formula'**: this is an extremely formal way of stating how the Act is to come into force. The general formula is as follows:

> BE IT ENACTED by the Queen's most Excellent Majesty, by and with the advice and consent of the Lords Spiritual and Temporal, and Commons, in this present Parliament assembled, and by the authority of the same, as follows—.

7. **Main body**: the main body of the Act is divided into sections, sub-sections, paragraphs, and sub-paragraphs. It provides the substantive law that the Act sets out to achieve. Dependent on their length, many statutes will be divided into chapters, parts, and headings.
8. **Commencement**: the commencement date will feature within the Act also. Generally, this is placed towards the end of the Act; however, some Acts may include the

commencement towards the start. In the **SGA 1979**, the commencement is situated in the last section (**s64(2)**), which states, 'This Act comes into force on 1 January 1980.'

9. **Schedules**: many statutes have one or more Schedules at the end. These Schedules often contains matters such as definitions, further provisions outside the main body, detailed and minor amendments to other pieces of legislation, and repeals of pre-existing legislation.
10. **Explanatory Notes**: post-1999, most Acts include Explanatory Notes. According to the Office of Public Sector Information:

> The purpose of these Explanatory Notes is to make the Act of Parliament accessible to readers who are not legally qualified and who have no specialised knowledge of the matters dealt with. They are intended to allow the reader to grasp what the Act sets out to achieve and place its effect in context.

For statutory instruments, such notes are known as 'Explanatory Memorandums'.

Reading legislation

As a hopeful lawyer, practising or not, you need to be aware of what exactly each part of a statute means. As an example, **s90 Companies Act 2006** concerns the re-registration of a private company as a public company. **Section 90** is divided into several parts, as shown in Table 3.6.

Table 3.6 How to read legislation

How written	How spoken
90	Section
(1)	Sub-section
(c)	Paragraph
(i)	Sub-paragraph
s90(1)(c)(i) = Section ninety, sub-section one, paragraph c, sub-paragraph one.	

Revision Lip

Avoid careless mistakes when referring to certain sources of law. The most common mistakes by students, which can annoy examiners, are the following:

- Act of Parliament—Whenever you refer to an Act in the context of legislation, it always has a capital A. Likewise, a Bill of Parliament has a capital B in the context of legislation.
- When referring to Parliament as the branch of government, ensure you spell it with a capital P.

Secondary legislation

Also known as delegated legislation, or subordinate legislation, this source of law is the most common instrument for implementing change within the UK. Parliament has neither the time, the resources, nor the expertise to deal with certain matters. It is for these reasons that the majority of legislation is made outside of Parliament.

Revision tip

When reading this section of the text, consider the advantages that secondary legislation has over primary legislation, and likewise, consider the disadvantages to using secondary legislation.

ADVANTAGES:

- It saves time.
- It is produced with specialist knowledge.
- Control is exercised by Parliament.

DISADVANTAGES:

- There is lack of oversight.
- There is lack of publicity.
- It is undemocratic.
- There is a risk of sub-delegation.

Looking for extra marks?

In an essay-style question, consider the use of the term 'subordinate legislation'. This term is used to denote that the courts can challenge the legislation and set it aside (something they cannot do with primary legislation). However, given that the majority of legislation passed in England and Wales is secondary, is it still correct to refer to such legislation as 'subordinate'?

Accordingly, Parliament may delegate such powers, through an Act of Parliament (known as the 'parent' or 'enabling' Act) to other bodies and institutions to implement. Such bodies often include the Privy Council, government ministers, local authorities, and other regulatory agencies. The three main types of secondary legislation are statutory instruments, statutory rules, and byelaws.

Statutory instruments

Statutory instruments (SIs) are regulated by the **Statutory Instruments Act 1946**, which lays down the procedural requirements necessary for their making.

Statutory instruments are now the most common form of legislation in the UK. Table 3.7 details the number of SIs when compared with Acts of Parliament as of the end of 2019. The figure is provided by www.legislation.gov.uk.

Table 3.7 Number of SIs compared with statutes

Year	Acts of Parliament (public and private)	Statutory instruments
2019	31	1408
2018	37	1387
2017	37	1289
2016	24	1243
2015	37	2058
2014	32	3480
2013	40	3290
2012	25	3327
2011	25	3131
2010	46	2967

As is obvious from Table 3.7, the majority of legislation passed during a parliamentary session is done by SI.

Like Acts of Parliament, SIs are set titles and SI numbers (also known as reference or 'running' numbers). You can spot an SI by the following example:

Criminal Justice Act 2003 (Categories of Offences) Order 2004, SI 2004/3346
The SI number '2004/3346' means that this SI is the 3,346th statutory instrument in the year 2004.

Statutory rules

The Rule Committees have delegated power to make procedural rules for the courts. As with Orders in Council (see below, under its own heading), although such rules do take the form of SIs, it is useful to separate them out due to the different institutions responsible for their creation. These rules state the procedure that must be followed when commencing a case in a particular court, the presentation of evidence at trial, and the routes for appeal.

Table 3.8 details the committees and their relevant procedural rules.

Table 3.8 Procedural rules and their committees

Rule committees	Procedural rules
Civil Procedure Rule Committee	Civil Procedure Rules (CPR)
Criminal Procedure Rule Committee	Criminal Procedure Rules (CrimPR)
Family Procedure Rule Committee	Family Procedure Rules (FPR)

Each of the procedural rules is accompanied by relevant Practice Directions (PDs), which offer further guidance and assistance on particular rules, an example being **r52 CPR 1998**, which concerns civil appeals. The rule provides a general procedure for appeals but is accompanied by five PDs, including **Practice Direction C**, which concerns specifically 'Appeals to the Court of Appeal'.

Byelaws

Byelaws (often seen written as 'by-laws') are a form of delegated legislation that allow local authorities to exercise power for the regulation, administration, and management of their local affairs. Byelaws are generally only created when there is no legislation dealing with particular matters of concern to local people. Byelaws are created under the **Local Government Act 1972**; however, they can only come into force once they have been affirmed by the relevant/appropriate minister. Common byelaws include matters such as waste collection, public car parking, littering offences, and many others.

Looking for extra marks?

Give plenty of examples when making a particular statement. For example, local councils may make byelaws regulating:

- public bathing (**s231 Public Health Act 1936**);
- Hackney carriages (Black Cabs) (**s68 Town Police Clauses Act 1847**);
- local nature reserves (**ss20, 21, and 106 National Parks and Access to the Countryside Act 1949**).

Orders in Council

The Privy Council may make an Order in Council. Such Orders are issued by and with the advice of the Privy Council and are approved in person by the Monarch.

Orders in Council

****

Revision tip

Do not confuse Orders **in** Council with Orders **of** Council. The latter are decisions of the Privy Council, which have the force of law. Unlike Orders **in** Council, Orders **of** Council do not require personal approval by the Monarch and can be made by the 'Lords of the Privy Council' (i.e. government ministers).

Orders in Council are divided into two broad categories, statutory and prerogative. According to the website of the Privy Council:

- Statutory Orders are made under any of the numerous powers contained in Acts of Parliament which give Her Majesty a power to make Orders;
- Prerogative Orders are made under the inherent power of the Crown to act on matters for which Parliament has not legislated.

This distinction is essential, as it will determine whether the Order is a form of primary or secondary legislation. As a result of **s1(1) Statutory Instruments Act 1946**, every power to make a Statutory Order in Council conferred by an Act of Parliament passed after 1 January 1948 shall be known as an SI. This means that Statutory Orders in Council are a form of secondary legislation and can be challenged by the courts. Examples of Statutory Orders in Council include:

- the **Burial Act 1853**, which provides that Her Majesty in Council may restrain the opening of new burial grounds, and order discontinuance of burials in specified places;
- the **Naval and Marine Pay and Pensions Act 1865**, which provides Her Majesty in Council the ability to determine the pay of the Navy, subject to such restrictions, conditions, and provision as directed by the Council.

A Prerogative Order in Council, however, has been declared by the House of Lords in ***R (Bancoult) v Secretary of State for Foreign and Commonwealth Affairs* (2008)** as primary legislation, similar to an Act of Parliament, 'in the sense that the legislative power of the Crown is original and not subordinate'. This does not mean, however, that Prerogative Orders are not reviewable by the courts. Rather, Lord Hoffmann at [35] of the judgment makes clear that such Orders remain reviewable by the courts despite their status as a form of primary legislation as it is an act of executive power alone which does not 'offend' the principle of parliamentary sovereignty. As a summary of this rather confusing matter, see Table 3.9.

These prerogative acts were formerly taken by the monarch in person; however, in more modern times, these are now taken by relevant ministers. In essence, the use of prerogative powers are now political decisions. The nature of prerogative powers has recently been reviewed by the Supreme Court, following the decision of Prime Minister Boris Johnson to prorogue Parliament. Prorogation of Parliament is an act which brings the current parliamentary session to an end and prepares for a Queen's Speech to formally open the new parliamentary session. Each parliamentary session lasts for around one year, meaning that prorogation is a common occurrence. In 2019, however, the government was successfully challenged over its decision to prorogue Parliament in ***R (Miller) v The Prime Minister* (2019)**. The Supreme Court declared that the advice given by the Prime Minister was justiciable (i.e. capable of being reviewed by the courts) and was also unlawful. The effect of this decision was that Parliament was not lawfully prorogued. This was a significant decision, which has caused much controversy on both sides, most notably from the Conservative Party, which indicated an intention to review the powers of the senior courts. See 'Key cases' below for a more in-depth discussion of ***R (Miller) v The Prime Minister***.

Table 3.9 Orders in Council

	Statutory orders	Prerogative orders
Primary legislation	✗	✔
Secondary legislation	✔	✗
Reviewable by the courts	✔	✔
Made under powers conferred through Acts of Parliament	✔	✗
Made under inherent powers	✗	✔

Customs and conventions

Customs and conventions are unknown to many, given their historic use outside of the more modern era. To this day, both customs and conventions still operate in the UK, and although they are not legally binding or enforceable, provide for a specific manner of operation in a given circumstance. Table 3.10 will assist in understanding these two sources of law.

Table 3.10 Customs and conventions

Type	Meaning	Examples
Customs	A custom is an understanding of a long-standing practice in a particular locality or region. It was defined in the ***Tanistry Case* (1608)** as 'such usage as has obtained the force of law'.	• Fishermen may dry their nets on private land. • Villagers may hold a fair in a certain place (***Wyld v Silver* (1963)**).

Type	Meaning	Examples
Constitutional conventions	A convention is an unwritten understanding about how something should be done.	• The Prime Minister must be a member of the House of Commons and not the Lords.
	Although not legally enforceable, conventions are generally observed.	• The Monarch must invite the party with the largest number of seats in Parliament to form the government. • The Monarch must give assent to legislation passed through Parliament.

Prerogative power

Also referred to as the Royal Prerogative, this historic power is officially vested in the Monarch. Dicey (1885) defined this power as:

> nothing else than the residue of discretionary or arbitrary authority which at any given time is legally left in the hands of the crown. The prerogative is the name of the remaining portion of the Crown's original authority . . . Every act which the executive government can lawfully do without the authority of an Act of Parliament is done in virtue of the prerogative.

Table 3.11 details the most important prerogative powers and divides these powers into domestic and foreign powers.

Table 3.11 Prerogative powers

Domestic powers	Foreign powers
The appointment and dismissal of ministers	Declaration of war
The dissolution of Parliament	Making of treaties

Importantly, the dissolution of Parliament must be distinguished from prorogation of Parliament, previously discussed under 'Orders in Council'. The former brings the parliamentary session to an end, resulting in members of the House of Commons ceasing to be MPs and the holding of a general election. Prorogation, however, brings that current parliamentary session to an end, to allow for the Queen's Speech, before the next parliamentary session begins.

Prior to 2011, the dissolution of Parliament and calling of elections would have been contained within the domestic powers section (see Table 3.11 above); however Parliament enacted the **Fixed-term Parliaments Act 2011**, which set a fixed period of five years before the next general election is to be called unless a motion is passed under **s2** by at least two-thirds of the House of Commons requesting an early election. On 29 October 2019, the Prime Minister, Boris Johnson, succeeded in his fourth attempt to call an early general election for 12 December 2019, with a majority vote of 438 votes to 20. The Conservative Party won 365 of the available seats, scoring a majority of 80 seats. In the Queen's Speech on 19 December 2019, it was read that the government would work to 'repeal the Fixed-term Parliaments Act'; no work has yet been done on this promise.

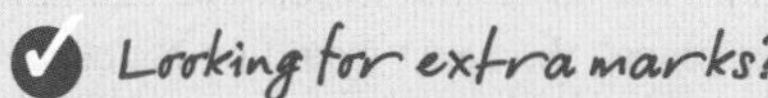

The majority of students can identify which sources of law are characterized as 'secondary legislation'. They can often list the advantages and disadvantages of such secondary sources; however, they may fail to comprehend the control of secondary legislation.

Control of legislation comes in two forms:

- parliamentary control; and
- judicial control.

Parliamentary control requires resolutions before the Houses of Parliament before the legislation can come into force. Parliament may control delegated legislation through the asking of questions, the requirement of publication of delegated legislation, and the removal of power from delegated bodies, should Parliament need to. Judicial control allows the judiciary to declare secondary legislation invalid through judicial review, which allows the courts to challenge delegated legislation on substantive and procedural grounds, as well as grounds of unreasonableness.

Statutory interpretation and rules of language

The courts in their distinct role are responsible for the application of the law, as implemented by the executive and legislature. Sometimes, however, such application is not possible, given the particular wording or language used within the statute. The language may be unclear, ambiguous, or just nonsensical. Bennion, in his seminal work *Bennion on Statute Law* (3rd edn, Longman 1990), listed certain factors which can cause ambiguity and difficulty in the meaning of statute. In our opinion, the three most prominent of these factors are:

- ellipsis (. . .): used when the draughtsman considers the words implied. Whether readers of the text understand what is implied, their own inference may be incorrect;
- unforeseen developments: where words bear little or no meaning in modern understanding of the language, it can often create problems in situations where the older use of the language does not accord with its modern usage;
- broad terms: the use of broad, vague, or generic terms may cause difficulties without further explanation or definition (especially words which may have multiple meanings); for example, the meaning of a 'house' or 'public place' (see later).

Other factors include political uncertainty, omissions, and other drafting errors.

As a result, the courts then take on their secondary function, which is to 'interpret' the law. The phrase often adopted is that the courts aim to find the 'intention or will of Parliament'. However, according to Lord Reid in ***Black-Clawson Ltd v Papierwerke AG* (1975)**, such a statement is 'not quite accurate'. His Lordship goes on to explain that the court is 'seeking the meaning of words, which Parliament used . . . not what Parliament meant but the true meaning of what they said'.

What this means is that the courts are concerned with the interpretation of the words in front of them, as opposed to the thought process behind the use of the words. For example, if a particular piece of statute used the words 'public place', the court would be concerned with interpreting those words and not the will of Parliament in using those words. It is for this reason that Fiona Cownie et al., *The English Legal System in Context* (6th edn, Oxford University Press 2013) argue that courts are not trying to find the true intention of Parliament's words, but rather, are 'selecting what *they decide* is the true meaning of Parliament's words' (emphasis added).

The judiciary interpret the law by use of certain 'workman tools' to assist them. These tools are:

- rules of construction/interpretation;
- rules of language;
- presumptions;
- aids to interpretation.

Revision tip

Statutory interpretation is one of the most popular topics to be examined, as it lends itself to both essay and problem-style questions. Be sure you understand each rule of interpretation and the aids to such construction. Do not ignore or discount a rule without explaining why you are discounting it. Examiners cannot read minds and if you fail to write why the **literal rule** is inappropriate (even if it is obvious), you could lose a substantial number of marks.

We shall now consider each of these tools in detail.

Rules of construction

Although they are referred to as 'rules' of construction/interpretation, such rules are more tools or apparatuses that lawyers and judges can use to interpret a particular statutory provision. Indeed, according to Smith, Bailey, and Gunn (2007) (see 'Key debates' at the end of the chapter), 'to call them "rules" is misleading: it is better to think of them as general approaches'.

The courts are generally free to choose the means they think is most appropriate to interpret the legislation. Although there is no strict priority or hierarchy between the rules, the courts are likely to follow the structure adopted in Figure 3.4

Figure 3.4 Process of the rules

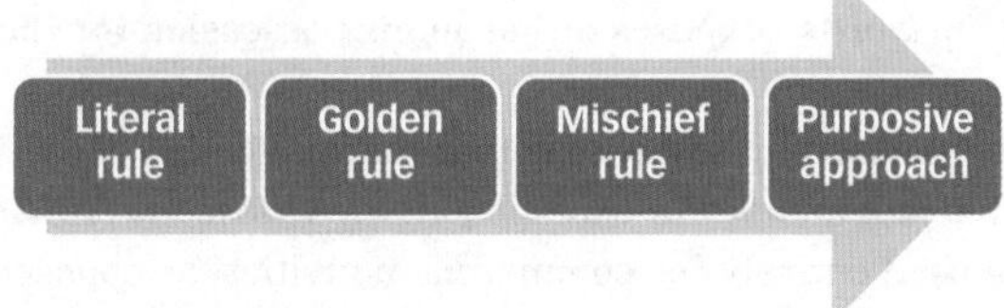

You may question the legitimacy of the power to use any tool of interpretation that the judge considers appropriate in the case. Indeed, Jacqueline Martin, *The English Legal System* (8th edn, Hodder 2016) argues that 'since any rules or approaches can be used, it can be suggested that judges simply use the rule that will give them the result they want in the case'.

Literal rule

The court will always look first at the literal rule. The literal rule requires courts to apply the 'natural and ordinary meaning' of the word (***Pinner v Everett* (1969)**, Lord Reid). In ***Duport Steels Ltd v Sirs* (1980)**, Lord Diplock explained that '[w]here the meaning of the statutory words is plain and unambiguous it is not for the judges to invent fancied ambiguities as an excuse for failing to give effect to its plain meaning'. The use of a dictionary will assist the court in finding the 'ordinary' meaning. Assistance has also been provided in this matter through use of the **Interpretation Act 1978**, which enables judges to seek definitions of words beyond the *Oxford English Dictionary*. See the section 'Aids to interpretation' below for more detail on these.

Often the use of the literal rule leads to harsh and absurd results; however, this is generally irrelevant if it can be made clear that such is the intention of Parliament.

***Whiteley v Chappell* (1868) LR 4 QB 147 (DC)**

FACTS: The defendant had impersonated a dead person and voted in an election in his name. A statute provided that it was an offence to impersonate 'any person entitled to vote' at an election.

HELD: Since the person impersonated was dead, he was not 'entitled to vote', and thus the defendant was not guilty. (In this case, the rule interestingly went against Parliament's intention.)

***Fisher v Bell* [1961] 1 QB 394 (DC)**

FACTS: The defendant advertised a flick-knife in his shop window with a price tag attached to it. The defendant was charged with 'offering for sale' a flick-knife, contrary to **s1(1) Restriction of Offensive Weapons Act 1959**.

HELD: The Divisional Court quashed the defendant's conviction on the basis that goods displayed in a shop window are not considered to be 'offers' according to the law of contract. Rather, they are to be considered 'invitations to treat'. The Divisional Court applied the literal interpretation of the words 'offering for sale' and found no liability could exist against the defendant.

Interestingly, Parliament overruled the decision in ***Fisher v Bell*** in the same year by enacting the **Restriction of Offensive Weapons Act 1961**, which amended the offence in the 1959 Act to include the words: 'exposes or has in his possession for the purpose of sale or hire'.

A point that is often missed by students is that the application of the literal rule can also lead to certain sensible judgments. For example, in ***Day v Hosebay*** **(2012)** the Supreme Court ruled that a building used entirely for commercial activities, as opposed to residential purposes, could not be considered a 'house' for the purpose of an enfranchisement claim under the **Leasehold Reform Act 1967**. That sounds pretty sensible to us, as we would not consider a 'house' to be a building that is not lived in. What do you think?

Golden rule

The literal rule, however, may give rise to ambiguity in interpretation. The golden rule therefore provides that words must be given their plain, ordinary, and literal meaning as far as possible, but only to the extent that they do not:

- produce absurdity; or
- result in a repugnant situation.

Zander (2015) (see 'Key debates' at the end of the chapter) has described the golden rule as 'an unpredictable safety-valve to permit the courts to escape from some of the more unpalatable effects of the literal rule'. Despite this, James Marson and Katy Ferris, *Business Law* (6th edn, Oxford University Press 2020) argue that the golden rule is rarely used so as not to compromise the principle of parliamentary supremacy by having to 'reinterpret what Parliament has already created'.

Adler v George **[1964] 2 QB 7 (DC)**

FACTS: The defendant was obstructing a member of Her Majesty's forces engaged in security detail at a Royal Air Force station. It was an offence under **s3 Official Secrets Act 1920** to obstruct the actions of the armed forces 'in the vicinity of' a prohibited place.

HELD: The offence took place 'in' a prohibited place rather than 'in the vicinity'. As a literal interpretation would be absurd (as it would have resulted in the defendant being discharged), the golden rule was used to give the true effect to the Act so that it read 'in or in the vicinity of'.

Re Sigsworth **[1935] 1 Ch 98 (DC)**

FACTS: This case involved a beneficiary of a dead person's estate. The beneficiary was the son of the benefactor, his mother. The son had murdered his mother in order to inherit her estate.

HELD: Use of the literal rule would give the murderer the right to claim the estate, but such a result would have been against public policy, as it would allow a murderer to profit from his crime. The court thus interpreted the statute by use of the golden rule to avoid the repugnant situation.

Mischief rule

The mischief rule, often known as the rule in ***Heydon's Case* (1584)**, is a tool where the court seeks to find the 'mischief' or the gap that the Act was enacted to deal with or cover. According to ***Heydon's Case***, four questions need to be asked in order to ascertain the mischief of a particular statute:

1. What the common law was before the making of the Act,
2. What the mischief and defect was for which the common law did not provide,
3. What remedy the Parliament hath resolved and appointed to cure the disease of the Commonwealth, and
4. The true reason of the remedy.

***Smith v Hughes* [1960] 1 WLR 830 (HC)**

FACTS: The **Street Offences Act 1959** was passed to stop prostitution in the 'street or public place'. A prostitute solicited from inside her house in an attempt to circumvent the law.

HELD: Under the literal rule, the defendant was not in a 'street or public place', nor was there any absurdity or a situation that was a situation that would be against public policy, though this point is debatable. The courts, therefore, considered the mischief that the Act intended to avoid, namely the mischief of prostitution. The Court, therefore, interpreted that 'street or public place' could include the defendant's home.

***Attorney General v Associated Newspapers Ltd* [1994] 2 AC 238 (HL)**

FACTS: A journalist published a newspaper article citing the reasons as to how a verdict was reached by a jury in a high-profile criminal trial. The information was passed on to the journalist by a third party who had obtained the information from a juror. The newspaper submitted that the **Contempt of Court Act 1981** applied only to 'direct contact by or with the jury'.

HELD: Lord Lowry, in the House of Lords, sought to identify the mischief which the Act was designed to remedy. Attention was given to two sources reaffirming the idea that the Act was designed to protect jury secrecy. On that basis, the argument raised by the newspaper was rejected.

Purposive approach

Based upon, but much wider than, the mischief rule, this approach looks beyond the words of the Act and interprets the legislation in line with the purpose of the Act, not just as a gap that the legislation wished to fill. A useful definition of the **purposive approach** was provided by Lord Simon in ***Maunsell v Olins* (1975)**, where his Lordship stated that:

> The first task of a court of construction is to put itself in the shoes of the draftsman—to consider what knowledge he had and, importantly, what statutory objective he had . . . being thus placed . . . the court proceeds to ascertain the meaning of the statutory language.

Under this approach, even if the result is to depart from the words used, judges will look at the reasons why the statute was passed and its purpose for enactment. This approach is used by the European courts when interpreting EU law, given the often broad and general expressions used by the draughtsman. This approach has more recently found favour with many judges dealing with the interpretation of domestic law. Indeed, in ***R (Quintavalle) v Secretary of State for Health* (2003)**, Lord Steyn in the House of Lords said:

> The pendulum has swung towards purposive methods of construction. This change was not initiated by the teleological approach of European Community jurisprudence, and the influence of European legal culture generally, but it has been accelerated by European ideas.

***Pepper v Hart* [1993] 1 All ER 42 (HL)**

FACTS: Mr Hart was a teacher at Malvern College, a public school. As a benefit of the job, his own children could attend the school at a discounted rate (one-fifth of the regular fees). The Inland Revenue wished to tax this benefit and Mr Hart claimed that no tax was payable given the statement made by a minister in Hansard.

HELD: The House of Lords referred to the statements of the Financial Secretary in Hansard. These statements revealed that the intention of Parliament was to tax employees on the basis of the additional cost to the employer of providing the concession.

***Jones v Tower Boot Co. Ltd* [1996] IRLR 168 (CA)**

FACTS: The complainant, a 16-year-old of mixed ethnic parentage, worked in a shoe factory and during his employment was subjected to both physical and verbal racial abuse from his work colleagues. He sued the company for damages under **s32 Race Relations Act 1976**, which said that the employer shall be held liable for racial discrimination of its employees 'in the course of employment'.

HELD: The company was liable even though it had never authorized the racial abuse and the abuse had nothing to do with the abusers' job, which the company argued meant they were not liable. The court thus gave a broad interpretation of 'in the course of employment' and awarded damages.

Revision tip

The mischief rule and purposive approach are similar in many respects; indeed, it is often said that the purposive approach is merely a more modern version of the mischief rule. Despite this, some subtle differences can be noted. In particular, the purposive approach is wider than the mischief rule in that it does not presuppose that statutes are passed for the purpose of overcoming a particular mischief in the law. The purposive approach looks past the mischief and looks towards parliamentary intention more generally.

Rules of language

In addition to the rules of construction, there are also rules of language which the courts may use. As above, these are tools to help the courts resolve any ambiguity. Steve Wilson et al.,

The English Legal System (4th edn, Oxford University Press 2020) comment that they are 'rules of grammar' as opposed to 'rules of law'. They are known as:

- ***ejusdem generis;***
- ***noscitur a sociis;***
- ***expressio unius est exclusio alterius.***

Table 3.12 explains these terms further.

Table 3.12 Rules of language

Language tool	Literal meaning	Explanation
Ejusdem generis	'Of the same type'	If a word with general meaning follows a list of particular words, then the general word applies exclusively to things of the same type, also known as *genus*, as the particular words. ***Powell v Kempton Park Racecourse*** **(1899)**
Noscitur a sociis	'Known by the company it keeps'	Words in a statute derive meaning from the words surrounding them. Words in a list have related meanings and are to be interpreted in context with the rest of the matters within the list. ***Muir v Keay*** **(1875)**
Expressio unius est exclusio alterius	'To express one thing is to exclude others'	To list a number of specific things within a specified class may be interpreted as impliedly excluding others of the same class. ***R v Inhabitants of Sedgley*** **(1831)**

Powell v Kempton Park Racecourse **[1899] AC 143 (HL)**

FACTS: The defendant was operating an outdoor betting ring. It was an offence to use a 'house, office, room or other place for betting'.

HELD: The words 'house, room, office or other place . . .' was held to refer to a class of indoor places. A racecourse fell outside this class and the defendant was not guilty.

Muir v Keay **(1875) LR 10 QB 594 (HC)**

FACTS: All houses open at night for 'public refreshment, resort and entertainment' required a licence. The defendant ran a café and argued that his café did not need a licence because he did not provide 'entertainment'.

HELD: Entertainment was interpreted as meaning the reception and accommodation of people, as opposed to musical entertainment. The defendant was required to have a licence by law.

R v Inhabitants of Sedgley **(1831) 2 B & Ad 65 (CKB)**
FACTS: A poor rate was levied on owners of 'lands, houses, tithes and coal mines'.
HELD: Those words impliedly excluded all other types of mines, specifically limestone mines, in this case by the specific mention of 'coal'. Therefore, the rate could not be levied on owners of limestone mines.

Presumptions

Further tools that the courts may use to aid their interpretation of a particular statute are the numerous presumptions that exist as a result of the common law. These presumptions assist in finding the intention of Parliament; however, they can often be rebuttable. The most prominent of these presumptions are listed in Table 3.13.

Table 3.13 Presumptions

Presumption against . . .	Explanation and example
Altering the common law	Parliament is empowered to change the existing common law; however, such an intention cannot be implied (***Beswick v Beswick*** **(1968)**).
Binding the Crown by an Act	Parliament is presumed not to bind the Crown unless it does so expressly or impliedly (e.g. **Equality Act 2010**).
Criminal liability without fault	For statutory criminal offences, Parliament is presumed to have intended no liability without proof of *mens rea* unless express words or implication can rebut the presumption and establish a strict liability or state-of-affairs case (***Sweet v Parsley*** **(1970)**).
Retrospective statutes	Statutes do not operate retrospectively, e.g. an individual cannot be liable for an offence that was legal at the time that the act was carried out. This presumption can be rebutted by the use of express words by Parliament (e.g. **War Crimes Act 1991**, which allows the prosecution of those suspected of committing acts of 'atrocity' during the Second World War).
Deprivation of liberty	Clear words must be used if Parliament intends to deprive a person of their liberty. There is a presumption against such deprivation; however, any clear words to the contrary will be construed so as to interfere with the individual's liberty as little as possible (***R (H) v London North and East Region Mental Health Review Tribunal*** (2001)).

Aids to interpretation

The final tools available to the judiciary to assist in the undertaking of statutory interpretation are what have become known as the 'aids' to interpretation. Such aids can be intrinsic (i.e. within the statute) and extrinsic (i.e. outside of the statute) in nature.

Intrinsic

The statute itself is the primary source of information. As a result, therefore, the statute must be read as a whole—with every word being considered—before looking outside of the statute. This intrinsic exercise will ensure the judiciary are as close to the intention of Parliament as possible before considering exterior factors. The most common intrinsic aids are listed in Table 3.14.

Table 3.14 Intrinsic aids

Intrinsic aid	Explanation and example
Short title	This is of little use due to its descriptive nature; however, some value may be gained from the short title to demonstrate the overall intention of Parliament in relation to the purpose of the statute.
Long title	This gives an indication of the purpose of an Act. In ***R v Bates* (1952)**, Donovan J held that upon reading the words of a section, should ambiguity or doubt arise, the long title may be considered in the hope of resolving the ambiguity.
Preamble	Preambles are rarely seen in modern statutes, since the inclusion of an 'introductory text'. However, they were much more common in older statutes, where they set out the reasons for the passing of the statute.
Marginal notes	A side note may be used to consider what the purpose of the section is. In ***R v Montila* (2004)**, the House of Lords stated that as side notes are not debated in Parliament, but rather, are included for ease of reference, they may be used to assist in interpretation but are to be conferred less weight.
Punctuation	Lord Reid in ***DPP v Schildkamp* (1971)** held that punctuation is to be considered like any other part of a statute and may be used as an aid to interpretation.
Examples	Statutes may provide examples to illustrate how the Act might work or how terminology within it might be used.
Schedules	The majority of statutes contain a schedule which often includes definitions of terms used in the Act.

Extrinsic

On many occasions, the statute itself is not entirely helpful. As a result, one must turn to the extrinsic aids. These are aids that feature outside of the statue itself but may be used nonetheless to assist in interpreting any ambiguities. Table 3.15 details the most prominent extrinsic aids. Please note that such aids are not exhaustive. In fact, the list could no doubt form its own book.

Table 3.15 Extrinsic aids

Extrinsic aid	Explanation and example
Interpretation Act (IA) 1978	The **IA 1978** is useful for the more common words that are found within statutes but that is the limit of its helpfulness. One particular use is **s6**, which provides that unless stated otherwise **(i)** where words used in an Act refer to the masculine gender they also include the feminine gender; and **(ii)** vice versa; and **(iii)** words appearing in the singular include the plural and words in the plural include the singular. The best example demonstrating an express statement to the contrary of the **IA 1978** is the offence of rape, which can only be committed by a man, given the requirement in **s1 Sexual Offences Act 2003** of penile penetration.
Dictionaries	It is permissible to consult a dictionary if the meaning of a word used in a statute is unclear; however, such uses are considered with caution (***Customs and Excise Comrs v Top Ten Promotions Ltd*** **(1969)**).
Explanatory Notes	These are guidance notes on the majority of statutes passed since 1999 prepared by the Government Legal Service. The intention is to make the Act accessible to laypersons; however, they can also be very useful in finding the intention of Parliament.
Hansard	Hansard is the official report of what was debated in the Houses of Parliament. The report is updated daily. Under previous law, the courts were not permitted to refer to records of parliamentary debate; however, the rule was relaxed in ***Pepper v Hart*** **(1993)**.
Academic writing	Academic writing, both in textbooks and journal articles, is more commonly cited in courts nowadays, for example, David Ormerod in matters relating to criminal law. Recently, in ***R (Purdy) v DPP*** **(2010)**, the House of Lords required counsel to supply written submissions on whether the points contained within an article written by Professor Hirst were correct. Also, in ***R v Dooley*** **(2005)**, the court referred quite often to Smith and Hogan's *Criminal Law*.

Revision tip

Pepper v Hart is a key case. Many examination questions, both problem and essay-style, are based on a ***Pepper v Hart*** scenario. Often essay questions will focus on whether the rule in ***Pepper v Hart*** ought to be upheld, whilst problem questions will ask whether certain parliamentary debates may be used in a given scenario. For the latter of the two, it is essential that you remember that the rule in ***Pepper v Hart*** only applies in certain cases (see below under 'Key cases').

Impact of the Human Rights Act 1998

Since the introduction of the **Human Rights Act (HRA) 1998**, in October 2000, the courts have been provided with an additional power when interpreting a statute. This power also entails an obligation on the courts to interpret legislation in accordance with the ECHR. In particular, **s3(1) HRA 1998** provides that '[s]o far as it is possible to do so, primary legislation and subordinate legislation must be read and given effect in a way which is compatible with the Convention rights'. If the courts are unable to find a compatible interpretation, then they may make a 'declaration of incompatibility' under **s4 HRA 1998**.

One of the most controversial uses of **s3** can be seen in the criminal evidence case of ***R v A (Complainant's Sexual History)*** **(2002)**.

R v A (Complainant's Sexual History) [2002] 1 AC 45

FACTS: This case concerned the admissibility of a complainant's sexual history evidence in a sexual offence case. Under **s41(1) Youth Justice and Criminal Evidence Act 1999**, there is a general restriction on the use of a complainant's sexual history within a criminal trial. This restriction is subject to a number of exceptions detailed in **s41(3)(a)–(c)**. The relevant section concerned was **s41(3)(c)**, which provided that evidence of the complainant's sexual history may be admissible if the evidence is 'so similar that it cannot be explained by coincidence'.

HELD: The question for the House of Lords was whether the defendant was guaranteed a fair trial, under **Article 6 ECHR**, where potentially relevant evidence to his defence was restricted by the operation of **s41**. The Court held, by a majority, that the defendant could not be afforded a right to a fair trial in the given circumstances and used their power in **s3** to 'read down' the legislation to create a brand new exception to the general restriction, namely where the evidence is 'so relevant that it ought to be admitted'.

The decision in ***R v A*** remains controversial given the quasi-legislative role taken on by the House of Lords. As a result of ***R v A***, the majority of applications to adduce sexual history evidence are now admitted under the 'so relevant' gateway. See also the case of footballer Ched Evans (***R v Evans (No. 2)*** **(2016)**).

An example of the operation of **s4** can be found in the case of ***Bellinger v Bellinger*** **(2003)**.

Bellinger v Bellinger [2003] 2 AC 467

FACTS: This case concerned the recognition of a gender status after the individual had undergone gender reassignment surgery. According to the law, Bellinger remained male and thus could not marry a man.

HELD: The House of Lords declared the non-recognition of gender reassignment for the purpose of marriage as incompatible with **Articles 8 and 12 ECHR**. This forced the government's hand which, as a result, introduced the **Gender Recognition Act 2004**.

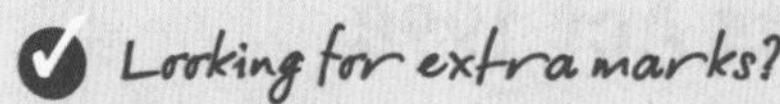

When revising the impact of the **HRA 1998**, don't forget to look for the most up to date and authoritative examples. Often these examples are also controversial. Here are two to get you started:

- prisoner voting rights (***Hirst v the United Kingdom (No. 2)*** (2005));
- mandatory life sentences (***Vinter and Others v UK*** (2013); ***AG's Reference (No. 69 of 2013)*** (2014)).

These decisions show the extent of the effect that **ss3 and 4 HRA 1998** have had in the field of statutory interpretation. In conjunction with the growing influence of EU law in the domestic courts, this impact has had the result that courts are now adopting a much less literal and formalistic approach to interpretation. The **HRA 1998** and the rights guaranteed under that statute are considered further in Chapter 5.

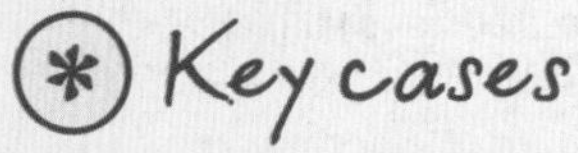

Case	Facts	Principles
***R (Miller) v The Prime Minister* [2019] UKSC 41 (SC)**	The Supreme Court was tasked with determining whether the Prime Minister's advice to the Queen on 27 or 28 August 2019 that Parliament should be prorogued from a date between 9 and 12 September until 14 October was lawful.	1. The advice given by the Prime Minister was justiciable (i.e. capable of review). 2. A decision to prorogue will be unlawful if the prorogation has the effect of frustrating or preventing, without reasonable justification, the ability of Parliament to carry out its constitutional functions as a legislature and as the body responsible for the supervision of the executive. 3. Prorogation was unlawful in this instance due to the significant time periods in which Parliament would be prorogued and without reasonable justification for such time period. 4. The advice to prorogue was unlawful; the Order in Council was thus void and had no effect.

Case	Facts	Principles
Pepper v Hart [1993] AC 593 (HL)	Mr Hart was a teacher at Malvern College, a public school. As a benefit of the job, his own children could attend the school at a discounted rate (one-fifth of the regular fees). The Inland Revenue wished to tax this benefit and Mr Hart claimed that no tax was payable, given the statement made by a minister in Hansard.	The rule against reference to Hansard as an extrinsic aid to interpretation was relaxed and is now permitted to be used in cases where (per Lord Oliver): (i) the legislation is ambiguous or obscure, or its literal meaning leads to an absurdity; (ii) the material relied on consists of statements by a minister or other promoter of the Bill together with such other parliamentary material as is necessary to understand such statements and their effect; and (iii) the statements relied upon are clear.

Topic	Literal rule
Academic	Michael Zander
Viewpoint	Describes the golden rule as 'little more than an unpredictable safety-valve to permit the courts to escape from some of the more unpalatable effects of the literal rule'.
Source	Michael Zander, *The Law Making Process* (7th edn, Bloomsbury 2015)

Topic	Presumptions against changing the common law
Academic	Stephen Bailey, Jane Ching, Nick Taylor
Viewpoint	Argue that the presumption against altering the common law is 'extremely controversial' and that it appears 'strange that there should continue to be a presumption that judge-made law will not normally be affected', given that Parliament is supreme and may legislate in what way it sees fit.
Source	Stephen Bailey, Jane Ching, Nick Taylor, *Smith, Bailey and Gunn on the Modern English Legal System* (5th edn, Sweet & Maxwell 2007)

Exam questions

****

Topic	Hansard and *Pepper v Hart*
Academic	Aileen Kavanagh
Viewpoint	Argues that restricting the use of Hansard to the comments of relevant ministers unavoidably distorts the position of Parliament and clouds the distinction between Parliament and the government in power.
Source	Aileen Kavanagh, 'Pepper v Hart and Matters of Constitutional Principle' (2005) 121 Law Quarterly Review 98

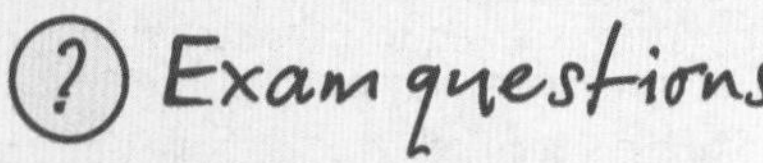

Essay question

'The legislative process does not allow for a full and systematic review of the Bill in question. The process is too heavily formulaic and party politics plays too great of a role.'

Critically discuss this statement considering the structure of the parliamentary process, the individuals involved in this process, and any potential reform of the system.

Problem question

Frank has been charged with an offence contrary to the Offensive Weapons Act 2015 (fictitious). The offence in question is contrary to s3 of the Act, which provides that 'It is an offence, triable on indictment, for a person to have in his possession an unlawful weapon without lawful justification in a public place.' On 19 November, Frank was practising aggressive manoeuvres on a dummy in the hallway of his flat complex. In practising these manoeuvres, Frank had in his possession a machete, which he was using to make a stabbing motion at the dummy. Residents of the complex were scared of Frank's actions and he was arrested.

- The Criminal Prosecution Service argues that Frank falls within the definition of the offence.
- Frank argues that the hallway is not a 'public place' within the meaning of the Act as it is private property, restricted by code-accessed gates accessible to only those who live there.

Advise Frank as to the likely interpretation of the Act. In advising Frank, consider the of rules of construction, the aids to interpretation, and any relevant presumptions.

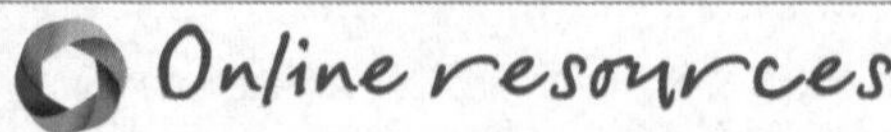

For an outline answer to this essay question, as well as multiple-choice questions and interactive key cases, please visit the online resources.

#4
Sources of Law II: Case Law

Key facts

- Case law, also known as the common law, is a set of judge-made rules that have either a binding or persuasive effect on future cases.
- Whether precedent is binding is dependent on whether there is a statement of law, as opposed to fact, certain reasoning for that decision (known as **ratio decidendi**), and the decision of a superior court.
- Certain courts are obliged to follow previous judgments, whereas others can ignore them due to their seniority.
- Judges act in a quasi-law-making capacity when developing judicial precedent.

Chapter overview

Precedent in England and Wales

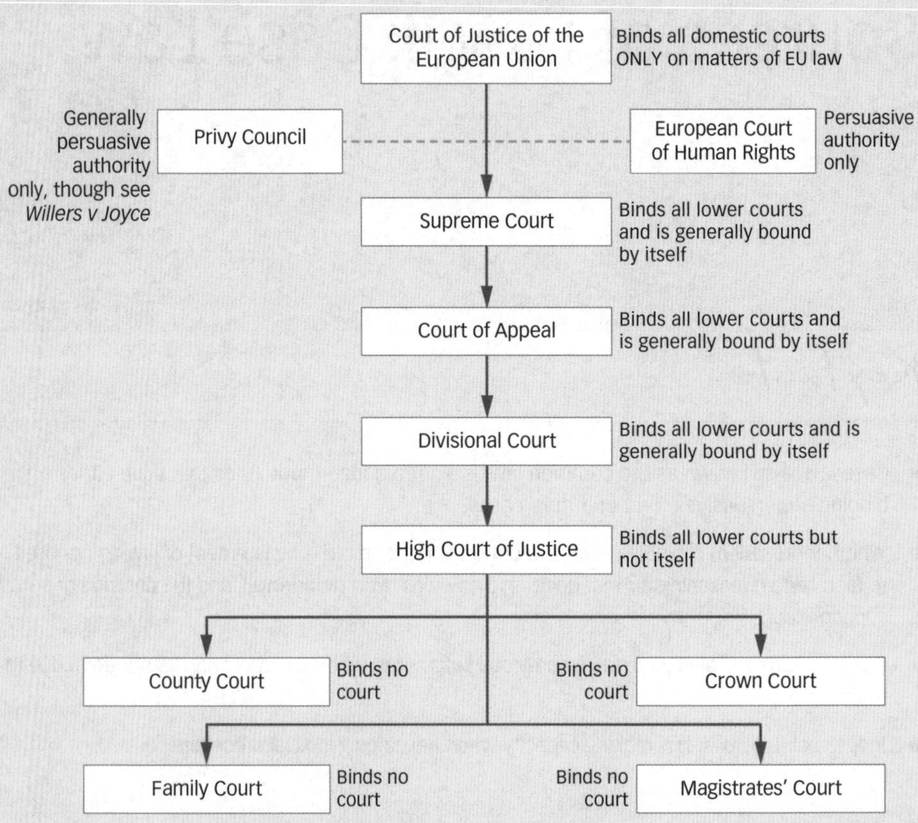

The common law

In Chapter 3 we spoke about the primary source of law, namely legislation. As a result of the doctrine of parliamentary supremacy, legislation is the superior source of law. However, England and Wales collectively are known as a common law society. Historically, the common law represented the law that was 'common' across England. In more modern terms, however, the common law is another way of speaking of case law and judicial precedent. Despite the enactment of legislation, case law is a major source of law providing for the interpretation of statutes and the application of law to particular circumstances. This chapter focuses on the meaning and operation of judicial precedent.

The common law: an introduction

An essential aspect of our legal system is the common law. Unfortunately, the phrase 'common law' has many different potential meanings:

- a common law system, compared with a civil law system;
- common law principles, compared with equitable principles;
- common law as case law.

Common law vs civil law

The first distinction that must be made is that of a common law system compared with a civil law system. Civil law is a European concept, developed from the Romano-Germanic legal systems, and can best be described as a system of rules that does not involve binding case law. Instead, a civil system adopts the use of 'codes' as a statement of law, with little influence from case law and little concept of precedent. Countries with civil law jurisdictions include states such as France and Germany. France is a particularly good example of a civil code, given that the law is coded almost to its entirety, whereas other countries such as the USA, operate a hybrid system with binding case law working alongside a code, namely the **US Constitution (1789)**, which incorporates the **US Bill of Rights (1789)**.

Common law vs equity

A frequent debate that is had by academics is the distinction between the common law and equity. Equity, itself, is a source of law; however, it is not a part of the common law. The principle of equity developed as a result of the harshness of the common law and its operation in fifteenth-century England. The Court of Chancery was established in 1474 as an entity distinct from the King's court. The Court of Chancery determined cases in accordance with the principles of **natural justice** and fairness. This became known as the law of equity, with rights and remedies available to the Court of Chancery that were not available in the King's common law courts. Nowadays, as a result of the **Supreme Court of Judicature Acts 1873 and 1875**, the operation and administration of the common law and equity is fused; however, it remains essential to distinguish the two. For more detail on the history of equity, and its fusion with the common law, see Iain McDonald and Anne Street, *Equity and Trusts Concentrate* (6th edn, Oxford University Press 2018).

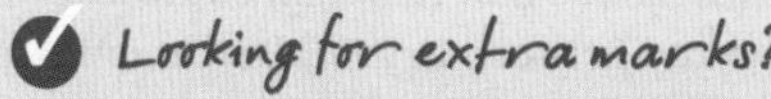

When discussing the development of equity, make sure you add plenty of detail and examples to your argument. For example, when discussing the rights and remedies available to the Court of Chancery but not the common law courts, discuss some of the equitable maxims, such as, 'He who comes to equity must come with clean hands' and 'Equity will not suffer a wrong to be without a remedy.' ➜

➜ On that last point, consider the equitable remedies that are available to an individual, namely injunctions or an order for specific performance. These examples will show the examiner that you are aware of a greater level of detail than that which is necessarily required of you.

Common law as case law

The final understanding of the common law, for our purposes, is that the common law refers to case law, i.e. law developed by judges through legal decisions. This is our focus on the term 'common law' in this chapter, which we shall proceed to discuss now.

Case law: general principles

Before proceeding into the meaning and operation of precedent, it is first useful to explain some of the core principles relevant to case law as a source of law.

Judge-made law

The first principle to exemplify is that the common law is judge-made. This means that a member of the judiciary has decided a case in a certain way, which has led to the development of that particular piece of law. The decisions of judges are known as judgments and, dependent on the level of authority, the judgment may be binding or persuasive. Both of these terms will be explored later in the chapter.

Revision tip

A legal decision made by a judge is spelled 'judgment' without an 'e' after the 'g'. This is a very common mistake, even amongst final year students. Ensure that you know the difference between judgment and judgement.

Judgment—a legal decision made by a judge. It is used specifically in relation to legal proceedings.

Judgement—when one passes judgement or opinion on another person. It is used outside of legal proceedings.

England remains the oldest common law jurisdiction in the world. Other common law jurisdictions include the USA and Australia. As an example of the operation of the common law in England and Wales, although the majority of criminal offences are now contained in statutory form, the offence of murder remains a common law concept. Defined famously by Sir Edward Coke CJ in 1628 (and subsequently updated to comply with modern usage) as 'The unlawful killing of a human being under the Queen's Peace, with malice aforethought, express or implied', this statement of law continues to operate in twenty-first-century England and Wales.

Forms of judgments

There are three forms of judgments that you must be aware of. Table 4.1 details these types of judgments.

Table 4.1 Forms of judgments

Judgment	Meaning
Unanimous	A unanimous judgment means that the court reached its decision in complete agreement.
Majority	A majority judgment means that the court could not reach a unanimous decision but could reach a majority, e.g. two to one in the Court of Appeal or three to two in the Supreme Court.
Dissenting	A dissenting judgment means the decision of the judge who was not present in the majority. This judgment will explain why the judge disagrees with the majority and may be persuasive in later cases to show a differing approach that may be adopted in the future.

Law reporting and case citations

As part of your studies, you will encounter many different cases from many different sources. It is essential that you understand what the law reports of England and Wales are and what a case citation means.

Should you find an authority that does not conform with the list below, we advise you to refer to www.legalabbrevs.cardiff.ac.uk. This website, set up by Cardiff University, contains a full database of most legal reports in the world. The useful search function makes searching for abbreviations an easy task.

Hierarchy of law reports

According to **Practice Direction (Citation of Authorities) (2012)**, there is a rigid hierarchy of law reports that must be followed by lawyers in practice (see Figure 4.1). It is advised that you understand this hierarchy and use it when writing any pieces of coursework and if you ever take up mooting.

We shall now explain what each of these abbreviations mean.

The Law Reports (Incorporated Council)

These are the most senior and authoritative of the law journals. Each report published by the Council is first checked and confirmed as accurate by the judge who delivered the judgment. Table 4.2 details the Incorporated Council's Official Law Reports.

Please note the following:

- The Appeal Cases Report does not cover all appeal court decisions. It only reports cases from the House of Lords, now the Supreme Court, and the Judicial Committee of the Privy Council.
- The Queen's Bench Report is different from the Queen's Bench Division (QBD) in that the reports of the Queen's Bench do not simply cover the QBD. More commonly, they cover judgments from the Court of Appeal.

- Where the Monarch is male, the report will change from the Queen's Bench, as it has been since 1952, to the King's Bench (KB).

Figure 4.1 Hierarchy of law reports

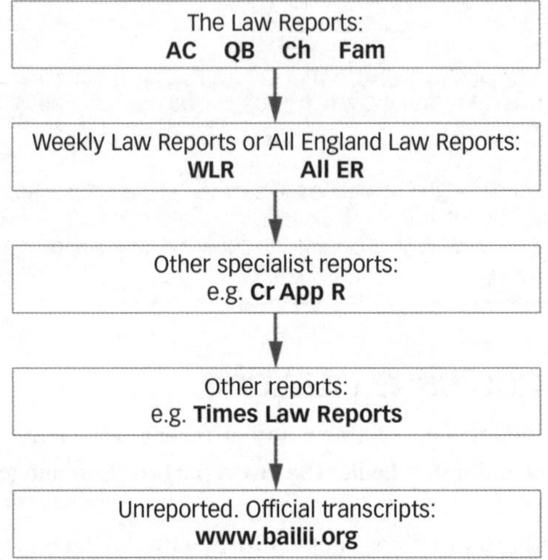

Table 4.2 The Official Law Reports

Abbreviation	Meaning
AC	Law Reports, Appeal Cases
QB	Law Reports, Queen's Bench
Ch	Law Reports, Chancery Division
Fam	Law Reports, Family Division

The Weekly Law Reports and the All England Law Reports

The Weekly Law Reports (WLR) are a part of the publication of the Incorporated Council; however, they are second preference to the Official Law Reports. The WLR are generally published weekly but there may be occasions where a Report is omitted. The All England Law Reports (All ER) are published by Butterworths/Lexis Nexis and operate on a similar basis to the WLR. Where a case is reported in both the WLR and the All ER, either may be cited.

Other specialist reports

These reports focus on the more specialized and narrow areas of law that the more senior law reports do not consider important enough. Table 4.3 details some of the many specialist reports.

Table 4.3 Other specialist reports

Abbreviation	Meaning
Cr App R	Criminal Appeal Reports
Crim LR	Criminal Law Review
FLR	Family Law Review
FCR	Family Court Reporter
HRLR	Human Rights Law Reports
UKHRR	United Kingdom Human Rights Reports
Lloyd's Rep Med	Lloyd's Law Reports Medical
BMLR	Butterworths Medico-Legal Reports
JP	Justice of the Peace Reports

Other reports

There are a number of reports that are placed towards the bottom of the hierarchy and are generally covered by newspapers and journals. Most prominently are the *Times Law Reports*, which are generally published on a daily basis. These reports have the advantage that they are produced normally within days of when a judgment was handed down. *The Independent* has recently begun its own law reporting service; however, that is of less prominence than the *Times Law Reports*. Other journals that report cases quickly are the *Solicitors Journal*, the *New Law Journal*, and the *Archbold Review* (formerly the *Archbold News*).

Unreported cases

There are a number of cases that go unreported. Since 11 January 2001, all cases have been prescribed what is known as a neutral citation (see next section); however, prior to this a case was simply reported by its name, the year of the case, followed by 'unreported' (e.g. ***R v Haider*, 22 March 1985 (unreported)** for the offence of handling stolen goods). Such citation was not helpful for a lawyer seeking to rely on a case and it resulted in lawyers relying upon transcripts of judgments, given that no law report was available.

BAILII (The British and Irish Legal Information Institute) is a private company that operates the website www.bailii.org and provides a comprehensive database of British and Irish cases. The cases are the transcripts of cases, as opposed to their reports (if they have one) and are useful where a case is unreported.

Table 4.4 Neutral citations

Abbreviation	Meaning
UKSC	United Kingdom Supreme Court
UKHL	United Kingdom House of Lords
EWCA Crim	England and Wales Court of Appeal, Criminal Division
EWCA Civ	England and Wales Court of Appeal, Civil Division
EWHC (Admin)	England and Wales High Court (Administrative Court)
EWHC (Fam)	England and Wales High Court (Family Division)
EWHC (Ch)	England and Wales High Court (Chancery Division)
EWHC (QB)	England and Wales High Court (Queen's Bench Division)

Neutral citations

From 11 January 2001 the neutral citation was introduced by way of **Practice Direction (Judgments: Form and Citation) (2001)**. The purpose of the neutral citation was to make it easier for those reading and researching case law to find a particular authority, especially online. It was originally restricted to the Court of Appeal and the Divisional Court but was later extended to the other divisions of the High Court, the Privy Council, and the House of Lords (now the Supreme Court). Table 4.4 details the most common neutral citations you will encounter.

Do not be confused, therefore, if you see a case before 2001 without a neutral citation. This merely reflects the change in practice since the Practice Direction. You may read a neutral citation and wonder what exactly it means. Table 4.5 details how to read a neutral citation.

[2016] vs (2016)

When reading cases, you may come across a different use of punctuation for different cases. For example, you may see the following: *R v Thomas* [2016] and *R v Thomas* (2016). Both cases are fictitious but demonstrate a key feature of case law in England and Wales. The majority of cases now firmly use square brackets, with parentheses (round brackets) being a thing of the past except in a small minority of law reports; however, it remains essential that you understand the distinction.

- The use of square brackets—[2016]—indicates that the date of the citation is an essential aspect of the citation (i.e. you require the date to find the case). By way of example, should you wish to find *Hindle Gears Ltd v McGinty* [1985] ICR 111, you would need to find the 1985 volume of the Industrial Court Reports and turn to page 111. You would not be able to find this case without the year.

- The use of parentheses—(2016)—indicates that the date is not an essential aspect of the citation (i.e. the date is not necessary to find the case). In these circumstances, the case citation will have a volume number which allows an individual to trace the judgment. By way of example, should you wish to find *Hindle Gears Ltd v McGinty* (1984) 81 LSG 3254, you would only need to find the 81st volume of the Law Society's Gazette and turn to page 3254. You can find the case without the year. In this regard, the law report and its respective volume number is essential! By way of example, the Criminal Appeal Reports (Cr App R) and the Butterworths Medico-Legal Reports (BMLR) are both law reports that make use of parentheses as opposed to square brackets.

Table 4.5 How to read neutral citations

***Hunter Kane Ltd v Watkins* [2003] EWHC 186 (Ch)**	
Components	**Meaning**
Hunter Kane Ltd and Watkins	These are the parties involved in the case. In the majority of cases, the first party listed is the 'claimant' and the second, the 'defendant'. In an appeal, the first party listed would be the 'appellant', whilst the second party would be the 'respondent'. These roles may switch as/if the case proceeds through the various courts.
[2003]	The date of the judgment
EWHC	The court where the case was heard; in this case, the High Court of Justice of England and Wales
186	The case number (i.e. the number at which the case was heard in the High Court in that year)
(Ch)	This is the Division of the court in which the case was heard. 'Ch' refers to the Chancery Division of the High Court. Not all courts have divisions.
Spoken as: Hunter Kane Limited and Watkins, the 186th case to be heard in the High Court of Justice for England and Wales, Chancery Division, for the year 2003.	

Preference should always be given to the square brackets, given that they designate the year of the particular law report. It is often the case that where a year is given in parentheses, that is likely to be the year that the judgment was delivered by the court, whereas the square brackets denote the year of the law report. Naturally, there will be a time lapse between the judgment date and the publication of the law report. This distinction is why you see the same case containing different citations with different years; for example, ***Hindle Gears Ltd v McGinty*[1985] ICR 111; (1984) 81 LSG 3254.**

Party names (criminal cases)

As part of your studies, you will come across many different cases, all of which feature different parties. You therefore need to appreciate these different party names and their meanings (see Table 4.6).

Table 4.6 Party names in criminal proceedings

Party name	Meaning
R	When a criminal case is reported, it is cited as 'R v Thomas'. The 'R' represents the reigning monarch, given that criminal cases are brought by the state (in the name of the Monarch) against an accused. The meaning of 'R' is dependent on whom the current monarch is: 'Regina' (pronounced 'Rejyna')—meaning 'the Queen', or 'Rex'—meaning 'the King'. When said orally, 'R' becomes 'the Crown', as opposed to the pirate version of 'argh'.
DPP	Many criminal cases are brought by the Director of Public Prosecutions; for example, a prosecution appeal by way of case stated from the magistrates' court to the Divisional Court would be reported as '*DPP v Thomas*'.
AG	The Attorney General may be a named party to a case in a number of circumstances. One example is where the Attorney General refers to the Court of Appeal sentences which he/she considers to be unduly lenient in line with **s36 of the Criminal Justice Act 1988**. These cases will be reported as an 'Attorney General Reference' and will feature a reference number for the year referred, e.g. ***AG's Reference No. 125 of 2004* (2005).**

It may be the case that the name of a private person will appear in a case citation (e.g. *Thomas v McGourlay*). Many students confuse this as being a civil case, given that the citation does not feature one of the above party names. However, all private persons have the ability to bring a private prosecution against an individual under **s6(1) of the Prosecution of Offences Act 1985**. This system is most commonly used by the RSPCA in prosecuting offences for cruelty to animals.

Party names (civil cases)

In the civil courts, however, the individual who brings the claim against the defendant is known as the claimant. Prior to the **Civil Procedure Rules (CPR) 1998**, the claimant was known as the plaintiff. Another example of a civil case name could be *Re Thomas (No. 2)* [fictitious]. 'Re' (pronounced 'ree') translates to 'about something' and when said orally means 'in the matter of' or 'in relation to'. Some older cases will be reported as *Ex parte Thomas* [fictitious]. 'Ex parte' simply means 'on the application of' and refers to cases where an application is made to the court without the presence of the other party. Following the **Civil Procedure Rules 1998**, such actions are now referred to as being 'without notice'.

When a civil case is reported, it is cited by the names of the parties involved in the dispute, e.g. *Thomas v McGourlay*. Like its criminal counterpart, the 'v' in the citation is said orally as either 'and' or 'against'.

Citing cases

Lawyers like to be specific. It is therefore essential that you understand how to cite cases and what the citations actually mean. Figure 4.2 gives an example that will help you understand how to cite cases and their meanings.

In Figure 4.2 there are four key elements:

Figure 4.2 Citing cases

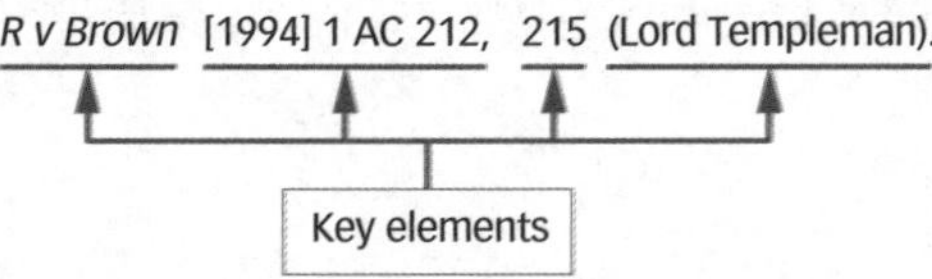

1. **Case name**—this informs the reader who the parties are and whether the case is a criminal or civil case. In this case, we have 'R', demonstrating that we are dealing with a criminal case, and 'Brown', which is the surname of the defendant. The 'v' in the middle of the party names stands for versus which translates from Latin as 'against'. When spoken, this would be said as 'The Crown and Brown' or 'The Crown against Brown'. Note that the following is NOT used when citing a case name:
   - R—as 'Arrr'; 'Regina' or 'Rex'.
   - V—as 'Vee' or 'Versus'.
2. **Citation**—this informs the reader where the case was reported, the year of the report, the report volume, and the page number it starts on. In this example, the case would be read aloud as 'The first volume of the Law Reports, Appeal Cases, for the year 1994 at page 212'.
3. **Page reference**—this informs the reader of the particular page reference that is being relied upon. Notice that there is no necessity to write 'p. 215' or 'page 215'. Often you see the use of square brackets in a citation, for example '[16]'. This designates 'paragraph 16' of the judgment, meaning that you need not write 'para' or 'paragraph'.
4. **Judge name**—this informs the reader of the name of the judge who provided the particular statement that is being relied upon. Often you see the phrase 'per Lord Templeman' being used. Although such a phrasing is perfectly acceptable, it is a part of the old legalese that modern lawyers wish to avoid. As such, according to the Oxford University Standard for the Citation of Legal Authorities (OSCOLA) you are advised to place the judge's name in parentheses as opposed to using 'per'.

Precedent—the principles

The doctrine of precedent denotes a system of case law, binding or not, that a lower court may or may not have to follow. When considering precedents, therefore, we must understand the general principles behind such a doctrine before then observing its application and operation. For a detailed and historical account of precedent, see Cross and Harris, *Precedent in English Law* (4th edn, Oxford University Press 1995).

> **Revision tip**
>
> Ensure you use the term 'precedent' as opposed to 'precedence'. The latter concerns the establishment of an order of hierarchy or importance, whilst the former concerns the establishment of a principle to be used at a later date to justify similar events. For our purposes, we are concerned with precedents.

Stare decisis

One of the first concepts to explore is the idea of binding and persuasive precedents. In England and Wales, there is a presumption known as stare decisis (pronounced 'stare-ay decisis') which means 'to stand by decisions'. This presumption exists only in cases of binding authority and does not apply to persuasive authorities. It is important to note at this stage that there is a difference between *stare decisis* and *res judicata*; the latter referring to the binding nature of the decision on the parties to that case, as opposed to other parties. The Latin phrase translates roughly to 'the matter has been settled' and refers to situations where the case has now concluded for those parties. Our focus, in this chapter, remains on the principle of *stare decisis*. A precedent is binding when certain conditions are met. Figure 4.3 outlines these conditions.

Figure 4.3 Requirements for a binding authority

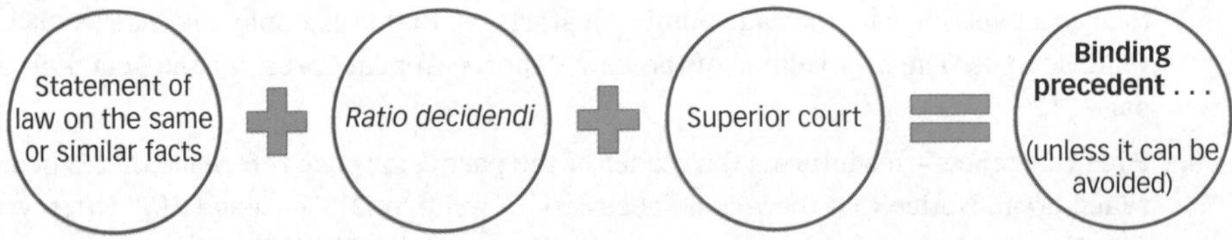

If any of these elements are missing, the case will be of a persuasive nature only. This means that the lower courts are not bound to follow the precedent, but they may use the precedent to influence their own decision.

Statement of law

The most basic requirement for a binding precedent is that the particular judgment must be concerned with a statement of law, as opposed to one of fact. Obviously, for a decision to be binding on the instant court, the facts of the instant case must be the same or similar to that of the previous case. Without such similarity, the case could easily be 'distinguished' (see 'To follow or not to follow . . . that is the question' later in this chapter on avoiding binding precedent).

The statement of law itself can be divided into the legal decision reached in the given case (the *ratio decidendi*) and other statements of law made (the obiter dictum). The following are the key terms we shall now consider:

- *ratio decidendi* (plural: *rationes decidendi*);
- *obiter dictum* (plural: *obiter dicta*).

Ratio decidendi

The *ratio decidendi*, often abbreviated to 'the *ratio*', is best defined as 'the reason for the decision'. The *ratio* informs the lower courts of the statement of law that is to be followed. Any statement that is not part of the *ratio* is called *obiter dicta*, often abbreviated to 'the *obiter*', which is best defined as 'other things said'.

Revision tip

It is often difficult for students to 'find' the *ratio* of a given case where they are reading the judgment in full. This is because the judge delivering judgment will not declare 'The *ratio* is . . .' and the decision may have numerous judgments with numerous apparent *rationes*. The important point to remember is that the *ratio* is not concerned with the outcome or the decision itself (e.g. guilty or not guilty) but, rather, it is concerned with the reasons for the decision. You can often find the reasoning by observing how the court has applied the law to the material facts in the case.

Table 4.7 Key definitions for binding precedent

Concept	Meaning	Example
Vertical *stare decisis*	All courts are bound by their superiors (i.e. the court that sits above them in the hierarchy).	The Court of Appeal is bound by the decisions of the Supreme Court.
Horizontal *stare decisis*	Certain courts are generally bound by their own previous decisions.	The Court of Appeal is bound by its own previous decisions unless it falls within a recognized exception (see 'Court structure' in 'Precedent—the operation' later).

Obiter dictum

As opposed to the *ratio*, which forms the key element of a binding precedent, the *obiter dictum* will not act as a binding statement of law. The *obiter* of a case may include examples given by the judge, hypothetical scenarios, discussion of broader principles etc. Whilst such statements may not be binding points of law, *obiter dicta* may still act as very persuasive authority for a future case where a similar legal issue has arisen. Often the *obiter dictum* from a previous case is cited by counsel in the hope that the court will follow those other things said and apply the *obiter* as part of their reasoning—thus creating a *ratio*.

Superior court

In order for a decision to act as a binding precedent, the judgment must be delivered by a superior court to the court where the present case is being heard. The court structure was considered in more detail in Chapter 2; however, for present purposes it is important to appreciate the two key definitions shown in Table 4.7. It will be helpful to refer back to the diagram in the chapter overview at this stage.

Further to this, a court is never bound by an inferior court (i.e. a court on the lower level of the hierarchy). For example, the Court of Appeal will never be bound by the Crown Court. We shall consider each court and the operation of precedent on that court in 'Precedent—the operation' below.

Each of these elements when added together amounts to a binding precedent. If one element is absent, the authority is not binding but, rather, is persuasive. Table 4.8 will help bring all of the information together on this topic.

It is necessary to appreciate that these categories are not mutually exclusive. For example, a decision may be persuasive only if it was heard in an inferior court but still provided a statement of law and a *ratio* for its decision. Likewise, a judgment may have been delivered in a superior court; however, unless that judgment includes a statement of law and reasoning for such a statement, it too will only amount to a persuasive authority.

Table 4.8 Binding vs persuasive precedent

Binding	Persuasive
The judgment provided a statement of law on the same or similar facts as the instant case.	The judgment provided a statement of law on dissimilar facts.
	The judgment provided a statement of facts on the same, similar, or dissimilar facts.
The judgment provided a *ratio* for the decision.	The judgment provided merely *obiter dicta* statements.
The judgment was delivered by a court more senior to that of the present court.	The judgment was delivered by a court less senior to that of the present court.

Other sources of persuasive law

It is appropriate at this stage to discuss briefly the other sources that may be of a persuasive nature to any court. Table 4.9 details these other sources.

Table 4.9 Other persuasive authorities

Authority	Level of persuasion
Dissenting/minority judgments	Not all judges in a case will agree! Where a decision is not unanimous, the judge who disagrees with the majority is said to be 'dissenting' or 'in the minority'. Whilst these judges may still make a statement which forms its own *ratio decidendi*, it will not amount to binding law, given that it is a minority statement. Minority judgments remain persuasive however, especially on appeals on contentious points of law.
Decisions from other countries	Ultimately it depends on the level of court and the origin. Some Commonwealth countries, such as Australia, may have a very persuasive effect on an English case. Likewise, some American authorities, as a common law system, have been persuasive in English cases (e.g. ***A v Secretary of State for the Home Department*** **(2005)**).
Academic commentary	As discussed in Chapter 3 in relation to statutory interpretation, academic commentary in the form of textbooks and journal articles may act as persuasive authority to an English court. The undergraduate textbooks are largely ignored; however, certain key texts such as *Treitel on The Law of Contract* and *Smith and Hogan's Criminal Law* are repeatedly cited in the appellate courts, even the most senior of those courts.
Books of authority	These differ from textbooks in that over time they have become accepted as an expert statement of the law in a particular area. For example, *Blackstone's Commentaries on the Law of England* and *Coke's Institutes of the Laws of England*.

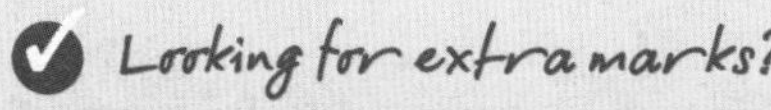

Don't forget about these other sources of law. They will be useful when answering problem questions or essay questions. These other sources vary in their persuasiveness and it is important to demonstrate this knowledge in a piece of work.

Precedent—the operation

Now that we understand the general principles behind the doctrine of precedent, it is essential that we put these principles into context and discuss the operation of precedent. This section reconsiders the court structure (from Chapter 2) but in much greater detail, dealing with each court in the hierarchy individually. The section then goes on to discuss how a lower court can 'avoid' a binding precedent from a superior court.

Court structure

In conjunction with Table 4.10, the diagram in the chapter overview should be consulted at this stage. In addition, it is advised that you revisit Chapter 2 and consider the overview of the court structure there. The key terms used above in 'Precedent—the principles' (vertical and horizontal *stare decisis*) will be used when discussing each key court. The general rule from **Broome v Cassell & Co. (1971)** is quite simple: senior courts bind inferior courts. As Lord Hailsham expressed: 'The fact is, and I hope it will never be necessary to say so again, that, in the hierarchical system of courts which exists in this country, it is necessary for each lower tier . . . to accept loyally the decisions of the higher tiers.'

Table 4.10 Checklist of precedent

Court	Vertical *stare decisis*	Horizontal *stare decisis*
Court of Justice of the European Union (whilst the UK remains in the EU)	✓	✗
Supreme Court (Formerly House of Lords)	✓	✓/✗
Privy Council (Judicial Committee)	✓/✗	✗
European Court of Human Rights	✗	✗
Court of Appeal (Civil Division)	✓	✓/✗
Court of Appeal (Criminal Division)	✓	✓/✗
Divisional Courts	✓	✓
High Court of Justice	✓	✗
Crown Court	✗	✗
Magistrates' court; Family Court; County Court	✗	✗

Court of Justice of the European Union

As a result of **s3(1) European Communities Act (ECA) 1972**, UK courts (and other courts within the Union) are bound by decisions of the Court of Justice of the European Union (CJEU) on matters of EU Law. By **Article 234 Treaty of Rome 1957**, the UK courts may refer a point of European law to the CJEU for interpretation. The CJEU is not bound by its own previous decisions, but the court is likely to follow them. In December 2019, Prime Minister Boris Johnson announced that the Withdrawal Agreement Bill, dealing with the exit of the

UK from the EU, will involve a provision that the lower courts will be able to 'roll back' EU laws after Brexit. It remains to be seen how this will work, but it appears that it will not simply be the Court of Appeal or Supreme Court that will be able to ignore and overrule CJEU judgments; the lower courts may also have this ability. This is of a particular concern in relation to employment rights.

Supreme Court (formerly House of Lords)

The Supreme Court (and all previous decisions of the House of Lords unless later overruled) binds all lower courts. Generally, the Supreme Court is bound by its own previous decisions. Indeed, prior to 1966, the House of Lords was bound absolutely to its own previous decisions. This was made clear by the Earl of Halsbury LC in ***London Street Tramways Co. Ltd v London County Council* (1898)**, where it was stated that:

> a decision of this House once given upon a point of law is conclusive upon this House afterwards, and that it is impossible to raise that question again as if it was *res integra* and could be reargued, and so the House be asked to reverse its own decision. That is a principle which has been, I believe, without any real decision to the contrary, established now for some centuries, and I am therefore of opinion that in this case it is not competent for us to rehear and for counsel to reargue a question which has been recently decided.

However, as a result of **Practice Statement (Judicial Precedent) (1966)** issued by Lord Gardiner LC, the House of Lords could depart from a previous decision where it appeared 'right to do so'. However, this power was to be used 'sparingly'. Following the creation of the Supreme Court in October 2009, it was questioned whether the Practice Statement applied equally to that Court or whether it was applicable only to the former House of Lords. In ***Austin v Mayor and Burgesses of the LBC* (2010)**, Lord Hope in the Supreme Court identified that it was not 'necessary to re-issue the Practice Statement as a fresh statement of practice in the Court's own name. This is because it has as much effect in that Court as it did before the Appellate Committee in the House of Lords.' ***Austin***, therefore, clarified that the Supreme Court will consider itself bound in the same way as the House of Lords was and may depart from previous decisions in the same circumstances also. On the Supreme Court directing the lower courts to follow them, see ***R v Barton* (2020)** in 'Key cases'.

British Railways Board v Herrington [1972] AC 877 (HL)

FACTS: A young boy was electrocuted, suffering severe burns, when he ventured from a play park onto a nearby live railway line. Although the railway lines were surrounded by a high fence, a small part of the fence had been pushed down, resulting in a gap in the fence used frequently as a shortcut. The defendant knew of the gap in the fence and failed to rectify it.

HELD: The House of Lords had to decide whether to follow their previous authority of ***Addie v Dumbreck* (1929)**, which ruled that an individual does not owe a duty of care to trespassers. The House of Lords departed from this previous decision, relying on the Practice Statement finding that individuals owe a duty of care to all persons, even trespassers.

Other case law examples include the following:

- ***R v G & R* (2003)** overruled ***MPC v Caldwell* (1982)** in relation to the test of recklessness in criminal law;
- ***Howe and Bannister* (1987)** overruled ***DPP for NI v Lynch* (1975)** in relation to the availability of the defence of duress to an accessory to murder;
- ***Pepper (Inspector of Taxes) v Hart* (1993)** overruled ***Davis v Johnson* (1978)** in relation to the use of Hansard as an aid to statutory interpretation;
- ***Hall v Simons* (2000)** overruled ***Rondel v Worsley* (1969)** in relation to the immunity of court advocates from being sued for negligent performance in court. However, please note that the House of Lords did not refer to the Practice Statement when departing from *Rondel*. This may indicate that use of the Practice Statement is not necessary to depart from a previous decision.

Privy Council (Judicial Committee)

The binding nature of decisions of the Privy Council on English and Welsh courts has been a matter of some confusion over the years. Following the Supreme Court decision in ***Willers v Joyce* (2016)**, the position has now been clarified. Lord Neuberger in ***Willers***, explained the following points of precedent:

- '[U]nless there is a decision of a superior court to the contrary effect, a court in England and Wales can normally be expected to follow a decision of the JCPC, but there is no question of it being bound to do so as a matter of precedent'.
- 'There is also no doubt that a court should not, at least normally, follow a decision of the JCPC, if it is inconsistent with the decision of a court which is binding'.
- '[T]he members of that panel can, if they think it appropriate, not only decide that the earlier decision of the House of Lords or Supreme Court, or of the Court of Appeal, was wrong, but also can expressly direct that domestic courts should treat the decision of the JCPC as representing the law of England and Wales.'
- Like the CJEU, the Privy Council is not bound by its own previous decisions but is likely to follow them.

The main part to take away from ***Willers*** is that if the Judicial Committee of the Privy Council consider decisions of the House of Lords, Supreme Court, and Court of Appeal to be wrong, they may direct all domestic courts to treat decisions of the Committee as binding on them and representing the law of England and Wales. To see an example of domestic courts taking favour of Privy Council decisions, see ***R v James* (2006)**, in which the Court of Appeal followed the Privy Council decision of ***AG for Jersey v Holley* (2005)**, as opposed to the binding House of Lords decision in ***R v Smith (Morgan)* (2001)**. The decision in ***Willers*** makes sense, given that the composition of that court (i.e. who sits in that court) is identical to that of the Supreme Court.

European Court of Human Rights

Decisions of the European Court of Human Rights (ECtHR) are extremely persuasive authority but do not bind any court in England and Wales, as the domestic courts are only required to 'take into account' any decision (**s2(1) HRA 1998**). See Chapter 5 for a further discussion on s2(1). The ECtHR is not bound by its own previous decisions but is very likely to follow them.

Court of Appeal (Civil Division)

The Court of Appeal is bound by decisions of the Supreme Court (though Lord Denning is particularly noteworthy for his attempts to circumvent this in the 1970s—see ***Broome v Cassell & Co.*** **(1971)**). The Civil Division binds all lower courts but is only persuasive to the Supreme Court. The Civil Division is generally bound by its own previous decisions (often referred to as the 'self-binding rule'); however, ***Young v Bristol Aeroplane Co. Ltd*** **(1944)** provided three exceptions to this rule.

Young v Bristol Aeroplane Co. Ltd **[1944] KB 718 (CA)**

FACTS: This case concerned the payment of workmen's compensation and whether the claimant was entitled to such compensation. The facts of the case are not relevant; more so, the question for the court was whether they had the ability to depart from a previous Court of Appeal case.

HELD: Lord Greene MR held that: the Court of Appeal is generally bound by its own previous decisions, or the decisions of its predecessor, subject to three exceptions:

1. Where there are two conflicting decisions of the Court of Appeal (in that case, it must choose which one to follow).
2. Where the previous decision of the Court of Appeal, even if not expressly overruled, conflicts with a House of Lords (now Supreme Court) decision (in that case, it must follow the superior court).
3. Where its previous decision was made *per incuriam* (meaning 'through lack of care' or without due regard to the relevant law) (in that case, it may create a new precedent).

A fourth exception can be said to exist following ***R (RJM) v Secretary of State for Work and Pensions*** **(2009)**. In particular, the House of Lords ruled that the Court of Appeal may depart from one of its own previous decisions where the Court considers that the previous decision is inconsistent with a subsequent decision of the ECtHR.

Davis v Johnson **[1979] AC 264 (HL)**

FACTS: The case concerned a non-molestation order under the **Domestic Violence and Matrimonial Proceedings Act 1976**. The majority of the court disagreed with previous Court of Appeal decisions on this area of law (one of which was made only a matter of days earlier); however, they were bound to follow it according to ***Bristol Aeroplane***. Lord Denning MR argued that the Court of Appeal ought to have the same power as the House of Lords in departing from an earlier decision of the same court.

HELD: The Court of Appeal was wrong to think that it was not bound by its own previous decisions. Lord Diplock concluded that, 'In my opinion, this House should take this occasion to re-affirm expressly, unequivocably [sic] and unanimously that the rule laid down in the ***Bristol Aeroplane*** case . . . as to *stare decisis* is still binding on the Court of Appeal.'

Court of Appeal (Criminal Division)

The Criminal Division binds all lower courts but is only persuasive to the Supreme Court. The Criminal Division is generally bound by its own previous decisions; however, according to ***R v Spencer* (1985)**, the ***Bristol Aeroplane*** exceptions also apply to the Criminal Division. As a result of ***R v Taylor* (1950)** and later ***R v Gould* (1968)**, the Criminal Division has a wider discretion than its civil counterpart, where 'the liberty of the individual is at stake'.

***R v Gould* [1968] 2 QB 65 (CA)**

FACTS: The defendant pleaded guilty to bigamy and later attempted to withdraw his guilty plea on the basis that he held a reasonable, but mistaken, belief that his first marriage had been successfully dissolved.

HELD: The Court of Appeal had to decide whether to follow their previous decision of ***R v Wheat* (1921)**. The Court of Appeal found that the Criminal Division held a wider jurisdiction to disapply the precedent of the previous court. Specifically, Diplock LJ went so far as to say that the Court of Appeal is 'bound to give effect to the law as [they] think it is'.

Revision tip

When answering a problem question which involves the Court of Appeal potentially departing from a previous decision, don't forget that the Criminal Division has a much broader scope to depart than their Civil counterpart, given the risk of loss of liberty for the defendant.

Divisional Court

The Divisional Court binds all lower courts (except the Crown Court—***R v Colyer* (1974)**) but is only persuasive to the Court of Appeal and to the Supreme Court. The Divisional Court is generally bound by its own previous decisions (***Huddersfield v Watson* (1947)**), unless an exception in ***Young v Bristol Aeroplane Co. Ltd* (1944)** applies. See also ***C (A Minor) v DPP* (1994)** and ***ex parte Tal* (1985)**.

High Court of Justice

The High Court is bound by all decisions of the Supreme Court, Court of Appeal, and Divisional Courts. The High Court binds all lower courts but is only persuasive to the superior courts. The High Court is not bound by its previous decisions (***Howard de Walden Estates v Aggio* (2008)**) but previous decisions can be extremely persuasive (***Willers v Joyce* (2016)**). In this respect, one judge in the High Court may not overrule his judicial brother/sister; instead they may only 'disapprove' of the judgment and refuse to follow it. This may result in decisions being contradictory, requiring resolution by the Court of Appeal.

Crown Court

The Crown Court is bound by decisions of the Court of Appeal and the Supreme Court. As noted above, the Crown Court is not bound by decisions of the High Court. The Crown Court binds no court but can act as persuasive authority to all courts, albeit slight. The Crown Court is also not bound by its previous decisions, despite it being a court of record; however, previous decisions can be extremely persuasive (especially where the trial judge is a High Court judge).

Magistrates' court; Family Court; County Court

The magistrates' court, Family Court, and County Court bind no courts and are unlikely to act as persuasive authority. These courts are bound by all superior courts, i.e. Divisional Court, Court of Appeal, and Supreme Court. These courts are also not bound by their own previous decisions and their decisions are unlikely to be persuasive to a future tribunal, given their focus on factual disputes.

To follow or not to follow . . . that is the question

Now that you understand which courts are bound to follow the decisions of other courts, it is essential to appreciate the actions that the superior and lower courts must or may take in relation to a precedent.

The superior courts

The superior courts, when confronted with an appeal, may take numerous avenues to determine the outcome of the case. The actions that may be taken by the superior courts when confronted with a precedent are detailed below:

- **Follow**: this means that when presented with an authority from its predecessor, the court can decide to follow that authority. The Supreme Court can decide to follow or depart from a case; whereas the Court of Appeal must 'follow' previous Court of Appeal decisions unless the case falls within one of the ***Bristol Aeroplane*** exceptions.
- **Affirm**: when a superior court has before it an authority that is not binding on them, they may 'affirm' or 'approve' the authority, which may then result in a binding precedent (subject to the conditions of *stare decisis* discussed in 'Precedent—the principles' earlier).
- **Consider**: a superior court may discuss the decision of another case, but may decide not to follow, apply, or affirm it.
- **Depart**: this means that the superior court can depart from a decision of their predecessors. As stated previously, the Supreme Court has the right to depart where it considers it 'right to do so' but the Court of Appeal may only depart from a previous decision within the exceptions laid out in ***Bristol Aeroplane***.
- **Doubt**: a superior court may decide not to depart from or overrule an earlier authority, but may have expressed doubt as to its validity/viability. This may apply where the superior court either does not think it necessary to overrule the authority, or does not have the authority to do so. 'Disapproving' is in a similar vein, but this is where the court expressly states that the decision or principle from a particular authority is wrong.
- **Overrule**: this means that the superior court decides that the previous precedent is incorrect and changes the precedent. The effect of overruling is to create a new binding precedent to be followed.

- **Reverse**: more often than not, this phrase is adopted when speaking of the factual matters involved in the case. For example, the Court of Appeal may reverse the decision of the High Court in relation to a personal injury matter.
- **Quash**: this phrase is more likely to be seen in a criminal law context and means that the decision of the lower court is removed. Normally, one speaks of 'quashing a conviction', meaning that an individual is no longer guilty of an offence. Usually, if a conviction is quashed a retrial will be ordered.

Looking for extra marks?

When answering an essay-style question on binding precedent, don't forget to consider whether, even if they have the power to do so, a particular court will actually choose to depart from an earlier decision. For instance, the Supreme Court (formerly the House of Lords) is permitted to depart from a previous decision where it considers it 'right to do so'. However, in practice, the right is rarely exercised, with an estimated thirty cases reported since 1966. Gain extra marks by including this detail and take it one step further by asking the question: 'Why is it rarely used?'

Revision tip

Many students struggle with distinguishing between the concept of overruling a case and reversing a case.

Overruling means that the precedent in a previous case (whether it be the same or a different case) is wrong and should not be followed in the future. This is concerned with the precedent itself.

Reversing means that the superior court has changed the decision of the lower court in the same case. This is concerned with the decision itself.

These two terms are not mutually exclusive as if a decision is overruled, it is likely that the decision of that court is also reversed.

The inferior courts

Given their inferior status, the avenues open to these courts are not as wide as those available to the superior courts. Superior courts are not bound by their inferiors, thus have no need to find a reason or way to 'avoid' the decision. However, there are numerous ways in which a lower court may 'avoid' a binding authority from their superiors. The actions available to the inferior courts, including the ability to avoid the authority, are detailed below:

- **Follow**: this means that when presented with an authority from its superior, the court must 'follow' or 'apply' that authority.
- **Distinguish**: this means that the court can avoid the binding nature of the precedent by arguing that the instant case is 'materially different' in facts to the binding precedent and thus has no application in the instant case. What the court will do instead is use an authority, if one is available, that more closely reflects the instant case on its facts (see, e.g. ***Balfour v Balfour* (1919)** and how it was treated in ***Merritt v Merritt* (1970)**).

Judicial law-making—overstepping the mark

We considered this topic briefly in Chapter 2 when discussing the interrelation between the legislature and the judiciary. However, it is also pertinent to appreciate that through the doctrine of precedent, judges may act in a quasi-legislative role by creating a binding precedent for the lower courts to follow. Whilst judges may not wish to admit that they 'make' law, such conduct is inevitable. In ***ex parte Evans* (2001)**, Lord Hobhouse explained that:

> [t]he common law develops as circumstances change and the balance of legal, social, and economic needs changes. New concepts come into play; new statutes influence the non-statutory law. The strength of the common law is its ability to develop and evolve. All this carries with it the inevitable need to recognize that decisions may change. What was previously thought to be the law is open to challenge and review; if the challenge is successful, a new statement of the law will take the place of the old statement.

By way of example, prior to 1991 marital rape was legal in England and Wales before the House of Lords ruled that such a law was abhorrent in modern society and held it to be unlawful (***R v R (Marital Rape Exemption)* (1991)**). In some circumstances this binding precedent will force Parliament's hand, that will then enact a piece of legislation to deal with this matter. On the other hand, the senior judges have shown restraint in certain circumstances where change is better within the remit of Parliament, as opposed to the courts. For example, the courts have repeatedly ruled that any change to the law on assisted suicide is a matter for Parliament, not for the courts (see ***R (Nicklinson) v Ministry of Justice* (2015)** and ***R (Conway) v Secretary of State for Justice* (2018)**).

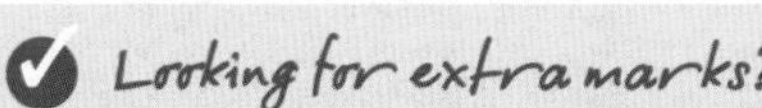

When discussing the role of judges as lawmakers, don't forget that law-making does not need to be a positive act (like in ***R v R***). Law-making may be a passive act also where the judiciary refuse to change the common law on the grounds that it ought to be a change made by Parliament. This statement, in essence, forces Parliament's hand, as in the case of ***C v DPP* (1995)**, where the House of Lords refused to change the principle of *doli incapax* (i.e. that a child between the ages of 10 and 14 cannot generally commit a criminal offence). This led to Parliament enacting **s34 Crime and Disorder Act 1998**, which abolished this rule. Now all persons over the age of 10 are capable of committing a criminal offence in the eyes of the law.

Review of precedent

Now that we understand the prominence of the common law and the operation of precedent in our legal system, it is worth briefly highlighting some of the advantages and disadvantages of precedent (see Table 4.11).

Review of precedent

Table 4.11 Advantages and disadvantages of precedent

Advantage	Explanation
Consistency and fairness	The operation of precedent ensures that all cases based upon similar facts and law are treated the same. This ensures fairness, justice, and transparency in the legal system.
Certainty	Lawyers are able to effectively advise their clients as to their thoughts or predictions on the outcome of a particular case, given the established precedent.
Modernization	Case law has the benefit of being able to develop and modernize to reflect societal norms.
Disadvantage	**Explanation**
Rigidity	The operation of precedent has been criticized for being too rigid—the exceptions to which the Court of Appeal must follow their own previous decisions and is bound by the superior courts is too restrictive. This rigidity may create injustice in a particular case.
Slow to change	Given that changes to the law by way of precedent may only be made when a particular point of law comes before the courts, the law is often slow to develop and adapt. Many areas of law are in need of reform and clarification, but without a platform to demonstrate this the law remains outdated.

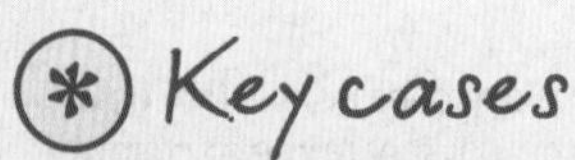

Case	Facts	Principles
***Young v Bristol Aeroplane Co. Ltd* [1944] KB 718 (CA)**	The question for the court was whether the Court of Appeal had the ability to depart from a previous Court of Appeal case.	The court may depart in three circumstances: **(i)** where there are two conflicting decisions of the Court of Appeal; **(ii)** where the previous decision of the Court of Appeal, even if not expressly overruled, conflicts with a House of Lords (now Supreme Court) decision; **(iii)** where its previous decision was made *per incuriam*.

Case	Facts	Principles
R v Barton **[2020] EWCA Crim 575 (CA)**	The defendant had exploited a number of care home residents into gifting him large sums of money. On appeal he alleged that the Court of Appeal were not bound by a decision of the Supreme Court which was merely *obiter dicta*.	The Court of Appeal ruled that where the Supreme Court directs that the lower courts are bound by its decision, even though strictly *obiter dicta*, the lower courts must be bound. The CA accepted that ordinary rules of precedent were slightly modified as a result. This principle would only apply where it was the unanimous view of the Supreme Court that it should bind lower courts.
R v Gould **[1968] 2 QB 65 (CA)**	The defendant wished to withdraw a guilty plea of bigamy. The Crown Court refused to allow the withdrawal on the grounds of a Court of Appeal decision (***R v Wheat*** **(1921)**). The question was whether the Court could depart from that case.	'If upon due consideration we were to be of the opinion that the law had been either misapplied or misunderstood in an earlier decision . . . we should be entitled to depart from the view as to the law expressed in the earlier decision notwithstanding that the case could not be brought within any of the exceptions laid down in Young v Bristol Aeroplane Co. Ltd.' (Lord Diplock)

Key debates

Topic	The exceptions in Bristol Aeroplane
Academic	Terence Prime and Gary Scanlan
Viewpoint	Argue that the Court of Appeal are developing a fourth exception to **Bristol Aeroplane** and are declining to follow a case where it was 'manifestly wrong'.
Source	Terence Prime and Gary Scanlan, 'Stare Decisis and the Court of Appeal: Judicial Confusion and Judicial Reform' (2004) 23 Civil Justice Quarterly 212, 220

Topic	Distinguishing cases
Academic	Bruce Harris
Viewpoint	Argues that **distinguishing** need not be restricted to factual differences, but can also include situations where 'societal factual circumstances have changed since [the precedent] was originally decided'.
Source	Bruce Harris, 'Final Appellate Courts Overruling their own "Wrong" Precedents: The Ongoing Search for Principle' (2002) 118 Law Quarterly Review 408, 411

Exam questions

****

Topic	Status of the judge re *stare decisis*
Academic	Andrew Ashworth
Viewpoint	Argues that the status of the judge should be 'irrelevant' to whether a non-binding precedent is persuasive to a court.
Source	Andrew Ashworth, 'The Binding Effect of Crown Court Decisions' (1980) Crim LR 402

Essay question

'The doctrine of precedent is essential to the English common law system; however, the development of the **Bristol Aeroplane** exceptions is making a mockery of the principle of *stare decisis*.'

Critically discuss this statement.

Problem question

The Supreme Court has just released a brand-new criminal judgment, *R v Thomas* [2017] UKSC 12 (fictitious). You are a criminal **barrister** and have been asked to present a paper on the effects of this case on all other courts.

Describe the effect the Supreme Court's decision will have on all courts, the manner by which the case is likely to be reported, and whether the decision can be avoided by any courts that disagree with it.

Would your answer differ if the judgment was delivered by the Court of Appeal (Criminal Division)? If so, how?

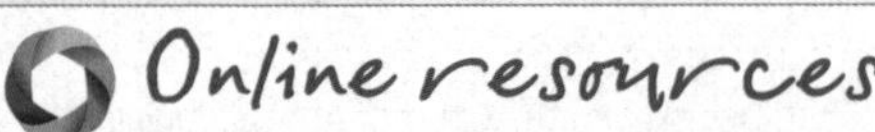

For outline answers to these exam questions, as well as multiple-choice questions, please visit the online resources.

#5 Sources of Law III: Effect of EU and International Law

Key facts

- The UK is a signatory to multiple international institutions. Each of these institutions sets a framework for the UK to operate within, granting certain rights, benefits, and obligations.
- Since joining the European Economic Community (EEC), now the European Union (EU), in 1972, parliamentary supremacy has been limited by the operation of EU law.
- On 23 June 2016, the UK voted to 'leave' the EU.
- International law governs the relationships between states regulating their conduct upon being granted consent to do so.
- The European Convention on Human Rights (ECHR) grants certain fundamental rights to the citizens of the state and the **Human Rights Act (HRA) 1998** allows them to enforce those rights in a domestic court.

Chapter overview

The bigger picture

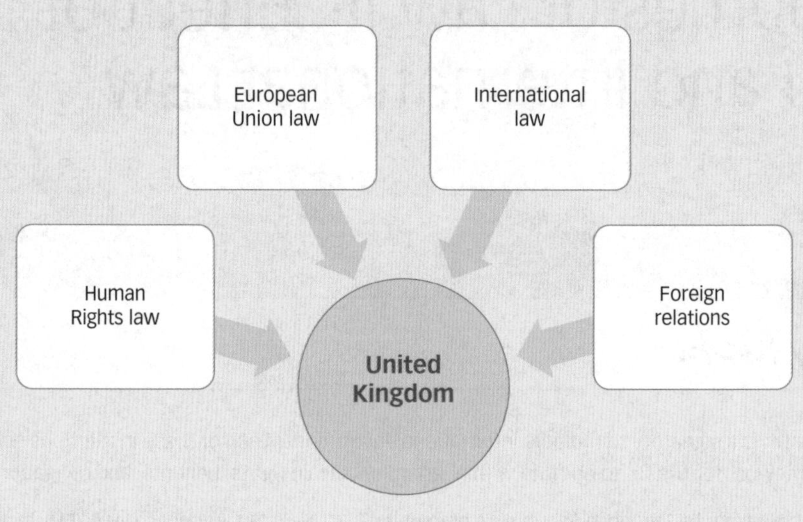

Introduction

The UK is a 'member' of a number of different conventions and institutions. This means that it is a part of a much bigger picture.

The most prominent institutions for the purposes of this text are:

- the European Union (EU);
- the European Convention on Human Rights and Fundamental Freedoms (ECHR); and
- the United Nations.

You will hopefully have noticed that above the word 'member' has been placed in quotation marks. This is intentional, given that the word 'member', although useful for our purposes, is not 100 per cent accurate. For instance, the UK is a 'member' of the EU but is not a 'member' of the ECHR. Instead, the UK is considered a 'signatory' of the ECHR. Further to this, the UK is a recognized 'state' for the purposes of international law and submits itself to international law where relevant and appropriate. We use 'member' in this chapter to refer to the affiliation or relationship that the UK holds with these different institutions.

Remember from Chapter 1 that we spoke of the 'dynamism' of the English legal system (ELS). In this context, you will need to appreciate that foreign relations will also have an effect on the way in which the ELS operates. Although the UK's continued involvement in the above institutions will have a direct impact on the operation of UK law, relations with other states, whether they be good or bad, will also shape the face of the ELS.

This chapter is devoted to focusing on the three key institutions listed above and how the UK's affiliation has affected the operation and administration of the ELS.

The European Union

UK membership and Brexit

As a consequence of the **European Communities Act (ECA) 1972**, Britain formally joined the European Economic Community on 1 January 1973 (which would then become the European Union) becoming the seventh Member State in this ever-growing community. As a result of this membership, the UK became bound by the laws of the EU and became obliged to follow them in all relevant cases. Some areas that are affected include:

- employment law;
- environmental law; and
- consumer law.

On 23 June 2016, the UK held a national referendum asking the question: 'Should the United Kingdom leave the European Union?' The holding of the referendum was legally underpinned by the **European Union Referendum Act 2015**.

By a vote of 52 per cent to 48 per cent (17,410,742 to 16,141,241), the UK voted to leave the European Union (popularly known as 'Brexit'). **Article 50 of the Treaty on European Union (TEU)** provides for the procedure where a Member State wishes to withdraw its membership from the Union. Specifically, **Article 50.2** provides that the Member State must provide notice to the European Council of its intention to withdraw from the Union. Upon notice being provided, the Member State shall officially withdraw from the Union immediately or within a two-year period starting from when notice to withdraw was provided. This is detailed in **Article 50.3**. The legal process of exiting the EU (referred to as 'triggering Article 50') officially began on 29 March 2017, with Britain's permanent representative to the EU, Tim Barrow, handing an official notice of the UK's intention to leave the EU to the then President of the European Council, Donald Tusk.

As a result of the vote to leave the EU, a number of challenges have been brought against the vote which require consideration. Two challenges will be discussed here:

- whether the UK government could lawfully ignore the result of the referendum; and
- whether Parliament could exercise prerogative power in order to leave the EU or whether some form of legislation was required before **Article 50 TEU** could be invoked.

With regard to the first challenge, it is worth remembering, as we know from Chapter 3, that Parliament is supreme and cannot be bound by itself or be questioned by outside bodies. In simple terms, therefore, although legislation can and did authorize the holding of a national referendum, no legislation is capable of requiring the government to be bound by such a decision. To bind the government would be contrary to the doctrine of continuing sovereignty and would have the effect of binding future Parliaments. Ian Loveland, *Constitutional Law, Administrative Law, and Human Rights: A Critical Introduction* (8th edn, OUP 2018), has made clear that Parliament can legally ignore the vote to leave the EU and have the power to set a second referendum on the topic; however, they are unlikely to do so, given the political effects it may have on the government at the time. This is the essential distinction between legal sovereignty (the power to do whatever Parliament wishes to do) and political sovereignty (the practical factors that will restrain Parliament from doing whatever it wishes to do). On 7 December 2016, the House of Commons voted on whether to respect the outcome of the referendum. The House voted in favour, by a large majority, of respecting the outcome of the referendum. As a result, although Parliament was not bound to accept the result, the outcome was nonetheless accepted.

The second challenge was first brought in the Administrative Court by Gina Miller, an investment banker, and others, and is reported as ***R (Miller) v Secretary of State for Exiting the European Union*** **(2017)**. The Administrative Court found in favour of the claimants, ruling that the government could not use prerogative powers to trigger **Article 50**. The *ratio* of this decision is made clear by the Court between [82–94] and [97–104] of the judgment. In summary, the Court ruled that whilst Parliament is supreme in that it can make or unmake any law, as it did with the **ECA 1972**, it is not possible or permissible for the government to use prerogative powers to change law enacted by Parliament. The Court reasoned that there is nothing within the writing of the **ECA 1972** justifying such a right of the government; further, to do so would contradict the constitutional principles of parliamentary sovereignty. The judgment of the Administrative Court was appealed by the government to the Supreme Court, which delivered its judgment on 24 January 2017.

R (Miller) v Secretary of State for Exiting the European Union **[2017] UKSC 5 (SC)**

FACTS: On 23 June 2016, the UK held a referendum asking the UK population whether they wished to leave the EU. With a majority vote, the UK voted to leave the EU. The question before the court concerned the steps which were required as a matter of law before the process of leaving the EU could be initiated.

HELD: The Supreme Court, by a majority of eight to three, dismissed the government's appeal (Lord Reed, Lord Carnwath, and Lord Hughes dissenting). In a joint judgment of the majority, the Court ruled that an Act of Parliament was required to authorize ministers to give notice of the decision of the UK to withdraw from the EU in accordance with **Article 50**. Each of the dissenting justices gave a separate judgment.

Between [78–82] the majority reasoned that withdrawal from the EU makes a fundamental change to the UK's constitutional arrangements. Simply put, it cuts off the source of EU law. Their Lordships furthered this by stating that such a fundamental change will be the 'inevitable effect' of a notice being served and the UK constitution requires such changes to be effected by parliamentary legislation. Their Lordships continued by explaining that the fact that withdrawal from the EU would remove some existing domestic rights of UK residents also renders it impermissible for the government to withdraw from EU treaties without prior parliamentary authority.

In response to the judgment of the Supreme Court, on 31 January 2017, the UK government introduced the **European Union (Notification of Withdrawal) Act 2017**. The process of leaving the EU has been a slow and controversial matter. In December 2019, the Conservative Party won the General Election with a large majority of seats, and since then have proceeded to pass the **European Union (Withdrawal Agreement) Bill 2019–20** in the House of Commons. The Bill had been originally defeated in the House of Lords on 20 January 2020, given the serious concerns the House had regarding some of the clauses of the Bill. Specifically, the House of Lords voted in favour of an amendment that would ensure that EU citizens be given physical proof of their right to remain in the UK post-Brexit. This amendment returned to the House of Commons but was rejected by the House. The House of Lords subsequently approved the Bill, despite failing to secure the desired change noted above. On Thursday 23 January 2020, the Bill gained royal assent and became law: the **European Union (Withdrawal Agreement) Act 2020**. As a result of this, the UK left the EU on 31 January. Technically, the UK remains a member of the EU until a withdrawal agreement has been made. The UK will either leave the EU with a deal, or without a deal. The Prime Minister, Boris Johnson, has said that, as the Conservative Party is likely not to accept the trade deals offered by the EU, the 'No deal' situation is likely to come back on the table.

Once the UK formally removes its membership of the EU, it will no longer be subject to the obligations, duties, and benefits that membership brings with it. Despite the fact the process of leaving the EU is now underway and soon to be complete, as part of your studies, you will still need to be aware of some of the key areas of EU law and its relationship with England and Wales. It is better, therefore, to accept that you need to be aware of the 'influences' of EU law on domestic law.

Introduction to EU law

According to Nigel Foster, *Foster on EU Law* (7th edn, Oxford University Press 2019), EU law can helpfully be divided broadly into three main components, these being:

- institutional law;
- procedural law; and
- substantive law.

This section is not concerned with either the procedural law or the substantive law element of the EU. Rather, it is dedicated to institutional law. Also known as 'constitutional law', this area observes how the UK's current (albeit close to ending) membership in the EU affects the UK at a domestic level. Institutional law includes such matters as the development of the EU, the sources of EU law, the different institutions of the EU, and the effect of the EU on domestic supremacy.

For a fuller account of EU law, including the substance of EU law, please consult Matthew Homewood, *EU Law Concentrate* (6th edn, Oxford University Press 2018).

History of the EU

The origins of the EU, as we know it, can be located in the **Treaty Establishing the Creation of the European Economic Community 1957 (Treaty of Rome)**, signed by the six founding states, which established the European Economic Community (EEC). This was the Treaty that set the foundations that the EU is built upon today. However, there were some earlier signs of unionization before the **Treaty of Rome**. In 1951, the **European Coal and Steel Community Treaty (ECSC) 1951 (Treaty of Paris)** created a single common market in coal and steel. The next steps saw the introduction of the 'common market' (now known as the 'internal market'), which entailed not only the free movement of goods, but also of persons with the signing of the **Treaty of Rome** in 1957. Also signed in 1957 was the **European Atomic Energy Community Treaty (Euratom Treaty)**, which regulated nuclear power.

As a result of the **Treaty on European Union (TEU) 1992 (Treaty of Maastricht)** the EEC was no longer, and arising from its ashes was the European Union (EU).

Revision tip

Be careful not to say that the EEC was 'renamed' as the EU. It was not. The EU was a brand-new entity created by the **Treaty of Maastricht**, which incorporated the existing communities and amended all existing treaties.

As a result of the **TEU**, the EU was now built on three pillars. The three pillars formed the structure/framework of the EU, which is demonstrated in Figure 5.1.

Figure 5.1 The three pillars of the EU

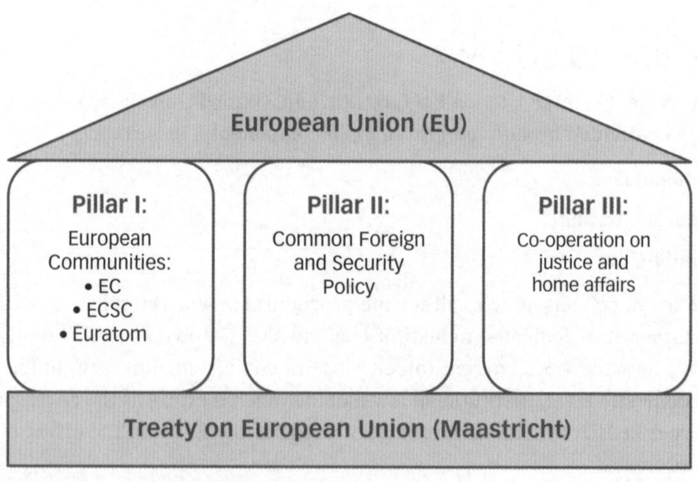

The EU developed further as a result of subsequent treaties. These treaties are listed below and it is advised that you go away and research their effects on the EU:

- **Treaty of Amsterdam 1997**;
- **Treaty of Nice 2001**;
- **Treaty of Lisbon 2007**.

Enlargement and the Member States

Between 1957 and the present date, there has been what is known as an 'enlargement' of the EU. In 1957, the EEC began with as few as six Member States (also known as 'Member Countries'). As of 2020, there are 27 EU Member States (now that the UK has invoked **Article 50 TEU**). Please see the online resources for a list of these Member States, the year in which they joined, their voting rights, and their number of seats in the European Parliament (EP).

Naturally, the EU is an ever-growing entity, as demonstrated by the continued increase in state membership. There are a number of countries that may, in the future, become EU Member States. The countries can be divided into three categories, namely: candidates; potential candidates; and frozen/withdrawn applications:

- **Candidates**: candidates relate to those states whose application has been confirmed by the EU, and with whom negotiations will then be undertaken.
- **Potential candidates**: potential candidates relate to those states whose application the EU has promised to consider, should one be made. Potential candidates must satisfy the **Copenhagen Criteria**.
- **Frozen/withdrawn applications**: frozen applications relate to those states whose applications have either been frozen pending investigation or withdrawn.

Figure 5.2 demonstrates the current states that fit into these categories.

Now that we understand the EU and its development, we can now consider what Foster (2016) refers to as the 'institutional' law of the EU.

EU institutions

As with England and Wales, which is comprised of three branches of government (legislature, executive, and judiciary), the EU is composed of several institutions that help ensure the efficient operation of the Union. This section considers those institutions, their role, and how they are governed. According to the official websites of the EU (http://europa.eu and http://eur-lex.europa.eu), the EU:

> has an institutional framework aimed at promoting and defending its values, objectives and interests, the interests of its citizens and those of its member countries.

The Union is comprised of seven key institutions. These institutions are listed in **Article 13 TEU 2007** and are detailed in Table 5.1. The roles of the different institutions were most recently amended by the **Treaty of Lisbon 2007** and are detailed on the Europa website.

Figure 5.2 Candidates, potential candidates, and frozen candidates for EU membership

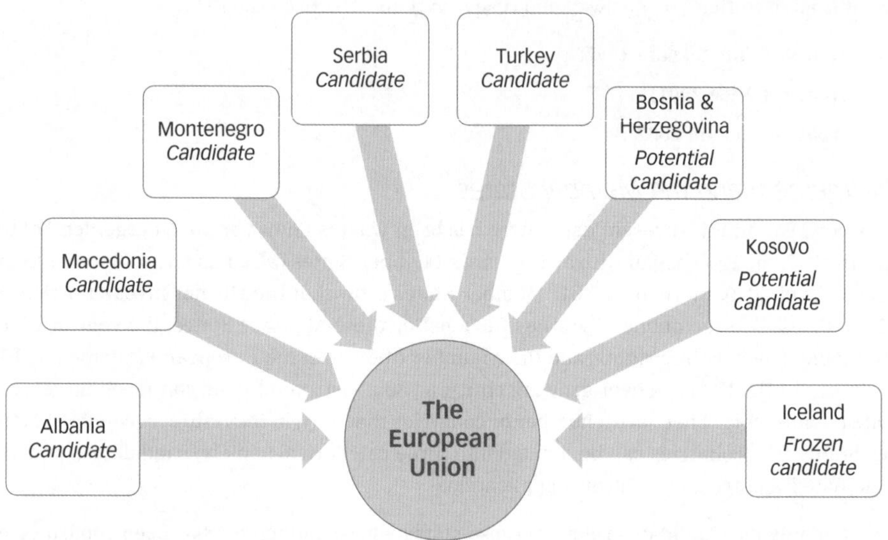

Table 5.1 EU institutions

The European Council (EC) Article 15 TEU; Articles 235–236 TFEU	
What is the institution?	**Role**
• The EC is comprised of the Heads of State or government of the 28 EU Member States, the President of the EC, and the President of the European Commission. For the UK, the Prime Minister attends. • Prior to the **Treaty of Lisbon**, the EC was not an EU institution. • The Treaty created the position of the President of the EC.	• The EC meets at least twice every six months (known as a 'European summit') and defines the EU's overall political direction and priorities for the EU's development. • The EC does not exercise any legislative function. It does, however, adopt 'conclusions' during EC meetings, which identify issues of concern and actions to take.
The Council of the European Union (The Council) Article 16 TEU; Articles 237–243 TFEU	
What is the institution?	**Role**
• The Council is the main legislative body of the EU institutions. • It comprises ministers of the Member States, with its membership fluctuating depending on the matter under debate (e.g. if employment matters are under consideration, the Council comprises national Ministers of Employment).	• The Council acts as final decision maker, alongside the EP, on the adoption of secondary legislation. • The Council can delegate power to the Commission to enact regulations. • The Council shares budgetary powers with the EP in voting on the annual budget.

The European Commission Article 17 TEU; Articles 244–250 TFEU	
What is the institution?	**Role**
• The European Commission is comprised of one Commissioner from each Member State, appointed for a five-year term.	• The European Commission proposes and enforces legislation. • The Commission manages EU policies and allocates EU funding. • The Commission may refer any infringement by a Member State to the CJEU (**Article 258 TFEU**).

The European Parliament (EP) Article 14 TEU; Articles 223–234 TFEU	
What is the institution?	**Role**
• The EP is a democratically elected body that represents the EU citizens. • Members of the EP (MEPs) are elected once every five years by citizens from across the 28 EU Member States. • The number of MEPs per country is set by the European Council. There are currently 751 MEPs. • Prior to Brexit, the UK held the third most votes with 72, behind France with 74 and Germany with 96.	• The EP acts as a co-legislator alongside the Council, based on European Commission proposals. • The EP has the power of control over the different EU institutions, in particular the Commission. • The EP shares budgetary powers with the Council in voting on the annual budget and approving the EU's long-term budget (the 'Multiannual Financial Framework').

The Court of Justice of the European Union (CJEU) Article 19 TEU; Articles 251–281 TFEU	
What is the institution?	**Role**
• The CJEU is divided into three bodies: **(i)** CJEU (one judge from each EU country, plus eleven Advocates General); **(ii)** General Court (one judge from each EU country); **(iii)** Civil Service Tribunal (seven judges).	• The CJEU ensures that EU law is interpreted and applied in the same way in every EU country. • The CJEU deals with requests for preliminary rulings from national courts. • The General Court rules on actions for annulment brought by individuals. • The Civil Service Tribunal rules on disputes between the EU and its staff.

The European Central Bank (ECB) Articles 282–284 TFEU	
What is the institution?	**Role**
• The ECB President represents the Bank at high-level EU and international meetings.	• The ECB sets the interest rates.

The European Central Bank (ECB) Articles 282–284 TFEU	
• The ECB has the three following decision-making bodies: **(i)** Governing Council; **(ii)** Executive Board; **(iii)** General Council.	• The ECB manages the eurozone's foreign currency reserves. • The ECB ensures that financial markets and institutions are well supervised by national authorities. • The ECB authorizes production of euro banknotes.
European Court of Auditors (ECA)	
What is the institution?	**Role**
• The ECA consists of court members who are appointed by the Council, for renewable six-year terms.	• The ECA looks after the interests of EU taxpayers. • It carries out three types of audit: **(i)** financial audits; **(ii)** compliance audits; **(iii)** performance audits.

Revision tip

Do not confuse the European Court of Human Rights (ECtHR) and the Court of Justice of the European Union (CJEU). The former sits in Strasbourg and is concerned with the enforcement of human rights guaranteed under the ECHR. The latter sits in Luxembourg and is concerned with the application and interpretation of EU law.

Further, do not confuse the Council of the European Union, the European Council, and the Council of Europe. The Council of Europe (although it includes Europe in the name) is not an institution of the EU. Rather, it is a separate body concerned with the enforcement of the ECHR.

EU law

Sources of law

Just as with English Law, EU law (formerly known as 'EC law') can be divided into primary and secondary sources (see Figure 5.3). You may come across the term *acquis communautaire* in your studies, which is used to describe the body of law of the EU in its entirety. We shall consider these sources of law in detail now.

1. **Treaties**:
   - Treaties are the primary source of law of the EU requiring all subsequent legislation to act in accordance with the Treaty obligations and objectives.

Figure 5.3 EU sources of law

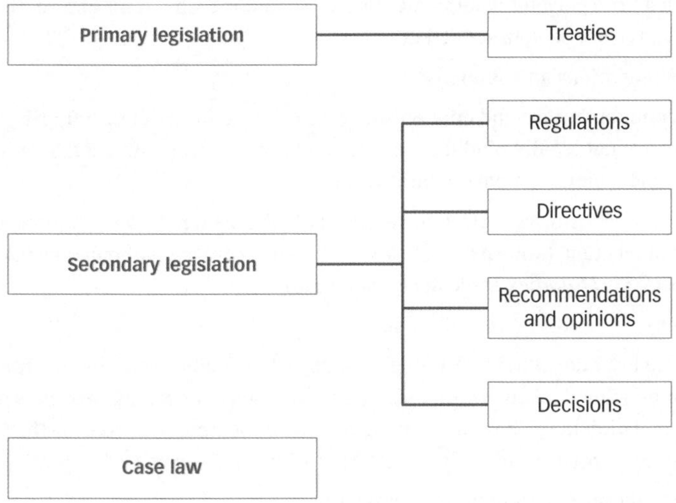

- The EU is founded on three Treaties, these being:
  - **Treaty of Lisbon**;
  - **Treaty on European Union** (also known as the **Maastricht Treaty**); and
  - **Treaty on the Functioning of the European Union (TFEU)**.

2. **Regulations**:
   - Regulations are defined in **Article 288 TFEU** as having 'general application . . . binding in its entirety and directly applicable in all Member States'.
   - They are designed to ensure the uniform application of Union law in all the Member States.
   - Regulations supersede national laws incompatible with their substantive provisions.
3. **Directives**:
   - Directives are also defined in **Article 288 TFEU** as 'binding as to the result to be achieved, upon each Member State to which it is addressed but leaving to the national authorities the choice of form and methods'.
   - What this means is that Member States must enforce a provision of EU law; however, it is in their discretion as to how it is implemented (known as 'transposing'). In the UK, this has normally been achieved by use of statutory instruments, though it may be done by way of an Act of Parliament.

- Directives, which lay down an objective or policy, are issued to the Member States with a time period for implementation. Should the time limit expire, the Directive will have vertical direct effect.

4. **Recommendations and opinions**:
   - Recommendations and opinions are also covered in **Article 288 TFEU**; however, they are not legally binding. Recommendations merely offer a line of action or provide a view on a particular question.
   - National courts are, however, required to take such recommendations into 'consideration' (known as 'soft law') when interpreting national law (***Grimaldi v Fonds des Maladies Profesionelles* (1989)**).
5. **Decisions**:
   - These are addressed to Member States or to specified individuals, for instance Commission decisions addressed to businesses concerning breaches of competition law. These are not, as may be expected, decisions of the Court of Justice of the European Union (CJEU)—for that, see point 6 below.
   - Decisions are binding in their entirety.
6. **Case law**:
   - The decisions of the CJEU are binding on each Member State, including their national courts.
   - The decisions of the Court are for reference only and it remains the role of the domestic court to issue a judgment in a given case.
   - The Court deals only with matters concerning EU law and has no jurisdiction for matters of a domestic-only nature.
   - The Court is generally responsible for the interpretation of both primary and secondary legislation.

Direct applicability and effect

The effect that the EU has on Member States is subject to whether the source of law is of 'direct application' and whether it has 'direct effect'. It is necessary to distinguish these two terms as both, although interrelated, require a distinction to be drawn:

- If a source of law is said to be 'directly applicable', this means that the law becomes part of the national law of the Member State immediately (it is 'self-executing') and without the necessity to transpose that law into domestic legislation.
- If a source of law is said to have 'direct effect', this means that individual rights are created and protected by that source of law. These rights can be enforced in the CJEU. There are two forms of direct effect, vertical and horizontal. Figure 5.4 explains this distinction.

Figure 5.4 Direct effect

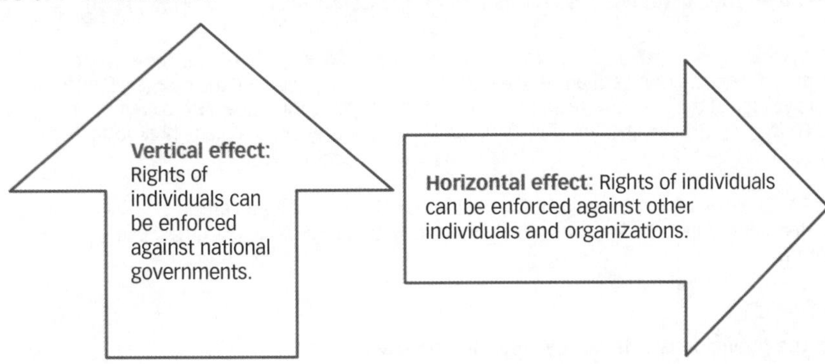

Looking for extra marks?

Show your knowledge of these terms by appreciating that, although related, these two terms are, in a sense, exclusive. This is because directly applicable EU law will not necessarily be directly effective (it is not automatic) and provisions that are not directly applicable are still capable of direct effect. The classic example of this are Directives which are not directly applicable, as they require implementation by the Member States; however, if they satisfy certain criteria (see paragraph 3 (Directives) in the following text), they may be directly effective.

Emily Finch and Stefan Fafinski, *Legal Skills* (7th edn, Oxford University Press 2019) quite helpfully distinguish **direct applicability** and direct effect by stating that 'direct applicability is concerned with the incorporation of EU law into the legal system of a Member State, whereas direct effect is concerned with its enforceability'.

We shall now consider the different sources of law and their status in relation to **direct applicability** and direct effect (see also Table 5.2).

1. **Treaties**:
    - Treaties are directly applicable as they require no further implementation on part of the Member State. They apply automatically.
    - Treaties are directly effective so long as they are 'sufficiently clear, precise and unconditional' and their implementation must not be dependent upon any implementing measure. These are known as the ***Van Gend*** criteria (see 'Key cases' at the end of the chapter).
    - If these conditions are met, treaties have both vertical direct effect (***Van Gend en Loos* (1963)**) and horizontal direct effect (***Defrenne v Sabena* (1976)**).

***Van Gend en Loos v Nederlandse Administratie der Belastingen* [1963] ECR 1 (ECJ)**
FACTS: In the Dutch court, Van Gend brought proceedings seeking refund of a customs duty charged on an import of goods from Germany to the Netherlands. Van Gend claimed the charge infringed the substantive right of the free movement of goods (**Article 30 TFEU**). It was argued by the defendant that claims concerning the infringement of EU law could only be brought in enforcement proceedings by the Commission or other Member States, directly in the Court of Justice. **HELD:** The European Court of Justice (ECJ), now the CJEU, held that for an article of legislation (whether it be a Treaty, Regulation, or Directive) to be directly effective, three conditions must be met (known as the '***Van Gend*** criteria'). These are that: (i) **the provision is sufficiently clear and precise;** (ii) **the provision is unconditional;** (iii) **the provision requires no further legislation in Member States**.

***Defrenne v Sabena* (Case 43/75) [1976] ECR 455 (ECJ)**
FACTS: Defrenne, an air hostess, sought an equal pay claim against her employer under what is now **Article 157 TFEU**, which concerned the right to equal pay for equal work. **HELD:** The Court of Justice ruled that 'the prohibition on discrimination between men and women applies not only to the action of public authorities, but also extends to all agreements which are intended to regulate paid labour collectively, as well as contracts between individuals'.

2. **Regulations**:
    - Regulations are directly applicable. **Article 288 TFEU** states that Regulations are of 'general application . . . binding in its entirety and directly applicable in all Member States'. Despite its binding nature, a Member State may still decide to legislate to transpose the law. For example, the **General Data Protection Regulation (EU) 2016/679** resulted in the UK enacting the **Data Protection Act 2018** to complement the Regulation and update the current UK law contained in the **Data Protection Act 1998**.
    - Regulations are directly effective, both vertically and horizontally, so long as the same *Van Gend* criteria are met (***Leonesio* (1971)**).
3. **Directives**:
    - Directives are not directly applicable as they require implementation by the Member State. It is made clear in **Article 288 TFEU** that implementation of the Directives is left to 'the national authorities . . . choice of form and methods'. For example, the UK transposed the **Trade Secrets Directive (EU) 2016/943** by way of statutory instrument: **Trade Secrets (Enforcement, etc.) Regulations 2018**.

- Directives can be directly effective so long as they are 'sufficiently clear, precise, and unconditional' (***Van Duyn* (1974)**) and its implementation deadline must have expired (***Pubblico Ministero v Ratti* (1978)**).
- Directives can have vertical direct effect; however, they cannot be relied upon horizontally (***Marshall* (1986)**).
- Where a Member State has failed to implement a Directive within the allotted time frame and this failure has caused a loss to a citizen, the state may be liable for damages according to the ***Francovich* (1992)** principle.

Van Duyn v Home Office **(Case 41/74) [1975] 2 WLR 760 (ECJ)**

FACTS: Van Duyn, a Dutch national, was refused entry into the UK on the public policy grounds that her membership in the Church of Scientology was 'socially harmful'. Van Duyn challenged this decision, arguing that any restriction can only be justified on the 'personal conduct' of the individual alone and such membership did not amount to 'personal conduct'. However, the UK had yet to implement the Directive responsible for this rule.

HELD: The Court of Justice held that Van Duyn could invoke the Directive before the national court.

Marshall v Southampton and South West Hampshire Area Health Authority **(Case 152/84) [1986] ECR 723 (ECJ)**

FACTS: Marshall sought to challenge her employer's compulsory retirement policy on the grounds that it was discriminatory. Her employers were the health authority, thus meaning her claim was vertical (as the health authority was held to be part of the state). Nevertheless, the Court of Justice took the opportunity to consider the issue of horizontal direct effect of directives.

HELD: Directives cannot be invoked horizontally against other individuals. They are restricted to being invoked vertically, against the state or a public authority.

Looking for extra marks?

Marshall has been extensively criticized for its contradictory nature. Marshall could invoke the Directive, as her employers were considered an arm of the state. However, other individuals who are not employed by the state cannot invoke the Directive against their private employer.

4. **Recommendations and opinions**:
   - Given that recommendations and opinions are not legally binding and are simply a form of soft law, such recommendations are neither directly applicable nor directly effective.
5. **Decisions**:
   - Decisions are directly applicable.
   - Decisions are also vertically directly effective, but only to those to whom the decision is addressed.

Table 5.2 Direct effect and sources of law

Source of law	Directly applicable?	Directly effective?	
		Vertical	Horizontal
Treaties	✓	✓	✓
Regulations	✓	✓	✓
Directives	✗	✓	✗
Recommendations and opinions	✗	✗	✗
Decisions	✓	✓	✗

Indirect effect

Before we move on to the supremacy of EU law, it is also worth considering a third term relating to the application of EU law, namely 'indirect effect'. According to the principle, national law must be interpreted in accordance with relevant EU law, with the qualification that the transposition deadline into national law must still have passed. This principle may prove useful to EU citizens in cases where the provision is not 'sufficiently clear, precise and unconditional', or because they cannot rely on the provision horizontally.

The principle of indirect effect was established in ***Von Colson* (1984)**, which concerned sex discrimination in the employment context (***Adeneler v ELOG* (2006)**).

EU supremacy

Although there is no express Treaty reference to supremacy, as a result of the **ECA 1972**, any UK enactment has effect subject to existing 'enforceable Community rights'. Given the lack of Treaty provision on this point, the CJEU has developed this doctrine, stating that supremacy is implied in the Treaty provisions. As a result, therefore, until the UK formally leaves the EU when a withdrawal agreement is reached, any legislation passed must not conflict with existing EU law. The case law history in this field is staggering, with cases as relatively recent as 2015 coming before the courts questioning the supremacy of the EU over domestic legislation. Naturally, we have to question the supremacy of the EU over the UK Parliament, given the recent vote to leave the EU. However, until the UK formally exits from the EU, it remains subject to EU law and must not conflict with such laws.

Table 5.3 details the development of jurisprudence in this area of EU law.

Table 5.3 EU supremacy

***Van Gend en Loos* (1963)**	The ECJ ruled that 'the community constitutes a new legal order of international law for the benefit of which the states have limited their sovereign rights'.
***Costa v ENEL* (1964)**	The ECJ ruled that 'the transfer by the states from their domestic legal system to the Community legal system of the rights and obligations arising under the Treaty carries with it a permanent limitation of their sovereign rights, against which a subsequent unilateral act incompatible with the concept of the Community cannot prevail'.
***Internationale Handelsgesellschaft GmbH* (1970)**	The ECJ ruled that: the law stemming from the Treaty, an independent source of law, cannot because of its very nature be overridden by rules of national law, however framed, without being deprived of its character as community law and without the legal basis of the Community itself being called in question, therefore the validity of a Community measure or its effect within a member state cannot be affected by allegations that it runs counter to either fundamental rights as formulated by the constitution of that state or the principles of a national constitutional structure.
***Factortame (II)* (1990)**	Lord Bridge stated that 'Whatever limitation of its sovereignty Parliament accepted when it enacted the ECA 1972 it was entirely voluntary . . . there is nothing in any way novel in according supremacy to rules of Community law.'

***R v Secretary of State for Transport, ex parte Factortame Ltd (II)* (Case 213/89) [1990] ECR 1-2433 (HL)**

FACTS: Spanish fishermen claimed that the UK **Merchant Shipping Act 1988** breached EU law. They sought a reference to the Court of Justice (***Factortame I***). ***Factortame II*** was concerned with the application for an interim injunction to prevent the UK government from setting aside the provision pending the outcome of ***Factortame I***.

HELD: EU law would be impaired if domestic law could prevent the grant of interim relief (in the form of an interim injunction) in relation to EU rights.

Citing EU law

In Chapters 3 and 4 respectively, we demonstrated the proper method of citing domestic legislation and case law. Here, we do the same but for EU law.

As we have seen, EU legislation may take various different forms: Treaties, Regulations, and Directives (see Table 5.4). Each of these are published in the *Official Journal of the European Communities*, often referred to as the *Official Journal* or OJ. The OJ consists of several series, the most important for our purposes being the 'L' series (Legislation)—which consists of the text of EU legislation, and the 'C' series (Communications and Information)—which consists of draft legislation, official announcements, and notices. Each series contains an issue and page number. We can use this information to understand the meaning of various EU sources. Our example below focuses on an EU Treaty; however, the same principles can be adopted for Regulations and Directives alike.

Table 5.4 Citing EU legislation

Consolidated version of the Treaty on European Union [2016] OJ C202/1	
Written text	**Meaning**
Consolidated version of the Treaty on European Union	Legislation title
[2016] OJ	Year of publication in the *Official Journal*
C202/1	C = Series of the OJ; 202 = issue number; 1 = page number

Citation of judgments of the EU courts depends on the court in which the decision is handed down. Judgments of both the CJEU and the General Court (prior to 2009, this was known as the Court of First Instance) are published in the *Official Reports of Cases Before the Court*, more commonly referred to as the *European Court Reports* (ECR). CJEU cases are reported in Volume one (ECR—I) whilst General Court decisions are reported in Volume two (ECR—II). Two examples will assist you in understanding how to cite EU cases (see Table 5.5).

Table 5.5 Citing EU case law

Case C-273/00 *Ralf Sieckmann v Deutsches Patent- und Markenamt* [2002] ECR I-11737	
Written text	**Meaning**
Case C-273/00	C = judgments of the CJEU 273/00 = case number
Ralf Sieckmann v Deutsches Patent- und Markenamt	Names of the parties
[2002]	Year the judgment was reported
ECR I-11737	ECR = name of the report; I-11737 = volume one of the ECR and the first page of the case judgment

Case T–344/99 *Arne Mathisen AS v Council* [2002] ECR II–2905	
Written text	**Meaning**
Case T–344/99	T = judgments of the General Court 244/99 = case number
Arne Mathisen AS v Council	Names of the parties
[2002]	Year the judgment was reported
ECR II–2905	ECR = name of the report; II-2905 = volume two of the ECR and the first page of the case judgment

European Convention on Human Rights

The **European Convention on Human Rights and Fundamental Freedoms 1950 (ECHR)** was established in the aftermath of the Second World War and the atrocities suffered in the concentration camps operated by Nazi Germany. The Treaty grants the protection of individual human rights and requires each signatory to the Convention (47 in total) to satisfy and abide by the obligations laid down in the Convention. Our discussion of the ECHR will be short. The Convention was signed in Rome in 1950, ratified by the UK in 1951, and came into force in 1953.

Revision tip

The UK is a 'signatory' to the ECHR; it is not a 'member' in the ECHR. Keep this distinction in mind.

For a more detailed account of human rights, see Bernadette Rainey, *Human Rights Law Concentrate* (4th edn, Oxford University Press 2017).

The ECHR and the EU

Although 'European' is in the title, the ECHR is not a part of the EU. The ECHR is a separate entity created by a Treaty of the Council of Europe, which is not an institution of the EU. The ECHR is concerned with the protection of fundamental human rights and freedoms, whereas the EU is concerned with the affordance of fundamental rights for EU citizens, including the free movement of goods and persons. Naturally, the divide is not entirely clear, with both the EU and the ECHR becoming involved in certain high-profile matters, such as prisoner voting rights and the deportation of individuals.

As we are now aware, the UK has voted to leave the EU. Upon exit from the EU, the UK will no longer be bound by the CJEU. However, because the ECHR is a separate institution, the UK would still be bound by the Convention, unless it decides to revoke its signature of the Convention also.

Suppose the alternative, however. Suppose the UK had voted to remain in the EU but wished to leave the ECHR. There is disagreement amongst experts as to whether this is possible. In determining membership in the EU, the Commission uses membership in the ECHR to demonstrate that the Member State has the appropriate respect for human rights. The Conservative government, upon election in 2015, announced their intention to revoke the **Human Rights Act (HRA) 1998** and replace it with a UK Bill of Rights. The question in this case would thus become whether the Bill of Rights would demonstrate a sufficient respect for human rights required to allow membership in the EU to continue. However, given that the UK has left the EU, this issue is—more or less—moot.

Rights guaranteed

The Convention grants certain rights and fundamental freedoms to the citizens of the Member States, with **Article 1 ECHR** providing that all 'High Contracting Parties must secure to everyone within their jurisdiction the rights and freedoms defined in the Convention.'

A distinction must be drawn, however, between rights that are absolute, rights that are limited, and rights that are qualified.

- **Absolute rights** are those where no derogation of those freedoms is permissible and any interference with those rights is incapable of being justified.
- **Limited rights** are those that do not allow explicit derogation or interference of those freedoms; however, there may be inherent limitations with the rights afforded.
- **Qualified rights** are those where interference is permissible so long as such interference or derogation is proportionate to achieve a legitimate aim.

Section 1 ECHR guarantees certain rights to individuals. Although the distinction between these different types of rights is not made in the Convention itself, application of these rights before the courts has made the distinction clear.

These rights are contained in Table 5.6, which also stipulates whether a right is 'absolute', 'limited', or 'qualified'.

Infringement of rights

By **s6 HRA 1998**, it is unlawful for public authorities to violate any Convention right or act in a way that is incompatible with a Convention right. 'Public authority' includes courts and tribunals, private individuals, and organizations performing public functions (**s6(3)(b)**) but does not include either Houses of Parliament (**s6(3)**). A person claiming infringement of Convention rights is known as a 'victim' (**s7**) and must be directly affected by the act or measure of the public authority before they are considered to have appropriate 'standing'.

Table 5.6 Convention rights

Article No.	Right guaranteed	Absolute or qualified?
2	The Right to Life (everyone's right to life shall be protected by law, except in times of war—**Article 15 ECHR**).	Absolute
3	Prohibition of Torture and Inhuman and Degrading Treatment	Absolute
4	Prohibition of Slavery and Forced Labour	Absolute
5	Right to Liberty and Security	Limited
6	Right to a Fair Trial	Limited
7	No Punishment without Law (prohibition of retrospective criminal law and penalties)	Absolute
8	Right to Private and Family Life	Qualified
9	Freedom of Thought, Conscience and Religion	Qualified
10	Freedom of Expression	Qualified
11	Freedom of Assembly and Association	Qualified
12	Right to Marry	Qualified

Enforcement of rights

The UK became a signatory state in 1951 upon the signing of the Treaty. This meant that UK citizens could enforce their rights when infringed in the European Court of Human Rights (ECtHR). However, until the introduction of the **HRA 1998**, which came into force on 2 October 2000 and which transposed the Treaty into national law, citizens were unable to claim such an infringement directly in UK courts. Instead, these citizens were required to take their case directly to the ECtHR, which sits in Strasbourg. Now, as a result of the **HRA 1998**, citizens may enforce their rights in UK courts, with all claims beginning in the High Court.

Derogation and justification

As stated earlier, certain rights can be derogated from and justified by the state. This power is in accordance with **s14 HRA 1998**. In assessing whether the derogation is a fundamental breach of the Convention, the domestic courts operate a tool known as 'the doctrine of proportionality'. In a nutshell, proportionality concerns the consideration of whether the interference with a Convention right was necessary and proportionate to achieve a legitimate aim. Prior to the enactment of the **HRA 1998**, the domestic courts relied on the traditional test of ***Wednesbury*** unreasonableness, asking the question as to whether an act or measure taken by a public authority was so unreasonable that no reasonable public authority could have made such a decision. Post **HRA 1998**, the UK adopted the test of proportionality, in human rights cases, as used by the ECtHR in adjudicating such matters. For more information on ***Wednesbury*** unreasonableness, see ***Associated Provincial Picture Houses Ltd v Wednesbury Corporation* (1948)**.

According to ***R (Daly) v Secretary of State for the Home Department* (2001)**, an act or measure by a public authority that interfered with the rights of an individual would be proportionate if:

1. the legislative objective is sufficiently important to justify the limitation of the right;
2. the measures taken to meet the objective are connected to it; and
3. the means used to meet the objective are no more than is necessary to meet the objective.

The essence of this test requires the courts to strike a 'fair balance' between the rights of the individual and safety or protection of the public at large. A similar situation is observed in relation to the addition of reservations under **s15 HRA 1998**.

A further tool used by the UK courts in adjudicating HRA matters, which sits alongside the doctrine of proportionality, is the idea of 'judicial deference'.

This term refers to the situation where the courts feel that they are not best placed to make a judgment on a particular matter before them. Often this is because the courts are not experts in a particular field, such as economic policy or national security, or the courts believe that such a matter is for a democratically elected body to determine. In such cases, the courts may defer (thus the term 'deference') to the judgment or decision of the public body concerned and find in favour of such body.

Such a principle is similar to that of the 'margin of appreciation', which concerns the consideration of the amount of discretion given to a signatory state by the ECtHR when adjudicating on qualified rights and their alleged infringement.

The role of the judiciary under the Human Rights Act 1998

The introduction of the **HRA 1998** also introduced new roles, duties, and powers for the judiciary in adjudicating human rights matters. These powers are contained in **ss2–4 and 8 HRA 1998** and are dealt with in Table 5.7.

For an in-depth discussion of the interpretation of statutes using **s3**, see Chapter 3.

Table 5.7 Roles/duties of the judiciary under the HRA 1998

Role/duty	Role/duty explained
Take account of ECtHR case law (**s2 HRA 1998**)	• When determining a question involving a Convention right, the domestic courts must take into account any 'judgment, decision, declaratory or advisory opinion' of the ECtHR. • In ***R (Ullah) v Special Adjudicator* (2004)**, Lord Bingham stated that 'The duty of national courts is to keep pace with the Strasbourg jurisprudence as it evolves over time: no more, but certainly no less.'
Interpretation (**s3 HRA 1998**)	• Primary and subordinate legislation 'so far as it is possible to do so' must be read and given effect to in a way which is compatible with Convention rights. • This provides the judiciary with a quasi-legislative role, allowing them to interpret legislation in light of the Convention; however, certain cases (such as ***R v A (Complainant's Sexual History)* (2002)**) arguably demonstrate the courts taking their role too far.
Declaration of Incompatibility (**s4 HRA 1998**)	• Where the court finds that legislation is incompatible with Convention rights, it may make a Declaration of Incompatibility. • The Declaration is a 'weapon of last resort' and should only be used where **s3** cannot be used (such as ***Bellinger v Bellinger* (2003)**). • When a declaration is made, Parliament must decide the appropriate action to take (e.g. repeal, amend, or ignore).
Remedies (**s8 HRA 1998**)	• Under **s8**, a court may grant such relief or remedy as it considers just and appropriate where it finds that an act by a public authority is unlawful. • The most common remedy is damages, which can only be awarded where it is necessary to afford just satisfaction (**s8(3)**).

Revision tip

Be careful when discussing the different roles and duties of the court when considering human rights matters. Do not overstate the role of the judiciary. Specifically:

- **Section 2** merely requires the court to 'take account' of ECtHR decisions. It need not *apply* or be *bound* by them.
- **Section 3** provides the judiciary with a quasi-legislative role in allowing interpretation of legislation; however, such a role is rarely exercised, with many courts ruling that Parliament remains the law-making body in the UK, especially where to interpret the provision a certain way would have the effect of creating a new law (see ***Bellinger v Bellinger* (2003)** on gender reassignment law).
- **Section 4** does not affect the validity of primary legislation (**s4(6)**), nor does it bind the parties; however, the courts can declare invalid subordinate (secondary) legislation (see ***A and Others* (2005)** on anti-terrorism legislation).

The role of the government under the Human Rights Act 1998

The government and relevant ministers were also affected by the changes introduced by the **HRA 1998.** Their new obligations and powers are contained in **ss10 and 19 HRA 1998** and are dealt with in Table 5.8.

Table 5.8 Role of the government under the HRA 1998

Role/duty	Role/duty explained
Remedial action (**s10 HRA 1998**)	• The relevant minister may amend primary legislation that is the subject of a declaration of incompatibility (under **s4**). • The relevant minister can do so without going through the full parliamentary procedure. • There are two ways to put through a remedial order: **(i)** the laying of an order subject to positive resolution; **(ii)** the laying of an order with immediate effect, which ceases to be law if it fails to be approved by positive resolution within 120 days. Examples of the use of **s10** can be seen in amending such legislation as the **Terrorism Act 2000 (Terrorism Act 2000 (Remedial) Order 2011**).
Statement of compatibility (**s19 HRA 1998**)	• When proposing legislation, the relevant minister in charge of the Bill must make either: **(i)** a statement of compatibility; or **(ii)** a statement of incompatibility. • The minister must do so before the second reading of the Bill.

Looking for extra marks?

Make your answer stand out by making clear that Parliament can pass an Act, regardless of whether it may be incompatible with Convention rights. This is because Parliament is supreme and may pass any Act it so wishes. The entire purpose of **s19** is not to grant supremacy to the ECHR, but rather, according to Rainey (2017), is 'designed to ensure proper human rights scrutiny of a Bill'.

The relevant minister also has the powers under **ss14–15** to derogate from Convention rights and add reservations to certain rights. See our earlier discussion in the section 'Derogation and justification'.

The future?

In their 2015 election manifesto, the Conservative Party vowed to 'scrap the Human Rights Act, and introduce a British Bill of Rights'. This policy was justified by the Conservatives on the ground that it would 'break the formal link between British courts and the European

Court of Human Rights, and make our own Supreme Court the ultimate arbiter of human rights matters in the UK'.

According to the Conservative Party manifesto, the Bill of Rights would 'restore common sense to the application of human rights in the UK'. Our signatory status was placed on a permanent backbench by the then Prime Minister, David Cameron, who considered there to be more important matters, such as the EU referendum, to deal with at the time. In August 2016, Liz Truss, the then Justice Secretary and Lord Chancellor, revealed that the Conservatives still intended to axe the **HRA 1998** in favour of a Bill of Rights. In particular, the Justice Secretary stated 'we are committed to that. That is a manifesto commitment.' In December 2016, the then Attorney General, Jeremy Wright, confirmed during questions in the House of Commons that the government would not attempt to repeal the **HRA 1998** until it had finalized Brexit negotiations. This statement was repeated by the then Prime Minister, Theresa May, in January 2019. It remains to be seen with Boris Johnson's new government what the status of the **HRA 1998** and the UK's signatory status in the ECHR is.

International law

We shall now briefly consider international law, looking at basic matters such as the meaning of international law, the doctrine of state sovereignty, and the distinction between public and private international law.

For a more detailed account of international law, see Ilias Bantekas and Efthymios Papastavridis, *International Law Concentrate* (4th edn, Oxford University Press 2019).

Meaning of 'international law'

According to the website of the United Nations (www.un.org), international law 'defines the legal responsibilities of States in their conduct with each other, and their treatment of individuals within State boundaries'. International law sets rules and policies that govern relations between international states and their citizens. Beginning with a membership of 51, the United Nations, amongst other bodies, is now responsible for addressing the needs of 193 Member States.

According to **Article 2, para 1 UN Charter 1945**, international law is 'based on the principle of the sovereign equality of all its Members'. Each Member State is thus considered equal and not subject to any form of supranational authority without the consent of the Member State concerned.

Coverage of international law

International law is a diverse and far-reaching subject. According to the UN website, international law:

> encompasses a wide range of issues of international concern, such as human rights, disarmament, international crime, refugees, migration, problems of nationality, the treatment of prisoners, the use

of force, and the conduct of war, among others. It also regulates the global commons, such as the environment and sustainable development, international waters, outer space, global communications and world trade.

Public vs private international law

Often the phrase 'international law' is thrown around by laypersons and the media to describe all matters involving foreign states or individuals. Although such is a correct statement, it is also a rather narrow and loose conception of the operation of international law. International law can be divided into:

- public international law; and
- private international law.

Public international law concerns the relations between sovereign states, often referred to as the 'law of the nations'. Private international law, on the other hand, is concerned with the so-called 'conflict of laws', which deals with relations between individuals and bodies in which the laws of more than one state may be applied, for example in the law of contract.

Legal personalities

As discussed above, public international law is concerned with the relations of states and other international legal personalities. *International legal personality* refers to the 'legal persons' that have rights and obligations under international law. The list below assists in understanding who these personalities are:

- **States**: a state is one recognized as such by other states in their own right. States are considered equal and hold sovereignty over their respective territory. In order to be considered as a 'state', four key characteristics must be present:
  - a permanent population;
  - a defined territory;
  - a government; and
  - the capacity to enter into relations with other states.
- **Organizations**: international organizations are established by sovereign states through international agreements. The powers of the organizations are limited to that conferred on them in the respective agreement document allowing them to enter into agreements and grant certain privileges and immunities to representatives of such organizations.
- **Individuals**: individuals are not regarded as 'legal persons' under international law. Instead, their status under international law is governed by the concept of nationality which is a matter to be determined by the sovereign states.

Sources of law

According to **Article 38(1) Statute of the International Court of Justice**, the following are sources of international law:

(a) international conventions (treaties), whether general or particular, establishing rules expressly recognized by the contesting states;

(b) international custom, as evidence of a general practice accepted as law;

(c) the general principles of law recognized by civilized nations;

(d) subject to the provisions of **Article 59**, judicial decisions and the teachings of the most highly qualified publicists of the various nations, as subsidiary means for the determination of rules of law.

International courts

Under international law, there are a number of courts that you must be aware of. We have spoken about two of these courts earlier in the chapter, namely the CJEU, which interprets EU law and observes uniformity of EU law across the Member States, and the ECtHR which deals with allegations of breaches of human rights under the ECHR.

Two further courts that you need to be aware of are:

- the International Court of Justice (ICJ); and
- the International Criminal Court (ICC).

International Court of Justice

The ICJ defines itself as the 'principal judicial organ of the United Nations'. Established by the United Nations Charter in 1945, the Court is responsible for settling legal disputes between states that have submitted themselves to the court's jurisdiction and offering advisory opinions on legal matters referred to it by other organs of the United Nations. The ICJ sits in The Hague in the Netherlands.

Judgments delivered by the ICJ in disputes between states are binding upon the states concerned. This is expressly provided for in **Article 94 UN Charter**, which provides that 'each Member of the United Nations undertakes to comply with the decision of [the Court] in any case to which it is a party'. These judgments are final, without the prospect of appeal.

International Criminal Court

Sitting in The Hague in the Netherlands, the ICC is responsible for the investigation and trial of crimes which are deemed to be of a concern to the international community. The ICC is particularly concerned with the prosecution of the following:

- **genocide**: the intentional and systematic annihilation of an ethnic, racial, or religious group;

- **war crimes**: violations of the international **Geneva Convention 1949** to protect prisoners of war (POWs); violation of other laws regarding international armed conflict;
- **crimes against humanity**: crimes that systematically exterminate, enslave, torture, rape, and persecute victims based on political, gender, religious, ethnic, national, or cultural differences.

The ICJ lacks jurisdiction to try individuals accused of such international crimes and, as such, the ICC is required to fulfil this role. Prior to the creation of the ICC, international matters of criminal law were dealt with by ad hoc international criminal tribunals including, for example the International Criminal Tribunal for the former Yugoslavia (ICTY) and the International Criminal Tribunal for Rwanda (ICTR). Such ad hoc courts were limited in efficiency and lacked a feature of deterrence to be truly effective. With this in mind came the creation of the ICC by way of the **Rome Statute 1998**.

Looking for extra marks?

There are a number of states that have refused to sign up to the jurisdiction of the ICC, most notably the USA and China. Justifications regarding their continued refusal include the fear that the ICC will try their soldiers for trivial or politically motivated reasons and that it may interfere with domestic sovereignty. You may wish to consider in an essay whether either of these 'excuses' stands up to scrutiny.

Key cases

Case	Facts	Principles
Costa v ENEL **(Case 6/64) [1964] ECR 585 (ECJ)**	Costa refused to pay his electricity bill, alleging it breached the **Treaty of Rome**.	EU law takes precedence over post-dating national legislation that conflicts with it.
Defrenne v Sabena **(Case 43/75) [1976] ECR 455 (ECJ)**	Defrenne sought to invoke a Treaty article in an equal pay claim.	Treaty articles are also capable of horizontal **direct effect**.
Marshall v Southampton and South West Hampshire Area Health Authority **(Case 152/84) [1986] ECR 723 (ECJ)**	Marshall sought to rely on a Directive in a sex discrimination claim.	Directives can only be invoked vertically, against the state or a public body, and cannot be invoked horizontally.
Pubblico Ministero v Ratti **(Case 148/78) [1979] ECR 1269 (ECJ)**	This claim concerned product labelling.	A Directive cannot be directly effective until its implementation deadline has passed.

Case	Facts	Principles
R v Secretary of State for Transport, ex parte Factortame Ltd (II) **(Case 213/89) [1990] ECR 1-2433 (HL)**	This was an application for an interim injunction.	National law must be set aside where it infringes EU law.
Van Duyn v Home Office **(Case 41/74) [1975] 2 WLR 760 (ECJ)**	Van Duyn challenged the UK's refusal to grant her entry into the country.	Directives are capable of **direct effect**.
Van Gend en Loos v Administratie der Belastingen **(Case 26/62) [1963] ECR 1 (ECJ)**	This was a challenge to a customs fee, arguing it breached the free movement of goods.	The principle of **direct effect** was established. A Treaty article is directly effective if it is 'clear, precise, and unconditional' and its implementation requires no legislative intervention by Member States.

Key debates

Topic	**Supremacy of EU law**
Academic	Joseph Weiler
Viewpoint	Argues that a foundational equilibrium exists between legal integration and political integration that guaranteed the success and viability of European integration in its early stage.
Source	Joseph Weiler, 'The Transformation of Europe' (1991) 100 Yale Law Journal 2403

Topic	**Human Rights Act 1998**
Academic	Tom Bingham
Viewpoint	Argues that the high number of cases being taken directly to the ECtHR was the main reason to incorporate the Convention into a domestic setting by way of the **HRA 1998**.
Source	Tom Bingham, 'Judicial Independence' in *The Business of Judging* (Oxford University Press 2002)

Exam questions

Topic	Formalizing the rules of international law
Academic	Jean D'Aspremont
Viewpoint	Puts forward his theory of 'ascertainment' and argues that the rules of international law need to be 'refreshed and revitalized' after certain advocates have attempted to de-formalize the identification of international law.
Source	Jean D'Aspremont, *Formalism and the Sources of International Law: A Theory of the Ascertainment of Legal Rules* (Oxford University Press 2011)

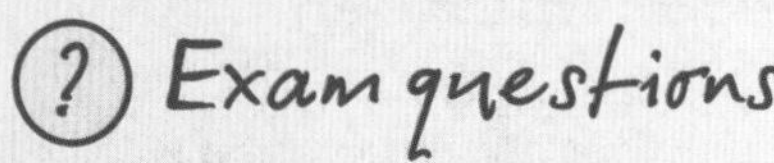

Essay question

Critically consider the position of parliamentary sovereignty in light of the United Kingdom's membership in the European Union.

Problem question

Adrian runs a small business in the UK, making watches specifically aimed at 10–15-year-olds. Adrian employs Mark, Helen, and Joy. Helen and Joy leave work early every day to pick up their children. Mark requests that he too can leave early; however, he has no children and Adrian refuses his request to leave early.

A recent EU Directive has been introduced which provides that it is unlawful to discriminate against an employee based on their parental status. The deadline for implementation was June 2015. It is now July 2017 and the Directive has not yet been implemented. Adrian still refuses to allow Mark to leave early.

Advise Mark as to whether he has any rights to enforce.

Would your answer be different if Mark was employed by the Ministry of Justice?

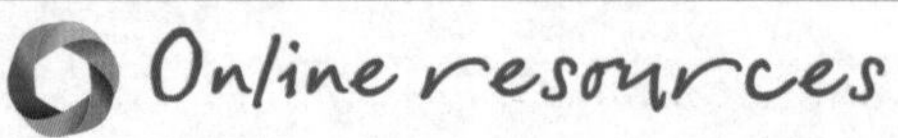

For outline answers to these exam questions, as well as multiple-choice questions, please visit the online resources.

#6 Personnel of the English Legal System

Key facts

- The English legal system (ELS) is composed of a multitude of different professionals, both legal and lay.
- Barristers and solicitors were traditionally two very distinct roles in the ELS. Nowadays, a fusion of roles has occurred, meaning that the two professions are not as different as they formerly were.
- Judges are not employees of the state; rather, they hold office.
- Lay personnel include juries and **magistrates** who are responsible for trying cases in the Crown Court and magistrates' court respectively.

Chapter overview

Key personnel of the English legal system

Introduction

Within this chapter we shall be concerned with the following:

- **legal professionals**—often referred to as 'lawyers', this category includes such individuals as solicitors, barristers, legal executives, and paralegals;
- **judiciary**—this refers to the various judicial 'offices' and 'office holders'. For the purposes of simplicity, this matter involves the discussion of judges;
- **law officers**—these are the individuals responsible for the operation of the ELS and include such persons as the **Attorney General** and the Solicitor General;
- **court staff**—these are the individuals who are involved in the day-to-day running of the ELS and include such persons as clerks, ushers, legal advisers, and many others;
- **laypersons**—this term is used to describe a special class of individuals, namely magistrates and juries. The ELS could not function without either of these classes, and thus they deserve their own category.

This chapter will now go on to consider each of these classes in turn.

Legal professionals

The legal profession, as it may be called, is concerned with those individuals often referred to as 'lawyers'. 'Lawyers' is a general umbrella term which traditionally covers two distinct professions, namely solicitors and barristers. In more recent times, two new and emerging professions (legal executives and paralegals) have increasingly become known as lawyers in their own right. The judiciary, for our purposes, is not considered within the category of 'lawyers' due to the holding of an office, as opposed to the holding of a practice (explained in greater detail in 'The judiciary' later in this chapter).

Each of these legal professionals may hold some form of advocacy rights. Advocacy refers to the ability of an individual to appear in court and present the case of their respective client. The phrase 'rights of audience' is often adopted to demonstrate whether a particular individual has the right to exercise advocacy in court. A further phrase that is used is that of 'higher' rights of audience, which refers to the situation that an individual holds advocacy rights in the lower courts (e.g. in the County Court or magistrates' court); however, they may not practise in the more senior courts (e.g. the Crown Court or the appellate courts) unless they obtain 'higher rights'. As will be demonstrated below, barristers hold these higher rights of audience from qualification; solicitors, on the other hand, must undertake specialist training which will allow them to 'appear' in the more senior courts. The advocacy rights of each professional will be dealt with later in this section.

Before considering these four legal professionals, it is first important to consider legal education and how one may become a legal professional.

Law students

In April 2017, the Solicitors Regulation Authority (SRA) announced that the pathway to becoming a solicitor would change. This has had a direct effect on the route to qualification for solicitors. In that respect, it is necessary to detail the traditional route to qualify. For the time being, the traditional route remains the same for a student who wishes to proceed to train to become a barrister.

Traditional route

Since the twentieth century, in order to practise as a 'lawyer', students must undertake a law degree (*Legum Baccalaureus*—LLB) and must complete the six 'foundations' of legal study. (There remains debate as to whether there are seven foundations of legal study (contract and tort being separate subjects) or six—the SRA contend that there are six, thus that is the approach taken here.) These are:

- criminal law;
- law of obligations (contract and torts) law;
- European Union (EU) law;

- equity and trusts law;
- land law;
- public law (constitutional and administrative law).

If a student has not completed an undergraduate law degree, but rather, has completed some other form of degree, such as History, they will be required to undertake a conversion course. This conversion course is known as the Common Professional Examination (CPE), which generally awards students a diploma (thus the title Graduate Diploma in Law (GDL)).

The GDL is an intense course focused on providing students with the knowledge of the foundational subjects in one year. Once the law degree or GDL is complete, the student may then proceed to their vocational study.

New SQE pathway

From autumn 2021, the SRA will introduce the **Solicitors Qualifying Examination (SQE)**. The new pathway allows any individual with an undergraduate degree (which need not be in law) to become a solicitor. In order to do so, the student must undertake and complete the Solicitors Qualifying Examination (SQE), which is designed in two stages:

- SQE1: consists of three multiple-choice-based assessments, covering 'functional legal knowledge' and two practical legal skills assessments. SQE1 is concerned with the substantive legal knowledge traditionally gained through an undergraduate law degree and the Legal Practice Course (LPC);
- SQE2: consists of vocational-based assessments, such as client interviewing and legal drafting. Students will undertake a total of 14 assessments in order to complete the SQE2 assessment.

The SQE is not a course (like an LLB or GDL); it is merely a set of assessments which are required to be undertaken to qualify. In that regard, many universities are creating, or considering the creation of, 'SQE-preparation courses'.

Figure 6.1 demonstrates the pathways that students may take upon completing their degree or conversion course.

In more recent times, there have been other methods by which individuals may come to practise in law. We shall consider legal executives and paralegals later.

Revision tip

Ensure that you are correct in your spelling of practise/practice.

- *Practise*—A verb. To practise.
- *Practice*—A noun. To have a practice.

Figure 6.1 Pathways of the law student

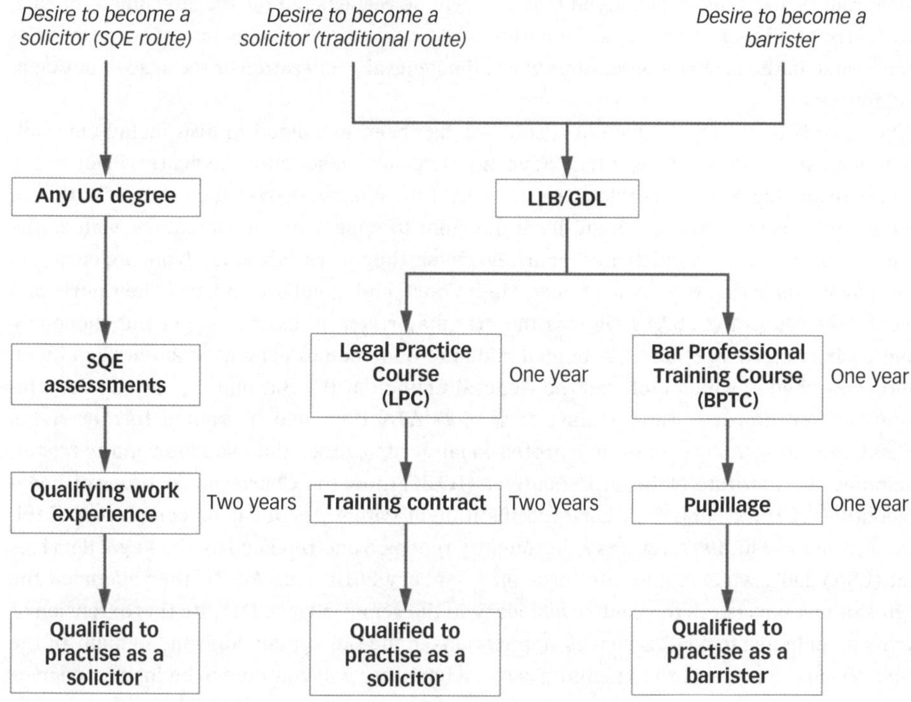

Solicitors

Solicitors are often the first point of contact for individuals seeking legal advice. Solicitors work in partnerships known as 'firms'. A qualified solicitor is admitted to the 'Roll of Solicitors' by the Law Society.

Role

Quite often, solicitors are considered as 'general practitioners' of the law, having an in-depth understanding of all areas of law, somewhat akin to a medical General Practitioner (GP). This could not be further from the truth, however, as solicitors generally specialize in one or two particular fields and their area of specialism often depends on the work of their firm in general, for example a criminal law firm, a family law firm etc. In addition, solicitors may engage in work which is 'non-contentious', such as conveyancing, wills and probate, or may engage in more 'contentious' work, such as criminal or family litigation. In this respect, one may also use the phrase 'litigious work' and 'non-litigious work'.

A solicitor's role was traditionally based in the office of the firm. We refer to their traditional role as 'pre-trial work', given that they will be responsible for the advising of clients, the drafting of legal documents, the gathering of evidence and collection of witness statements, and, in the case of contentious work, the general preparation of the case in anticipation for trial.

Nowadays, however, the role of a solicitor has been expanded to also include an ability to appear in the courts as a trial advocate (known as a solicitor advocate). Prior to the **Access to Justice Act (AJA) 1999**, barristers held the monopoly over the rights of audience in the senior courts. Solicitors did have the right to appear in certain courts such as the County Court and the magistrates' court; however, they were forbidden from appearing in the senior courts (i.e. the Crown Court, High Court, and appellate courts). The **Courts and Legal Services Act (CLSA) 1990** was the first major step in extinguishing this monopoly held by barristers. **Section 27** extended rights of audience to persons granted such by an 'authorized body', which included the General Council of the Bar and the Law Society. Intake was low, however, thus leading to **ss37–38 AJA 1999**, which granted further rights of audience to solicitors and other professional groups, other than solicitor and barrister, including the Institute of Legal Executives (ILEX) (now the Chartered Institute of Legal Executives (CILEx)) and the Chartered Institute of Patent Agents, upon completion of relevant training. The **1999 Act** was subsequently repealed and replaced by the **Legal Services Act (LSA) 2007**, which came into force on 1 January 2010. This Act further extended the rights of non-barristers to practise advocacy in the senior courts. Despite this extension of rights of audience to non-barristers, applications to the Bar remain high and in many of the most serious, complex, or challenging cases, a barrister will continue to be instructed over his higher-right advocate counterparts. Figure 6.2 provides a useful timeline of the higher rights of audience granted to solicitors.

Qualifications (traditional route)

As noted above, as a result of the introduction of the SQE, the qualification route for a solicitor is now rather more complex. It was traditionally the case (and remains the case for a few more years) that in order to practise as a solicitor, an individual must first undertake their law degree or GDL and then undertake the Legal Practice Course (LPC). The LPC is a year-long (full time) intensive course instilling hopeful solicitors with the necessary knowledge

Figure 6.2 Higher rights of audience timeline

for their first few years in practice. The LPC is comprised of certain 'core modules', such as criminal and civil litigation, solicitors' accounts, and drafting. It is also comprised of certain 'optional modules', such as family law, employment law, and commercial property law. Many students first seek funding before they undertake their LPC. Funding is available by scholarship at some institutions, but is generally provided by the firm with whom they will undertake their training contract, should they be lucky enough to secure one. Should a student undertake the LPC without a training contract, they run the risk of being disappointed after the work and money they have invested in the course, given that the training contract is a key requirement of the qualification process.

Once the student has completed the LPC, they must then undertake a training contract (TC), which generally lasts for two years. The student will be supervised throughout their TC by Associates and Partners within the firm. Also, during their TC, an individual must undertake the Professional Skills Course (PSC). Introduced in 1994, the PSC is designed to build on the foundations laid by the LPC. Trainees must complete 48 hours of tuition on core elements of training, such as financial and business skills and advocacy skills. Having completed all of the above requirements, an individual may then adopt the title of 'solicitor', having been added to the 'Roll of Solicitors' and may then practise in England and Wales. If an individual fails to complete any of the above requirements, they are not entitled to hold a practising certificate and may not be entered onto the Roll. This traditional route is still available to any student who commences a law degree, GDL, or LPC before September 2021. The student will have until 2032 to complete the route and qualify as a solicitor. They may, however, if they wish, choose to qualify through SQE.

Qualifications (SQE route)

With the introduction of the SQE, a number of changes can be noted from the above text:

- Students no longer require a law degree or GDL in order to become a solicitor. As long as the student has an undergraduate degree (or equivalent) in any subject, they will be able to undertake the SQE.
- The LPC will be disbanded and replaced with SQE-preparation courses, which are designed to prepare students for the SQE assessments. There is no obligation on students to undertake the SQE-preparation courses; they may sit the assessments outright.
- The requirement for a training contract will be removed and replaced with a requirement of 'qualifying work experience'. Students will still need to undertake two years' work experience; however, unlike a training contract, this two-year experience may be split amongst up to four firms and can include any other relevant work experience (e.g. time spent in a Law Centre).

Regulation, representation, and ethics

All lawyers are regulated by the Legal Services Board; however, there are eight separate regulators responsible for the different types of lawyer on a day-to-day basis. Figure 6.3

Figure 6.3 Regulation of lawyers

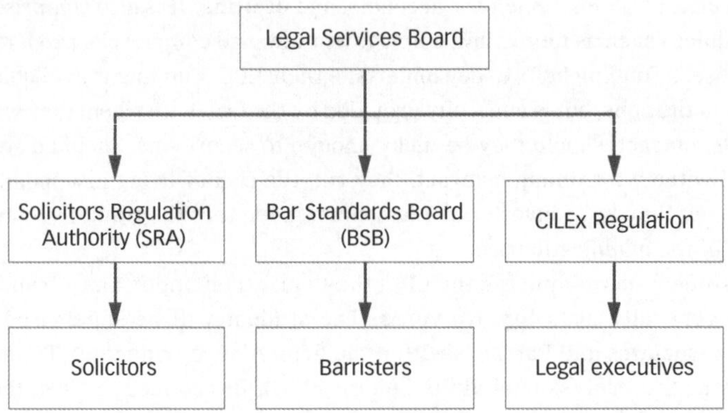

demonstrates this distinction for the three most relevant lawyers for our purposes. Other lawyers regulated by different bodies include patent and trade mark attorneys, costs lawyers, notaries, and legal conveyancers.

Solicitors are regulated by the Solicitors Regulation Authority (SRA), which is responsible for ensuring that all practising solicitors (i.e. those solicitors holding a practising certificate) abide by the **Solicitors' Code of Conduct 2007**, the **SRA Code of Conduct 2011**, and the **SRA Principles 2011**. One key principle, linked with the concept of legal ethics, is that of 'client care'. Solicitors must act independently and with integrity in the interests of their clients and also in the wider public interest.

Solicitors are represented in the public eye by the Law Society, which essentially acts as a trade union for solicitors. Its role is to 'represent and support [its] members, promoting the highest professional standards and the rule of law'. The Law Society formerly acted as the professional regulation body for solicitors; however, this function was removed by the **Legal Services Act 2007**.

Should a solicitor have acted in a manner inconsistent with the Code of Conduct, a claim may be brought against them in the Solicitors Disciplinary Tribunal (SDT), which is an independent body entirely separate from that of the SRA and the Law Society (**s46 Solicitors Act 1974**). Ninety per cent of cases are referred to the Tribunal and prosecuted by the SRA; however, claims may also be brought by the public directly.

Suing your lawyer

Upon retaining a solicitor, a contract is formed between solicitor and client. Should the solicitor breach such contract, the client may sue for damages. Solicitors may also be liable in tort law for negligence causing a loss to the client or even a third party (***White v Jones* (1995)**).

Barristers

Barristers are the specialist advocates whom solicitors instruct to represent a client during trial. Barristers can helpfully be divided into two categories:

- self-employed barristers; and
- employed (in-house) barristers.

Unlike solicitors, barristers cannot work in partnerships with other barristers. Rather, self-employed barristers work collectively in a set, known as 'chambers', whilst employed barristers often work within the government, or in an international legal firm. Practising barristers are known to practise at the 'Bar'.

The Bar in England and Wales is divided into six regions (also known as 'circuits'). The circuits provide support, advice, and representation for barristers practising in those particular areas. The circuits of England and Wales are as follows:

- Midland circuit;
- Northern circuit;
- North-Eastern circuit;
- South-Eastern circuit;
- Wales and Chester circuit; and
- Western circuit.

Role

According to the General Council of the Bar ('Bar Council'), barristers are best classified as 'specialist advocates and advisers'. Unlike solicitors, a barrister's role has always been focused on trial advocacy. They hold a right of audience in all courts in England and Wales and, in the majority of cases, are unlikely to be found undertaking the work traditionally done by solicitors. Most often encountered in the senior courts (see Chapter 2), barristers are independent and objective and hold specialist knowledge and experience in their respective area of law. A barrister's knowledge can cover broad areas of specialism, including the likes of criminal law, personal injury, and family law. Each of these categories can, itself, be subdivided into even more categories of specialism; for example, a barrister may specialize in sexual offences within the law of crime, or with adoption cases in family law.

A key distinction between the role of a barrister and that of a solicitor is the operation of the 'cab rank rule'. Unlike a solicitor, a barrister must accept any case that comes before him where the instructions are appropriate, taking into account the experience, seniority, and/or field of practice. This rule is irrespective of the identity of the client; the nature of the case to which the instructions relate; whether the client is paying privately or is publicly funded; and any belief or opinion which the barrister may have formed as to the character, reputation, cause, conduct, guilt, or innocence of the client. There are, of course, exceptions to the cab rank rule; these are listed in the Code of Conduct for the Bar and include such matters as:

- where the barrister lacks sufficient experience or competence to handle the case;
- where a barrister has been asked to accept instructions outside the field of his practice; and
- where, having regard to his other professional commitments, the barrister will be unable to do or will not have adequate time and opportunity to prepare that which he is required to do.

Looking for extra marks?

Be sure to make it clear that the term 'advocacy' does not simply relate to oral advocacy, i.e. standing up and speaking in court. Advocacy can also come in written form, requiring a barrister to draft legal documents, pleadings, and writing opinions (advice) to their instructing solicitors. As such, barristers are required to be specialist advocates both on paper and in speech.

In England and Wales, there are two types of practising barrister:

- junior barristers; and
- **Queen's Counsel (QC)**.

Junior barrister refers to any barrister, of any length of service, who is not a Queen's Counsel. Therefore, an individual could have practised at the Bar for 40 years and still be a junior barrister. In this event, they are often referred to as a 'senior junior'.

Queen's Counsel (QCs) refers to those barristers who have reached a level of outstanding ability and experience (generally a minimum of 15 years) such that they can justify charging higher fees. In order to become a QC, a barrister must apply to the QC Selection Panel, who will then recommend appointment to the Lord Chancellor. QCs are only instructed in very serious or complex cases and enjoy certain rights over their junior counterparts, including the wearing of silk robes (thus the phrase 'to take Silk') instead of the standard court dress, and the provision of sitting on the front bench (front row) in a courtroom, with junior barristers sitting behind them, and solicitors sitting behind the barristers.

Looking for extra marks?

Make clear in any answer on this topic that solicitors can become Queen's Counsel also. It is just a rarer occurrence for this to happen. In January 2020, 114 new appointments as Queen's Counsel were made, only four of which were solicitors. Why is this? Is the QC Selection Panel attempting to keep the ranks of QC within the Bar? Do solicitors consider that the rank of QC should remain within the Bar?

Naturally, the name Queen's Counsel will change dependent on the gender of the monarch at the time. At the point in the future when a King sits on the throne, silks will be thereafter known as 'King's Counsel'.

Looking for extra marks?

Look at the statistics and observe the number of barristers in practice and the number of Queen's Counsel. You will see that the number has dropped in recent years; for instance, since 2009 there has been a 15 per cent drop in the number of Queen's Counsel.

Ask yourself, 'Why is this?' Use the answer to this question to strengthen your answer and reach a higher mark.

The statistics can be accessed at: www.barstandardsboard.org.uk/media-centre/research-and-statistics/statistics.

The provision of a barrister's work is supplied and managed by their clerks. Barristers' clerks are operated and regulated by the Institute of Barristers' Clerks (IBC) and are tasked with ensuring their barristers are provided with work and are paid the appropriate fee for work undertaken. Barristers are not permitted to negotiate fees or accept fees from their instructing solicitors and thus all business must be conducted through their legal clerk.

The Bar remains predominantly a referral profession. This means that barristers are 'instructed' by solicitors to take on a certain case and that a member of the public may not directly approach a barrister to 'take on their case'. Rather, they must first 'retain' a solicitor, who will then instruct a barrister, if they feel such instruction is necessary. Figure 6.4 provides an illustration of this principle.

There are a number of barristers who can be directly instructed by members of the public to deal with their cases. These are known as 'public access' barristers, who require appropriate training and experience before they may offer public access services. This grants barristers the ability to start the case from scratch, allowing them to investigate and collect evidence, take witness statements, conduct correspondence etc. More information on public access barristers can be found on www.DirectAccessPortal.co.uk.

Qualification

In order to practise as a barrister, an individual must first undertake their law degree or GDL and then undertake their vocational training. Until September 2020, students wishing to become a barrister must undertake the Bar Professional Training Course (BPTC), formerly

Figure 6.4 Procedure for instructing a barrister

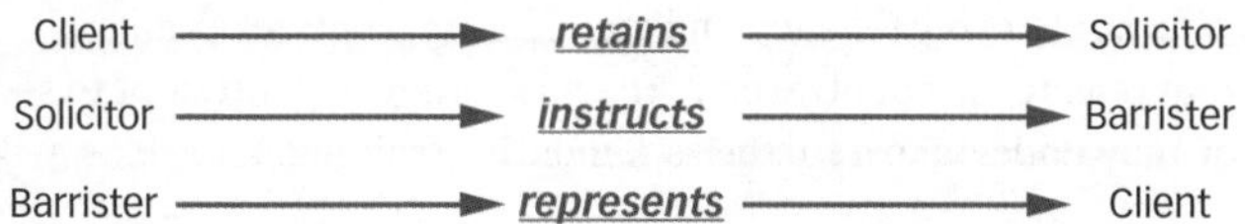

known as the Bar Vocational Course (BVC). Like its solicitor counterpart, the BPTC is a year-long (full-time) intensive course comprised of 'core modules' and 'optional modules'. From September 2020, the Bar Standards Board (BSB) will not prescribe a particular course that has to be undertaken for students wishing to complete the vocational part of their studies. Instead, individual institutions will be able to secure validation for their own version of the Bar course. For instance, Nottingham Law School will launch their Bar Training Course (BTC) and BPP University will launch their Barrister Training Course in September 2020.

Before a student may formally start the Bar course, they must first join one of the four Inns of Court. The Inns of Court are professional organizations with the responsibility for providing student barristers and practising barristers with extensive support through a range of educational activities, lunching and dining facilities, access to common rooms and gardens, and the provision of various grants and scholarships. The four Inns of Court are as follows:

- Middle Temple;
- Inner Temple;
- Lincoln's Inn;
- Gray's Inn.

Each Inn is formally named 'The Honourable Society of . . .'; however, they are commonly referred to by the names listed above as a matter of shorthand.

As part of their vocational education, student barristers must engage in 12 qualifying sessions (also known as 'dining sessions'). Each qualifying session may span a number of hours over a morning, afternoon, or evening and often involves activities such as dining in Hall, lectures, advocacy workshops, and residential weekends.

Upon successful completion of the vocational studies, the student shall be 'called to the Bar' (referring to the literal bar that separates counsel and the judge from other individuals), which then allows them to undertake pupillage.

Pupillage is a year-long apprenticeship where the pupil barrister shadows barristers of the chambers (known as tenants) where the pupillage is being undertaken. Chambers shall award the pupil a minimum of £12,000 per annum to cover their daily expenses. Some chambers pay well in excess of this amount; for example, some chambers offer their pupils figures up to £80,000.

Dependent on the set, the pupil is likely to have either one or two 'pupil supervisors', also known as 'pupil masters'. Pupillage is divided into two six-month periods. Table 6.1 details how the division is organized.

Once the pupil completes their pupillage, the tenants of the chambers shall then decide whether they wish to offer the pupil tenancy, meaning they become a fully fledged practising barrister, or decide not to offer tenancy and consider alternative options.

In the event that tenancy is not offered to the pupil, they may attempt to secure tenancy at a different set or may undertake a further six months' training, known as a 'third six'.

Table 6.1 Stages of pupillage

First six months	Second six months
Pupils can shadow tenants but have no right to appear in their own name.	Pupils can undertake work and earn a wage in their own name.
Pupils can undertake a 'noting brief', but only with consent of their pupil supervisor.	

Revision tip

Be sure to use the correct terminology to describe a barrister during the different stages of their career.

- When undertaking their vocational qualification, they are referred to as 'student barristers'.
- When undertaking their pupillage, they are referred to as 'pupil barristers'.
- When they have secured tenancy, they can simply be referred to as 'barristers' or 'tenants' (the latter only works in the context of their chambers).

Looking for extra marks?

Show your understanding of the legal terminology by demonstrating the circumstances when a person can and cannot refer to themselves as a barrister. According to the BSB, an individual may refer to themselves as a barrister having not obtained pupillage or a practising certificate. The rules are clear in that a person is entitled to use the term 'barrister' in such circumstances where they are *not* offering legal services. To offer legal services without a practising certificate, however, is a criminal offence.

Regulation, representation, and ethics

Barristers are regulated by the Bar Standards Board (BSB), who are responsible for:

> setting standards of conduct for barristers and authorising barristers to practise; monitoring the service provided by barristers to assure quality; setting the education and training requirements for becoming a barrister as well as setting continuing training requirements to ensure that barristers' skills are maintained throughout their careers; and handling complaints against barristers and taking enforcement or other action where appropriate.

All barristers, including non-practising ones, are subject to professional rules contained in the *BSB Handbook* (Version 4.4 2020). The Handbook is divided into six parts, the most important being Part 2, which concerns the Code of Conduct for barristers.

Like their solicitor counterpart, barristers are also represented in the public eye by an independent body. This body is the General Council of the Bar ('Bar Council') and its role is to represent members of the Bar and promote 'the Bar's high quality specialist advocacy and advisory services, fair access to justice for all, the highest standards of ethics, equality and diversity across the profession, and the development of business opportunities for barristers at home and abroad'. The Bar Council formerly acted as the professional regulation body for barristers; however, this function was removed by the **Legal Services Act 2007**.

In addition to the Bar Council, barristers are further represented by 'Specialist Bar Associations' (SBAs), which are dedicated to the interests of groups of barristers within a specific area of practice. At present, there are 24 SBAs, including the Criminal Bar Association (CBA) and the Employment Law Bar Association (ELBA), which help to promote their members' interests by, for example, responding to proposals for changes to regulations, and offering support to their members through networking events and mentoring schemes.

Complaints against a barrister are dealt with by the BSB and the Inns of Court, which have a large role in administering disciplinary tribunals to deal with serious complaints against barristers.

Suing your lawyer

Unlike their solicitor counterparts, no contract exists between a barrister and a lay client. Therefore, a client cannot sue under contractual principles. Prior to 2000, barristers also enjoyed immunity from suit by disgruntled clients for damages for any loss incurred as a result of the barrister's negligence in representing the client in court. The House of Lords removed this immunity in ***Hall v Simons* (2002)** and set a precedent which has effect in all proceedings, both criminal and civil, and at any stage of practise. Therefore, all barristers, of any age and length of practise (yes, even pupils) are open to claims of negligence.

***Arthur JS Hall and Co. v Simons* [2002] 1 AC 615 (HL)**

FACTS: Three claims were brought in a conjoined appeal to the House of Lords. In all three cases it was claimed that a firm of solicitors had been negligent in their advocacy. The firm attempted to rely on the case of ***Rondel v Worsley* (1969)**, which established the rule that an advocate is immune from any claim of negligence.

HELD: It was held that it was contrary to the public interest to allow advocates, whether they be solicitors or barristers, to not be held liable for negligent advocacy when such negligence caused a loss to an individual or third party.

Legal executives

In 1963, the Law Society created the Institute of Legal Executives which, in 2012, became the Chartered Institute of Legal Executives (CILEx) as a result of being awarded a Royal Charter. Originally thought of as solicitors' assistants, legal executives hold limited rights of audience in court and are permitted to undertake litigation work in their own right. Before you may be called a legal executive, you must first become a Fellow of CILEx. As opposed to barristers and solicitors, legal executives need not hold any form of legal education background, as all legal training is provided 'on the job'. Following qualification, Continuing Professional Development (CPD) is compulsory for legal executives and is determined by their level of seniority:

- Fellows—16 hours minimum;
- Graduate Members—12 hours minimum;
- Associate Members—eight hours minimum.

Legal executives will specialize in a specific area of law and will practise only in civil law, for example in conveyancing, wills, or matrimonial matters. Alisdair Gillespie and Siobhan Weare, *The English Legal System* (7th edn, Oxford University Press 2019), however, note that 'there is no reason why they could not, for example, also qualify as accredited police-station representatives'.

A rather large incentive for Fellows of CILEx is that as a result of their qualifications and experience they may become a solicitor without the need to undertake a training contract, given that the necessary experience to become a Fellow is equivalent to a training contract.

Paralegals

A paralegal is a 'fee earner', meaning that they are able to conduct a limited caseload for the company or firm that they represent. The type of work undertaken will ultimately depend on the qualifications and experience of the paralegal, but often includes the preparation of legal documents and limited advocacy experience in tribunals. Although it is not necessary to hold any legal qualifications to become a paralegal, in practice, the majority of firms expect applicants to have completed an appropriate vocational qualification. Further to this, the paralegal profession is largely unregulated, meaning that the exact number of paralegals in England and Wales is unknown. However, many paralegals belong to a regulated service provider, for example, the Institute of Paralegals, the National Institute of Licensed Paralegals, and the Society of Specialist Paralegals.

The judiciary

The 'judiciary' is a term to describe the numerous judicial offices and the holders of such office in England and Wales.

The judicial office

It is common for the layperson to think that a judge is an employee of the state, in that they are a representation of the Crown. However, a judge does not work under a contract of employment; rather, a judge is the holder of a judicial office for the duration of his tenure. It is for this reason that we do not characterize the judiciary as 'lawyers', given that upon taking office as a judge, they cease to practise in law and instead enforce the law. It is this distinguishing feature that sets judges apart from the common 'lawyer'.

As is to be expected, there is a fixed hierarchy of judicial offices in England and Wales and this hierarchy can be laid out into two distinct divisions: senior judges and inferior judges.

A third division is suggested by Gillespie and Weare (2019), who argue that there is a middle ground between the senior judges, who operate administrative functions in addition to their judicial role, and inferior judges, who operate limited jurisdiction and often sit only in courts of first instance. They label this category as 'superior judges'. Although this title is not to be found in statute or in practice, it is a useful way of dividing these classes of judges and will be adopted below.

Senior judges

Section 60(1) Constitutional Reform Act (CRA) 2005 defines the 'senior judges' of England and Wales. These judges are considered senior, given their combined functions in a judicial capacity and an administrative/leadership capacity.

Figure 6.5 details, in hierarchical order, the most prominent 'senior judges' for our purposes. Table 6.2 expands upon the role of these senior judges. For a full breakdown of the senior judges, visit www.judiciary.uk.

Figure 6.5 The senior judges and their roles

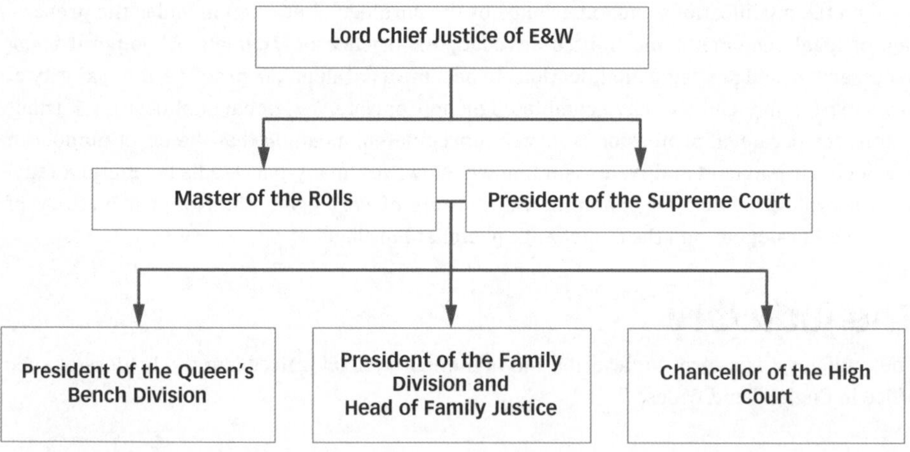

Superior judges

Gillespie and Weare (2019) describes 'superior judges' as those who have 'unlimited jurisdiction in that their jurisdiction is not limited specifically by statute'. This means that they may use their inherent jurisdiction in a manner they see fit, so long as it does not contradict a rule of law or statutory provision. All superior judges are to be referred to as 'My Lord/My Lady' in court. Figure 6.6 details the relevant 'superior judges'. Table 6.3 expands upon the role of these superior judges.

Table 6.2 Senior judicial posts

Judicial office and title	Key facts
Lord Chief Justice (LCJ) 'The Right Honourable, The Lord . . .'	Holds the office of President of the Courts of England and Wales and Head of the Judiciary of England and Wales (**s7(1) CRA 2005**). Also holds the office of Head of Criminal Justice (and thus is the Head of the Queen's Bench Division) (**s8(2) CRA 2005**). Can sit in any of the following courts (**s7(3), (4)**): • Court of Appeal; • High Court; • Crown Court; • County Court; • magistrates' court. *Mode of address in court*: My Lord/My Lady.
President of Supreme Court (PSC)	Created by **s23(5) CRA 2005** along with a deputy. Responsible for the judicial operation of the Supreme Court. Has the power to issue rules and practice directions (**s45 CRA 2005**). Responsible for allocating the justices who will sit on each case. *Mode of address in court*: My Lord/My Lady.
Master of the Rolls (MR) 'The Right Honourable, The Master of the Rolls . . .'	Ranks joint second, with the PSC, to the LCJ in precedence. Holds the office of Head of Civil Justice (**s62(1) Courts Act (CA) 2003**). The 'Rolls' in his title signifies his traditional role as the clerk responsible for maintaining the records of the Chancery Court. *Mode of address in court*: My Lord/My Lady.
President of QBD 'Sir . . .' or 'Madam . . .'	Created by the **CRA 2005**, each Head of their respective Division is responsible for overseeing the management of the Division; ensuring judges are adequately trained in each Division; and allocating resources for those Divisions. The Presidents are led by the LCJ. *Mode of address in court*: My Lord/My Lady.
President of Fam 'Sir . . .' or 'Madam . . .'	
Chancellor of HC 'Sir . . .' or 'Madam . . .'	

Figure 6.6 Superior judges

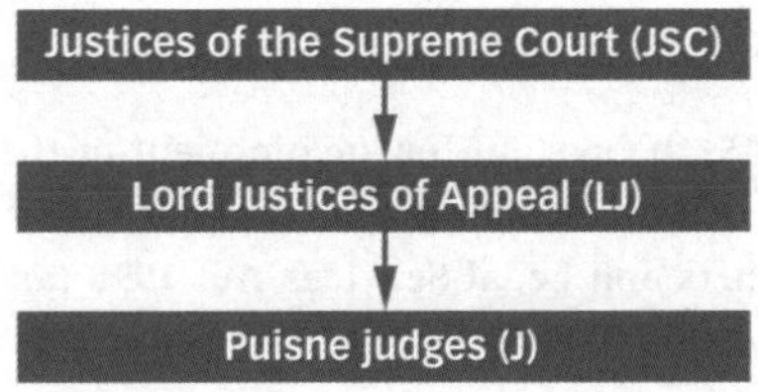

Table 6.3 Superior judicial posts

Judicial office and title	Key facts
Justices of the Supreme Court (formerly known as 'Lords of Appeal in Ordinary', or 'Law Lords' in the House of Lords)	Consists of 12 justices (judges) (**s23(2) CRA 2005**). Headed by the President and Deputy President. Appointed by the Queen upon recommendation from the Lord Chancellor. These judges also sit in the Judicial Committee of the Privy Council.
Lord Justices of Appeal 'Lord/Lady Justice . . .'	These are the 'ordinary judges' of the Court of Appeal who hear the cases. They generally sit in threes and must sit in an uneven number (to avoid stalemate).
Puisne Judges 'The Honourable, Mr/Mrs Justice . . .'	Pronounced 'puny' and meaning 'lower ranking', these are the ordinary judges of the High Court. These judges sit in the High Court and in the more serious cases in the Crown Court. Puisne judges may be invited to sit in the Court of Appeal. The judges are assigned to one of the three Divisions of the High Court. They are entitled to the prefix 'The Honourable'. They are knighted or made a Dame upon appointment.

Inferior judges

Inferior judges do not exercise unlimited jurisdiction. Rather, their powers are defined in statute. Where the statute does not advocate a certain authority, the judges may not exercise such authority, thus the term 'inferior'. Figure 6.7 details the relevant 'inferior judges'. Table 6.4 expands upon the role of these inferior judges.

Figure 6.7 Inferior judges

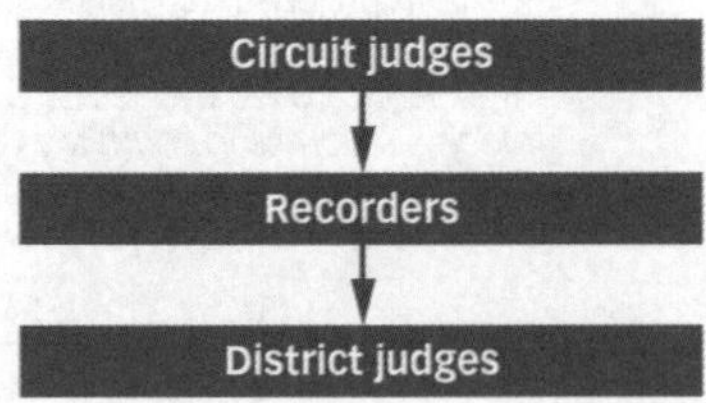

Appointment

As a result of the **CRA 2005**, the system for appointment of the judiciary was overhauled. Prior to the **2005 Act**, the Lord Chancellor played a major role in the appointment of judges in accordance with the **Courts and Legal Services Act 1990** (as amended by the **Tribunals, Courts and Enforcement Act 2007**).

Table 6.4 Inferior judicial posts

Judicial office and title	Key facts
Circuit judges 'His/Her Honour Judge . . .'	Created by **s16 Courts Act (CA) 1971**. They are appointed to one of seven regions of England and Wales. They sit in the Crown Court and County Court within their particular region. They must be lawyers who have held a 'right of audience' for at least ten years. They should have served either part-time as a recorder on criminal cases or full-time as district judges on civil cases before they can be appointed. They are appointed by the Queen, on the recommendation of the Lord Chancellor. *Mode of address in court*: Your Honour.
Recorders 'Mr/Mrs Recorder . . .'	Created by **s21 CA 1971**. They are appointed by the Queen on the recommendation of the Lord Chancellor, for a renewable period of five years. They have a part-time judicial role, expected to sit for 30 days a year in the County Court and Crown Court. *Mode of address in court*: Your Honour.
District judges (magistrates' court) 'District Judge . . .'	Formerly known as a 'stipendiary magistrate' or colloquially as 'stipes'. They are entitled to sit in the magistrates' court, Youth Court, and Family Court. They must have been a professionally qualified barrister or solicitor for at least five years. Additionally, they will have sat as a Deputy District Judge for two years. They generally sit in inner London. *Mode of address in court*: Sir/Madam.
District judges 'District Judge . . .'	They act solely as a civil judge, sitting in the County Court. They are appointed by the Queen on the recommendation of the Lord Chancellor. They are not to be confused with district judges (magistrates' courts). They hear procedural matters and nearly all small-claims court matters. *Mode of address in court*: Sir/Madam.

Judicial Appointments Commission

The **CRA 2005** established the Judicial Appointments Commission (JAC), which is responsible for the appointment of the judiciary. **Schedule 12 CRA 2005** (as amended by the **Crime and Courts Act (CCA) 2013**) states that the JAC consists of 15 members. The composition of the members is detailed in Table 6.5.

According to **sch 12, para 13**, the commissioners are appointed for a term of office no longer than five years at a time and may not hold office for periods totalling more than ten years.

Table 6.5 JAC composition

Type of member	No. of members	Description
Chairman	One	Chairman of the Commission.
Lay members	Five	A lay member is a person resident in England or Wales who has never held a listed judicial office or been a practising lawyer.
Judicial members	Five	There must be one of each: – Lord Justice of Appeal; – Puisne judge of the High Court; – either a Lord Justice of Appeal or a Puisne judge of the High Court; – Circuit judge; – District judge of a County Court.
Professionals	Two	May be either: – a practising barrister in England and Wales; or – a practising solicitor of the Senior Courts of England and Wales; or – a Fellow of the Chartered Institute of Legal Executives. Both commissioners must be different professionals.
Lay magistrate	One	A lay justice member is a justice of the peace who: – holds no other listed judicial office; – is not a practising barrister in England and Wales; and – is not a practising solicitor of the Senior Courts of England and Wales.
Tribunal member	One	Judge of either the first-tier or upper-tier tribunal.

Judicial qualities

The JAC has laid down five key qualities and abilities that a candidate is required to provide evidence of:

- intellectual capacity;
- personal qualities;
- an ability to understand and deal fairly;
- authority and communication skills;
- leadership and management skills.

Recommendations and appointments

The Commission will recommend the names of individuals who should be appointed to the Lord Chancellor. The Lord Chancellor has three options under **s94C CRA 2005**:

- accept the recommendation;
- reject the recommendation;
- ask the panel to reconsider the selection.

Please note that the Lord Chancellor may only reject a recommendation for a candidate once. Should the JAC maintain its recommendation, the Lord Chancellor must accept. Where the Lord Chancellor has accepted the recommendation, he shall then forward the names to the Monarch, who will formally appoint the individuals to the judiciary.

Training

As a result of the **CRA 2005**, the LCJ is responsible for arrangements for training the courts' judiciary in England and Wales. He does so through the Judicial College (JC). The former system of training was provided by the Judicial Studies Board (JSB), which was restricted solely to criminal matters. Prior to the establishment of the JSB in 1979, little, if any, training was provided for new and existing judges. Indeed, Lord Devlin was noted for stating that when he was appointed to the High Court in 1948: 'I had never exercised any criminal jurisdiction and not since my early days at the Bar had I appeared in a criminal court . . . Two days after I had been sworn in, I was trying crime at Newcastle Assizes' (David Pannick QC, *Judges* (Oxford Univesity Press 1987)).

The JC, however, is now responsible for the training of both criminal and civil judges. The JC is governed by the Board of the Judicial College, which is headed by a Chairman.

Independence

According to the then LCJ, Lord Phillips, in 2007, 'A judge should value independence above gold, not for his or her own benefit, but because it is of the essence of the Rule of Law.' The Rule of Law was discussed in Chapter 1 and you are advised to revisit that chapter.

In particular, judges must be independent from:

- political pressures;
- pressures from the media;
- personal motivations.

Section 3 CRA 2005 guarantees the principle of judicial independence and requires the Lord Chancellor and respective ministers to uphold this independence. The judiciary too, however, must ensure their own independence by avoiding conflicts of interests and personal bias. The key example in this respect concerns cases where a judge is disqualified by the principle of natural justice from sitting on a case in which they have some form of interest, whether proprietary or personal, in the outcome. For an example of this in practice, see ***ex parte Pinochet Ugarte (No. 2)*** **(1999)**.

If you are interested in this topic, we advise you to read: John Griffith, *The Politics of the Judiciary* (5th edn, Fontana Press 2010).

Removal/retirement

The ability to remove members of the judiciary from office depends on the seniority of judge. The first point to note is that as a result of the **Act of Settlement 1701** (renamed the **Senior Courts Act 1981** in 2009) the offices of the judiciary should be maintained '*quamdiu se bene gesserint*' ('while they behave themselves'). Essentially, the judiciary hold a form of tenure in their legal position:

- circuit and district judges can be removed for 'misbehaviour' or on the grounds of 'incapacity' by the Lord Chancellor, who may only do so where the LCJ agrees (**s17(4) Courts Act 1971**);
- judges of the High Court and Court of Appeal cannot be removed from office without a petition to the Queen from both the House of Commons and House of Lords (**s11(3) Senior Courts Act 1981**).

The latter of the two has never been used in England and Wales, but has been used in Ireland. Specifically, Sir Jonah Barrington was removed from office as a judge of the Irish High Court of Admiralty in 1830 for corruption (he misappropriated £700 paid into the Admiralty Court of Ireland).

The former has been used on two occasions. The first use was in 1983, when a judge was caught smuggling whisky from Guernsey into England; the second in 2009, for a variety of inappropriate behaviour. For a more detailed account of inappropriate judicial behaviour, see Graeme Williams QC, *A Short Book of Bad Judges* (Wildy Classics 2013).

All judges are required to retire from their office at the age of 70 (**s26(1) Judicial Pensions and Retirement Act 1993**).

Law officers

The law officers, formally known as the 'Law Officers of the Crown' are the chief legal advisers to the Crown. The officers are responsible for advising central and local government and they themselves must be Members of Parliament (MPs).

In England and Wales, the chief law officer of the Crown is the Attorney General. He is assisted by his deputy, the Solicitor General.

In accordance with **s1(1) Law Officers Act 1997**, 'Any function of the Attorney General may be exercised by the Solicitor General' and vice versa.

The Attorney General, who must be legally qualified, is responsible for overseeing several departments, including:

- the Crown Prosecution Service (CPS) (headed by the Director of Public Prosecutions (DPP);
- the Serious Fraud Office;
- Her Majesty's Crown Prosecution Service Inspectorate; and
- the Government Legal Department.

The Solicitor General is a 'support role' and he is responsible for:

- such matters as the Attorney General delegates to him; and
- providing support to the Attorney General on civil litigation and advice on civil law matters and on the public interest function.

Legal personnel

'Legal personnel' is a more formal way of referring to court staff; these individuals are the life and soul of the ELS. Without these staff members involved in the day-to-day running of the courts and legal sector, the ELS would not function. These staff are employed by the Ministry of Justice (MoJ) and are involved in the running of all three major types of courts, namely criminal, civil, and family courts. In addition to the court managers and administrative staff, the key legal personnel for our purposes are listed in Table 6.6.

Table 6.6 Court staff and their roles

Court staff	Role
Legal adviser (magistrates' court), also known as a **justice's clerk**	They provide advice to magistrates on applicable substantive, evidential, and procedural laws. They ensure that magistrates' court proceedings run smoothly by explaining procedures to defendants and witnesses in order to avoid disruptions. They must be a qualified barrister or solicitor.
Court clerks	They are responsible for assisting the judge and managing the courtroom. They ensure that the court runs smoothly and that everyone is in the right place at the right time. They implement any updates and inform the judge, and prepare all the case papers for the judge to make sure they are fully prepared for court.
Ushers	They are the first point of contact for all individuals involved in a case and are responsible for preparing the courtroom, checking that witnesses, defendants, and lawyers are present, calling defendants and witnesses into court, and administering oaths.

Court staff	Role
Stenographer	As a court of record, the Crown Court must have all of its proceedings recorded. Historically, this was to be completed by a stenographer (a court typist). In modern times, they have been recorded using tape recorders. The stenographer remains a role in the ELS, but is now responsible for ensuring that the recording equipment is functioning and transcribing the recording at a later date.
Security officers	They are responsible for control of access doors and gates; conducting entry searches of persons entering court buildings via public entrances, and preventing and dealing with security incidents. Bailiffs who sit with a defendant in the dock in criminal matters fall within this section.

Laypersons

Within this section we shall discuss two forms of layperson within the ELS, namely:

- juries; and
- magistrates.

Each form is essential to the operation of our legal system, with the latter dealing with 99 per cent of criminal cases and the former appointed to try the 1 per cent that makes it to the Crown Court.

Juries

Described by Lord Devlin in 1956 as 'the lamp that shows that freedom lives', trial by one's peers remains a hallmark of the ELS. This is so despite the fact that only 1 per cent of criminal cases are dealt with by way of trial by jury.

Jury trials are commonly associated with criminal trials (and indeed that is their key role); however, juries may also feature in Coroners' Courts and in civil proceedings, albeit rarely. Prior to the **Common Law Procedure Act 1854**, all civil trials were determined by judge and jury. Post 1854, a judge could determine a civil law matter without the need for a jury, where the parties agreed to such. Now, as a result of **s69 Senior Courts Act 1981**, the use of a jury in civil trials is restricted to four circumstances, detailed in Table 6.7. A jury may also feature in the specialist Coroners' Court in the circumstances listed in **s8** (see Table 6.7). Such trials are referred to as inquests and involve the jury acting as the arbiters-of-fact, whilst the Coroner acts as the arbiter-of-law. The jury's role is not to establish the guilt or innocence of a particular individual—that is a matter for the criminal courts. Instead, a jury is simply required to decide how the particular death was caused.

Table 6.7 Jury usage outside of criminal law

Civil Proceeding (s69 Senior Courts Act 1981)	• Defamation. • False imprisonment. • Malicious prosecution. • Fraud.
Coroners' Court (s8 Coroners Act 1988)	• Where the death appears to have occurred in prison, police custody, or where death followed an injury caused by the police. • Where the death is required to be reported by law to a government department or to the Health and Safety Executive (HSE).

The most highly reported jury inquest in recent times is that of the so-called 'Hillsborough stadium disaster', where a jury found that 96 persons were 'unlawfully killed' in 1989. As a result of the common usage of juries in the criminal trial, that will be the focus of this section. For completeness, however, Table 6.7 details some of the cases outside of criminal law where a jury may sit.

Role

The role of the jury is one based on fact. The jury must decide, unanimously or by a majority (see Chapter 7 for the meaning of 'majority'), whether a defendant is 'guilty' or 'not guilty'. They must only do so on the evidence presented before them and may not rely upon other means of reaching that conclusion. It is for this reason that jurors are known as 'arbiters-of-fact'. For example, in ***R v Young* (1994)**, four members of the jury relied upon the use of a Ouija board during their overnight stay in a hotel in an attempt to contact one of the victims of the alleged murder. The Court of Appeal quashed the defendant's conviction on the grounds that:

> there was a real danger that what occurred during this misguided Ouija session may have influenced some jurors and may thereby have prejudiced the appellant.

This was an abuse of the jury's role and a retrial was ordered, where the defendant was found guilty for a second time.

The trial judge is the arbiter-of-law alone and the jury are responsible for applying that law to the facts with the support and guidance of the judge. Further to this, the jury plays no part in a ruling of law, nor does it play a part in the sentencing of defendants whom it has found guilty.

Looking for extra marks?

Demonstrate your knowledge of the criminal justice system by making clear that although the jury have no part to play in the sentencing of a defendant, they do have a residual privilege to add a recommendation of mercy to their verdict, although such is a rarity and judges are advised to not inform the jury of such privilege (***R v Black* (1963)**).

Laypersons

****

Qualification and summons

Section 1(1) Juries Act (JA) 1974 provides for a general presumption that all persons shall be qualified to serve as a juror. Table 6.8 lists the necessary 'qualifications' required to sit on a jury.

Table 6.8 Jury qualifications

Section No.	Qualification
s1(1)(a)	• Registered on the electoral register. • Not less than 18 years old. • Not more than 75 years old (see the 'Looking for extra marks?' section below).
s1(1)(b)	• Has been ordinarily resident in the United Kingdom for any period of at least five years since attaining the age of 13.
s1(1)(c)	• Is not a 'mentally disordered person'.
s1(1)(d)	• Is not disqualified.

Looking for extra marks?

The age limit for jurors was raised from 70 to 75 on 1 December 2016. The government justified this increase by stating that the increase 'will better reflect the healthy life expectancy of people in England and Wales and mean juries are more representative of the communities they serve'. In an essay-style question, show the examiner that you are up to date on current issues such as this and demonstrate that you understand why such changes have been introduced. Take your answer even further by offering your own reasoned opinion as to what you think of the increase in age.

For a full list of 'disqualified' persons, see **sch 1 JA 1974**. The list is divided into individuals who are disqualified for this trial alone, individuals disqualified for life, and individuals disqualified for ten years. Table 6.9 details these disqualified persons further.

Before the **Criminal Justice Act (CJA) 2003**, a list of persons existed who were entitled to avoid jury service, or for whom it was thought 'inappropriate' that they should sit on a jury. These individuals were referred to as being 'ineligible' and included:

- doctors;
- teachers;
- lawyers;

Table 6.9 Disqualified persons

Length of disqualification	Reason for disqualification
That trial	On bail pending criminal proceedings against them.
Life	A person who has at any time been sentenced to: – life imprisonment; – detention at Her Majesty's pleasure or during the pleasure of the Secretary of State; – imprisonment for public protection or detention for public protection; – an extended sentence; or – a term of imprisonment of five years or more or a term of detention of five years or more.

Ten years	A person who at any time in the past ten years has:
	– been found guilty of jury misconduct; or
	– served any part of a sentence of imprisonment or a sentence of detention; or
	– had passed on him/her a suspended sentence of imprisonment or had made in respect of him/her a suspended order for detention; or
	– had made in respect of him/her:
	  – a community order;
	  – a community rehabilitation order;
	  – a community punishment order;
	  – a community punishment and rehabilitation order;
	  – a drug treatment and testing order; or
	  – a drug abstinence order.

- police officers;
- judges.

It was viewed that these individuals were ineligible due to a potential risk of bias and because their duty was considered to be done elsewhere, i.e. in an operating room or out protecting the streets. As a result, therefore, it became commonplace for middle-class individuals to avoid jury service, leaving all other categories of individuals required to serve. As a result of the **Review of Criminal Courts** by Auld LJ, the **CJA 2003** had the effect of removing the majority of the previous categories of individuals who could avoid jury service. Naturally, as can still be seen from Table 6.9 above, notable exceptions still apply, including the mentally incapacitated and individuals who hold certain criminal convictions. A further exception applies to serving members of the armed forces who have their excusal certified by their commanding officer.

Looking for extra marks?

Consider whether it is appropriate for legal professionals to be eligible to sit on a jury. The purpose of a jury is that they are laypersons focusing on the facts before them. Is it not possible that a legal professional will take their role as a juror too far and begin to question the case from a legal angle?

On that basis, could you justify the previous exemptions?

In response to this, see Auld LJ's response in his **Review of the Criminal Courts** in 2001, where he comments that, 'The variety of prejudices that jurors can have are almost unlimited.' Therefore, he concluded that there is no reason why the risk of prejudice is any greater among those excluded than with anyone else sitting as a juror.

As a result of the abolition of excusal by status, the right to a fair trial in circumstances where a juror is a police officer or a member of the CPS is a matter of great importance. As a starting point, the House of Lords in ***R v Abdroikov* (2007)** noted that the key principle following the **CJA 2003** reforms is that 'justice [has] to be seen to be done'. Certain general principles have arisen as a result of the judgment of the European Court of Human Rights (ECtHR) in ***Hanif v UK* (2012)**. These include:

- the fact a police officer is on the jury does not make the trial automatically unfair;
- a police officer should not sit on a jury where they know or are friends with prosecution or defence witnesses; and
- a Crown prosecutor must not sit in the same area as they practise.

The Lord Chancellor now holds the responsibility to publish guidelines on certain matters of public importance, for example, directions to the judiciary should they be required to sit on a jury.

Summons

Jurors are selected for jury service by a centralized computer system. According to Sally Lloyd-Bostock and Cheryl Thomas in Vidmar's *World Jury Systems* (Oxford University Press 2000), this has been the case since 1981. The responsibility of summoning a juror for duty is vested in the Jury Central Summoning Bureau (JCSB), based in London. Its role is to select individuals randomly from the electoral register, check for any criminal records, issue the summons, and liaise with the courts as to how many jurors are required. The power to summon is solely that of the JCSB and no person or institution has the power to interfere with this, including the judge himself.

Attendance and excusal

Section 7 JA 1974 provides that a person summoned under this Act 'shall attend for so many days as may be directed by the summons or by the appropriate officer, and shall be liable to serve on any jury at the place to which he is summoned, or in the vicinity'.

There are, of course, circumstances where a potential juror cannot or should not attend for service. These circumstances are prescribed in **s8(1)**, which provides that a juror may be excused if he/she shows to the satisfaction of the appropriate officer, or of the court:

- that he has served on a jury, or duly attended to serve on a jury, in the past two years; or
- that the Crown Court or any other court has excused him from jury service for a period which has not terminated.

Furthermore, **s9(2)** provides that if any person summoned under this Act shows to the satisfaction of the appropriate officer that there is 'good reason' why he should be excused from attending in pursuance of the summons, the appropriate officer may excuse him from so attending. The same test of 'good reason' applies when an individual seeks a deferral of jury service (**s9A(1)**).

Some of the most common 'good reasons' include:

- illness;
- prior commitments, such as pre-booked holidays;
- work/child commitments;
- personal involvement in the case.

Jury vetting

The topic of **jury vetting** has long been an issue in the ELS. Compared with our American counterpart, English law does not include a formal process of jury vetting. In the USA, advocates (known as Counsellors) are entitled to ask the jury a number of questions to ascertain whether they are suitable (or 'favourable') for that particular jury. In the UK, such vetting and investigation is forbidden.

The Attorney General published a **Practice Note on Jury Checks** in 1988. These Guidelines specified certain exceptional circumstances when jury vetting would be permitted. These exceptional circumstances include, but are not limited to:

- the juror being a risk to security; and
- the juror being susceptible to improper influence.

Looking for extra marks?

Look into the proposals that have been made on jury vetting in the UK over the years. For instance, Alfred Denning in *What Next in Law* (OUP 1982) suggested vetting the background and education of all potential jurors. This included the drawing up of a list of persons 'recommended' for jury service.

The process of vetting is taken in two stages and must be distinguished:

- Stage One: police checks using the standard Criminal Records Bureau (CRB) check;
- Stage Two: an 'Authorised Jury Check', which involves a more in-depth CRB check (an 'enhanced CRB check'), a Special Branch records check, and a Security Services check.

The former is now standard practice (***R v Mason* (1981)**) and is automatic during the selection process for jurors. The latter is a special form of vetting exercise used only in cases involving national security (i.e. alleged terrorism cases). This form of background check must be first authorized by the Atorney General, following recommendation by the DPP. See *Jury vetting: right of stand by guidelines* published by the Attorney General (last updated 30 November 2012).

Challenging jurors

The right to 'challenge' a juror is available to both the prosecution and the defence. There are two forms of challenge available in English law, these being:

- challenge for cause (prosecution and defence right);
- stand-by (prosecution right only).

Prior to the **Criminal Justice Act (CJA) 1988**, there was a third form of challenge, known as a peremptory challenge. This granted the defence the right to challenge jurors without cause. This challenge was abolished by **s118(1) CJA 1988**.

Section 12(1) JA 1974, as amended by the **CJA 1988**, provides that a defendant charged on indictment may challenge all or any of the jurors *for cause*, and any challenge shall be tried by the judge in the instant case.

Two key terms need to be addressed at this point:

- challenge to the array—a challenge to the whole jury;
- challenge to the polls—a challenge to an individual juror.

Procedurally, a challenge may only be made after the juror's name has been drawn by ballot and before he is sworn. Challenge for cause is used where it is suspected that a juror might be biased (***Porter v Magill* (2001)**).

Bias may arise where:

- the juror has been subject to pre-trial publicity;
- the juror has personal feelings regarding the type of offence the defendant is charged with (e.g. a mother may have very strong feelings regarding the trial of a suspected pederast);
- the juror may be motivated by politics and partisanship.

To challenge for cause, counsel merely says 'challenge' before the juror takes the oath. In the straightforward case of the defendant knowing the juror, counsel will state this and the judge will ask the juror to leave the box. If the matter is more complicated, a *voir dire* (simply meaning a 'mini trial' within the main trial) may be held in absence of the jury.

The second form of challenge, open only to the prosecution, is known as 'standing by'. In this case, the prosecutor will simply state 'stand by' and does not have to provide reasons for such. The **Attorney General's Practice Note (1988)** has provided that the stand-by challenge ought to be used 'sparingly' and only where:

- a person is manifestly unsuitable to sit on a jury; and
- where the juror has previous convictions, which have only just come to light.

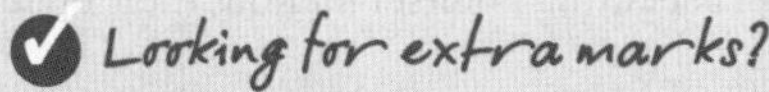

Ask yourself why the prosecution have the right to challenge a juror without cause, whereas the defence must provide a reason. Is there an inequality of arms present in this procedure? Compare this with the procedure in the USA, where each side is granted a number of challenges without cause which varies according to jurisdiction and type of case.

The judge in the trial also has the power to stand a juror by; however, this power is also to be used 'sparingly'. The judge has no power to stand a juror by in order to create a racially balanced jury (***R v Ford*** **(1989)**; ***R v Smith*** **(2003)**).

Looking for extra marks?

Look into the Auld Report and the **Royal Commission on Criminal Justice 1993**, which recommended that in cases where race is of relevance, a scheme should be devised to allow a selection of up to three ethnic minority jurors. This scheme was rejected by the government in their Report, Justice for All (2002). Look at some of the justifications for racially balancing a jury and come to a conclusion of what you think is the most appropriate way forward.

In coming to your conclusion, look at research conducted by Thomas 'Are Juries Fair?' in 2010 (see 'Key debates' below) and see whether your justification is hindered by the results found by Thomas.

Empanelling the jury

The clerk of the court will first assemble and list the names of a group of potential jurors (known as 'jurors in waiting') from the waiting area and will bring them into court. This list is known as a 'panel'. The panel will consist of more than 12 jurors (often 15) to allow random selection to continue even at this stage of proceedings. The clerk of the court first calls 12 jurors from the panel in the following manner:

> Members of the jury in waiting, please answer to your names and step into the jury box as you are called.

He then calls each juror by name and informs the defendant:

> The names that you are about to hear called are the names of the jurors who are to try you. If therefore you wish to object to them, or to any of them, you must do so as they come to the book to be sworn, and before they are sworn, and your objection shall be heard.

If the defendant is represented, any challenge will be made by his counsel.

All jurors are required to take an oath or affirmation in **open court** to 'faithfully try the defendant and give a true verdict according to the evidence'. They must do so in the presence of one another. When a full jury has been sworn, the defendant is placed within the 'charge' of the jury, with the clerk of the court addressing the jury as follows:

> Members of the jury, are you all sworn? The defendant stands indicted for that he, on the [stating the substance of the offences charged in the indictment]. To this indictment he has pleaded not guilty and it is your charge to say, having heard the evidence, whether he be guilty or not.

It is at this point that the trial proper can begin, with prosecuting counsel making their opening speech (see Chapter 7).

Dismissal of jurors

A jury must always start with 12; however, by **s16(1) Juries Act 1974**, up to three jurors may be discharged from the trial by reason of death, illness, or other reason. If more than three jurors are to be discharged, the trial must be abandoned and a fresh one must be ordered. The entire jury may be discharged in several circumstances:

(i) where they cannot agree on a verdict;

(ii) where the jury hears evidence that is inadmissible and prejudicial to the defendant;

(iii) where an individual juror has been discharged and there is a risk they have 'contaminated' the rest of the jury.

> **Looking for extra marks?**
>
> **Section 6(1)** provides that if it appears to the court that a jury to try any issue before the court will be, or probably will be, incomplete, the court may, if the court thinks fit, require any persons who are in, or in the vicinity of, the court, to be summoned (without any written notice) for jury service up to the number needed to make a full jury.
>
> This means that where the court is likely to dismiss several jurors, or did not have enough jurors to begin with, they can pick individuals up off the street to act as a member of the jury (often referred to as 'praying a tales').

Jury deliberations and secrecy

Section 71 Criminal Justice and Courts Act 2015 amends the previous law of jury deliberations found in **s8(1) Contempt of Court Act 1981. Section 8** previously prescribed a criminal offence, namely contempt of court, where an individual aimed to 'obtain, disclose or solicit any particulars of statements made, opinions expressed, arguments advanced or votes cast by members of a jury in the course of their deliberations'. Breaking this section down, it meant that it was a criminal offence for:

- a member of the jury to disclose details of what was said in the jury room; and for
- any person to attempt to obtain such information from a member of the jury.

The present law is now to be found in the **Juries Act 1974**, as amended by the **2015 Act** noted above. The new offences, although similar to the old provisions in **s8**, are now much broader and detailed. The offences include:

- researching the case that he or she is trying during the trial period for reasons connected to that case (**s20A Juries Act 1974**);
- intentionally disclosing information to another member of the jury that had been obtained by research in contravention of **s20A** and the information has not been provided by the court (**s20B Juries Act 1974**);

- intentionally engaging in conduct, during the trial period, from which it may reasonably be concluded that the person intends to try the issue otherwise than on the basis of the evidence presented in the proceedings on the issue (**s20C Juries Act 1974**);
- intentionally disclosing information about statements made, opinions expressed, arguments advanced, or votes cast by members of a jury in the course of their deliberations in proceedings before a court, or to solicit or obtain such information (**ss20D, 20E, 20F, and 20G Juries Act 1974**).

A few examples from the case law can be provided to show the operation of this area of law. Although decided under the previous **s8** provision, the outcome is likely to be the same:

- ***AG v Fraill and Seward* (2011)**: a juror and the defendant communicated during the trial via Facebook. Both were convicted of contempt.
- ***R v Hewgill* (2011)**: jurors were caught discussing the case in a local pub with other patrons and the defendant himself.

These examples show that individuals can be liable for offences of divulging information discussed in the jury room. However, what about the circumstances where information is not divulged, but there is a likelihood or possibility that the jury reached their decision by wrongful means? We have already discussed the case of ***Young* (1994)** in relation to the Ouija board. That is but one example. Other examples include:

- ***Vaise v Delaval* (1785)**: the jury reached their decision by the tossing of a coin;
- ***Harvey v Hewitt* (1840)**: the jury reached their decision by drawing lots;
- ***R v Thompson* (1962)**: the jury had relied on a list of previous convictions, that they were not entitled to know about, in order to convict the defendant;
- ***R v Qureshi* (2002)**: allegations were made that certain members of the jury had determined the defendant's guilt at the outset of the trial based on his race.

In each one of these cases, the court could not interfere with the decision of the jury, as to do so would be contrary to the common law, and **s8**, that jury deliberations cannot leave the jury room. What we hope these cases show is that a defendant may be convicted by a jury, despite evidence that they reached their decision in a manner totally unacceptable to the fairness of trial. This rule appears harsh to a defendant, and has led to stark controversy over the years. For instance, Lord Steyn in ***R v Connor and Mirza* (2004)** commented that:

> In my view it would be an astonishing thing for the ECHR to hold, when the point directly arises before it, that a miscarriage of justice may be ignored in the interests of the general efficiency of the jury system. The terms of article 6(1) of the European Convention, the rights revolution, and fifty years of development of human rights law and practice, would suggest that such a view would be *utterly indefensible* [emphasis added].

The position of the English courts was, however, endorsed by the ECtHR in ***Gregory v UK* (1997)**, where the Court ruled that:

> the rule governing the secrecy of jury deliberations is a *crucial and legitimate* feature of English trial law which serves to reinforce the jury's role as the ultimate arbiter of fact and to guarantee open and frank deliberations among jurors on the evidence which they have heard [emphasis added].

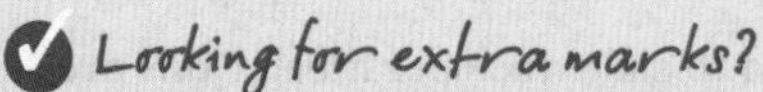

Make clear to the examiner that although research into 'real' juries is forbidden, research can be undertaken in so-called 'mock juries'. For instance, look at the research conducted by Thomas, 'Avoiding the Perfect Storm of Juror Contempt' (2013) and Darbyshire et al, 'What can the English Legal System learn from Jury Research published up to 2001?' (2001) (see 'Key debates' below).

A further matter that can be discussed under the heading of jury deliberations are the so-called, 'perverse decisions'. Perverse decisions refer to a jury's conclusion that has come about by agreement of the jury but is not consistent with the law or the facts presented before them. It is also referred to as 'jury equity' to designate that some juries refuse to apply the law when they believe that to follow it would lead to an unjust verdict. Examples of such perverse decision can be seen in the following two cases:

- ***R v Owen* (1992)**: the victim killed the defendant's son through careless driving. As a form of retribution, the defendant attacked the victim with a shotgun, causing multiple injuries. The jury acquitted him, and some members later congratulated him on what he had done.
- ***R v Blythe* (1998)**: the defendant cultivated cannabis for the purpose of supplying it to his wife, who was dying with multiple sclerosis. The judge directed the jury that no defence existed and yet the jury found the defendant not guilty.

The authors refer to this as 'jury justice' (others refer to it as 'jury equity'). Earlier, we discussed whether the jury, in acting outside their remit, were causing a detriment to the defendant. Surely, the same principle applies in the context of perverse decisions, but specifically for the prosecution and the alleged victim.

Jury verdicts

For a discussion of jury verdicts, see Chapter 7.

Effectiveness of the jury

As a final point on the jury system, it will be useful to briefly summarize some of the pros and cons of the system, as set out in Table 6.10.

Table 6.10 Pros and cons of the jury system

Pro	Con
The use of 12 jurors should mitigate or remove any potential bias by individual jurors.	Jury secrecy means that it will never be known what the true motives of the jury are, and whether the jury are biased in a particular way. Media coverage may influence a jury's verdict (even though they are directed to avoid any relevant media coverage).
Perverse verdicts enjoy public respect.	Perverse verdicts undermine the principle of justice and the rule of law (and are actually very rare).
Perverse jury verdicts can provide a 'criminal equity'.	Jurors may be tempted to reach a quick verdict in order to complete their jury service early.
Involvement of laypersons. Trial by peers.	Law on jury secrecy could allow the innocent to remain convicted rather than make reasonable enquiries into how the verdict was obtained and the reasons for the verdict.
Balances state intervention in criminal trials.	Juries are not representative; they are not racially balanced.

Looking for extra marks?

When considering the role of the jury in the ELS, observe the trends in recent times towards arguing for a reduction of the number of jurors in trials (from 12 to nine), the issues of social media and warnings to the jury regarding social media, and the concept of fixing a jury to ensure it is 'representative'.

Magistrates

Described by Lord Bingham as 'a democratic jewel beyond price', the use of lay magistrates is a further major hallmark of the ELS.

The role played by magistrates in the ELS can be traced as far back as 1195. It was in that year that Richard I commissioned certain knights to preserve the King's Peace in 'unruly areas'. It was at this point that the phrase 'Keepers of the Peace' was first adopted.

Another form of terminology used to describe a magistrate was to describe them as 'Justices of the Peace' (JPs). The phrase, first seen in 1361, during the reign of Edward III, remains in popular use today and is now synonymous with the more modern term of 'magistrate'.

Laypersons

****

Revision tip

The term 'magistrate' covers both lay magistrates and stipendiary magistrates (district judges). Ensure that you understand the distinction between the two and make such distinction clear in any answer you give.

District judges have been considered under the heading 'The judiciary'.

Magistrates are represented by the Magistrates Association and, as of 2019, there are approximately 14,000 magistrates sitting in around 330 magistrates' courts (figures from the Judicial Diversity Statistics 2019).

Role

Magistrates are unpaid volunteers acting as the arbiters of both fact and law. Magistrates are most commonly known for their role in adult criminal proceedings. However, magistrates may also sit, with specialist training, in the Youth Court and in the Family Court. Some magistrates also sit in a civil capacity, dealing with matters such as licensing and council tax repayments. In criminal matters, magistrates sit as a panel of three, and are required to reach a unanimous or majority verdict of guilty or not guilty on the evidence presented before them by the prosecution and defence.

Upon a finding of guilt, magistrates must then sentence the defendant according to the Sentencing Guidelines provided for magistrates. Magistrates' sentencing powers are contained in the **CJA 2003**.

Their powers will vary dependent on the offence or type of offence that is in question. Table 6.11 provides further details on this, specifically in relation to their powers of imprisonment.

Table 6.11 Magistrates' imprisonment powers

Type of offence	Sentence provision
A single summary offence	If punishable by imprisonment, the maximum sentence is six months or that prescribed by the statute which creates the offence, whichever is less.
A single either-way offence	The maximum sentence is six months' imprisonment.
Multiple summary offences	The court may order those sentences to be served concurrently or consecutively but with a maximum aggregate of six months.
Multiple either-way offences	The court may order those sentences to be served concurrently or consecutively and may sentence to a total aggregate of 12 months.

Magistrates may also issue fines, which are set on a 'standard scale' under **s37 Criminal Justice Act (CJA) 1972**. These fines are detailed in Table 6.12.

Table 6.12 The 'standard scale'

Level on the scale	Amount of fine
1	£200
2	£500
3	£1,000
4	£2,500
5	£5,000

Magistrates most commonly sit on criminal matters; specifically, they deal only with the less serious criminal offences. This process is described further in Chapter 7.

Magistrates are required to sit for at least 13 days/26 half-days each year, or 35 half-days if they also sit in the youth or family courts.

Appointment and eligibility

Prior to October 2013, the Lord Chancellor was responsible for the appointment of lay magistrates under **s10 Courts Act (CA) 2003**. As a result of **sch 13, para 39 Crime and Courts Act 2013**, which amended the **CA 2003**, the statutory power to appoint magistrates is now vested in the LCJ, who delegates the function to the Senior Presiding Judge for England and Wales. Appointments are made after consultation with and recommendation from the local Advisory Committee, which consists of a network of 30 committees, one in each county. The hopeful magistrates must either live or work in or near that justice area and must not be excluded from appointment as a result of criminal convictions, undischarged debts, or any other reason which could be viewed as bringing the magistracy into disrepute.

Magistrates can be appointed from the age of 18 to 65 and retire at 70 and require no legal training or qualification. Candidates must, however, demonstrate six 'key qualities'. These key qualities reflect key personality traits necessary to sit as a magistrate. Figure 6.8 details these six key qualities.

Training

Although magistrates require no form of legal education or qualification, training is provided for all magistrates before they undertake their role. Training is supervised by the Judicial College and costs the state £500 per trainee.

Figure 6.8 Key qualities of magistrates

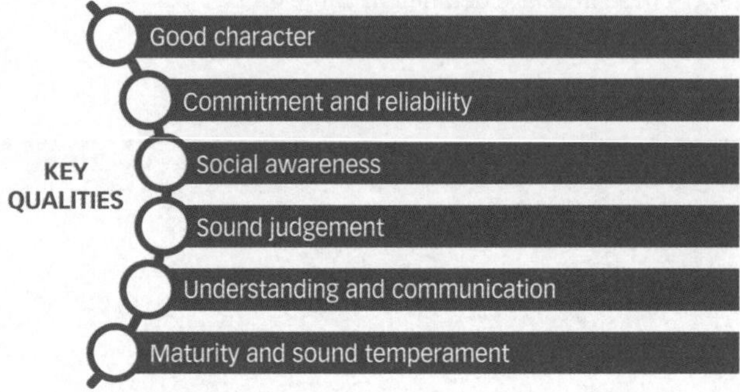

The training is based on three key competencies:

1. **Managing Yourself**: dealing with self-management;
2. **Working as a Member of a Team**: dealing with the team aspect of making decisions; and
3. **Making Judicial Decisions**: dealing with impartial and focused decision making.

There is a fourth competence dealing with 'managing judicial decision making'; however, this applies only to the chairman of the bench. The list below details a breakdown of the training received by magistrates:

- **Initial training**: introductory training on the basics of the role;
- **Mentoring**: each new magistrate has a specially trained magistrate mentor to guide them through their first months. There are six formal mentored sittings in the first 12–18 months, where the new magistrate will review learning progress and talk over any training needs.
- **Core training**: further training involving visits to penal institutions takes place to equip magistrates with the key knowledge they need.
- **Consolidation training**: at the end of the first year, consolidation training builds on the learning from sittings and core training;
- **First appraisal**: about 12–18 months after appointment, when both mentor and magistrate agree he/she is ready, the new justice is appraised. The appraisal observes whether the new magistrate is demonstrating that he/she is competent in the role, against the competencies.

Composition

Magistrates sit on a panel of three. The panel is composed as follows:

- one Chairman, who speaks in open court; and
- two wingers, less experienced magistrates who assist the Chairman.

All three magistrates carry equal weight in the decision-making process and play a full part in the discussions held in the magistrates' retiring room.

Removal/retirement

Once a magistrate turns 70, they must 'retire' from the bench. The word 'retire' is phrased in inverted commas given that such individuals are placed on a 'supplemental list' under **s13 CA 2003**, as opposed to formally retiring. Lay magistrates are no longer qualified to sit on a bench upon being placed on this list.

Alternate to retirement, a magistrate may decide to leave the bench of their own free will, should they wish to do so (**s11(1) CA 2003**). In addition, there are, of course, situations whereby a magistrate may be removed from the bench before they turn 70. These circumstances are prescribed under **s11(2) CA 2003** (as amended by the **Crime and Courts Act 2013**), which grants the LCJ the power to remove lay magistrates in certain specified circumstances. These circumstances are:

- on the grounds of incapacity or misbehaviour;
- on the ground of a persistent failure to meet such standards of competence as prescribed; or
- if he/she is satisfied that the lay justice is declining or neglecting to take a proper part in the exercise of his functions as a justice of the peace.

Natural justice

As part of their role, magistrates must act in accordance with the principle of natural justice; specifically, they must act without bias or apparent bias and must ensure that justice is seen to be done. Numerous cases demonstrate this apparent bias that may be held to the detriment of a defendant; the most prominent of these being ***ex parte Jowitt*** **(1974)**.

R v Bingham JJ, ex parte Jowitt [1974] The Times, 3 July (HC)

FACTS: The defendant exceeded the speed limit and his evidence contradicted that of a police officer. In finding the defendant guilty, the Chairman of the panel commented: 'My principle in such cases has always been to believe the evidence of the police officer.'

HELD: The Divisional Court held that this remark would cause any reasonable person to suspect that the Chairman was biased towards the police officer and that the defendant had not been granted a fair trial.

Natural justice does not solely involve the requirement to avoid bias. It also includes the duty to ensure fairness and attention to the defendant and the trial as a whole. This was clear in ***R v Weston-Super-Mare JJ, ex parte Taylor*** **(1981)**, where, during the defendant's trial, the Chairman appeared to be asleep. The defendant's solicitor suggested that the Chairman should withdraw from the case, but she declined to do so. The Divisional Court ruled that the Chairman must ensure their full attention is given to the trial and the defendant.

Use of local knowledge

One of the benefits of the use of magistrates is the ability to use and refer to their own local knowledge when trying a case. The key authority on this is the case of ***Bowman v DPP* (1991)**.

***Bowman v DPP* [1991] RTR 263 (HC)**

FACTS: The defendant drove at high speed around a multi-storey car park. He did so shortly after midnight and whilst heavily intoxicated. The magistrates were required to consider whether the car park was 'a public place' within the meaning of the Act that he was charged under.

One magistrate lived near the car park and a second magistrate used it regularly. Through this knowledge, they were aware that the barriers were raised at night, allowing motorists to use it freely. This meant that the car park was a public place for the purposes of the Act. The magistrates convicted.

HELD: The Divisional Court ruled that magistrates have the 'right and duty' to use their local knowledge where appropriate, though it is always wise for them to make their intention known so that the parties can comment.

This case was qualified by a later Divisional Court ruling in ***Norbrook Laboratories v Health & Safety Executive* (1998)**, which held that magistrates may use their knowledge but they must '*always* make this intention known to the parties and allow them a chance to comment on it before the decision is made' (emphasis added).

Assistance of the legal clerk

Magistrates are assisted in the performance of their role by the legal clerk, also known as the legal adviser (see above under 'Legal personnel'). The role of the legal adviser is detailed in the **Criminal Practice Directions 2015**. In particular, **Practice Direction (PD)24A, para 5** states:

> It shall be the responsibility of the justices' clerk or legal adviser to provide the justices with any advice they require to perform their functions justly, whether or not the advice has been requested, on:
>
> (a) questions of law;
> (b) questions of mixed law and fact;
> (c) matters of practice and procedure;
> (d) the process to be followed at sentence and the matters to be taken into account, together with the range of penalties and ancillary orders available, in accordance with the relevant sentencing guidelines;
> (e) any relevant decisions of the superior courts or other guidelines;
> (f) the appropriate decision-making structure to be applied in any given case; and
> (g) other issues relevant to the matter before the court.

What you should gather from the above list is that the legal adviser must not advise the panel on a matter of fact. This is made clear in **PD24A.12**, which states that 'A justices' clerk or legal adviser must not play any part in making findings of fact.' The clerk must therefore not retire to the deliberation room with the magistrates.

This rule is demonstrated in the *ex parte Ahmed* (1994) case.

R v Birmingham Magistrates' Court, ex parte Ahmed [1994] COD 461 (HC)
FACTS: The defendant was accused of deception and handling stolen property. The magistrates retired to consider their verdict; the clerk had retired with them, without being invited to do so in open court.
HELD: Suspicion was created that the clerk was taking part in the decision of guilt, given that no point of law arose. Such suspicion led to a retrial, given the fact that the legal clerk should not be involved in the decision.

Effectiveness of lay magistrates

As a final note on the magistrates' system, it will be useful to briefly summarize some of the pros and cons of lay magistrates (see Table 6.13).

Table 6.13 Pros and cons of lay magistrates

Pro	Con
Use of local knowledge assists decisions	'Middle-Class, Middle-Minded, Middle-Aged'
Three magistrates allows for a balanced view Use of a legal adviser allows the magistrates to focus on questions of fact	Higher conviction rate in magistrates' court than Crown Court
Cheaper than using professionals	Inconsistency in sentencing
Deal with the majority of cases	Rely too heavily on the legal clerk
Greater public confidence in magistrates than the judiciary	Case-hardened and biased

For a more in-depth look at the pros and cons of magistrates, see Penny Darbyshire, *Darbyshire on the English Legal System* (11th edn, Sweet & Maxwell 2014).

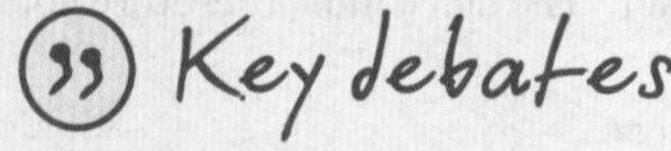

Topic	Jury selection
Academic	Penny Darbyshire
Viewpoint	Argues that the electoral roll is problematic. Specifically argues that 'It is not accurate, because of population mobility, house moves, death, and people not registering specially to evade council tax.'
Source	Penny Darbyshire, A Maughan, and A Stewart, 'What can the English Legal System Learn from Jury Research published up to 2001?' (Kingston Law School 2002)

Topic	White jurors
Academic	Cheryl Thomas
Viewpoint	Undertook research and found that verdicts of all white jurors did not discriminate against black and minority ethnic (BME) defendants. She argues that racially balanced juries are 'unnecessary for fairness', but did raise concerns of the 'appearance of fairness' with an all-white jury and BME defendants.
Source	Cheryl Thomas, 'Are Juries Fair?' Ministry of Justice Research Series 1/10

Topic	Cab rank rule
Academic	David Pannick
Viewpoint	In response to the argument that the cab rank rule operates as a restriction of freedom and that it cannot be justified, Pannick argues that 'any lawyer who does not understand [the purpose of the rule] really has no business being an advocate'.
Source	David Pannick, *Advocates* (Oxford University Press 1992)

Topic	Solicitor advocates
Academic	Penny Darbyshire
Viewpoint	Undertook research on the working lives of judges, and found that many judges do not appear to believe the quality of advocacy is the same between solicitors and barristers.
Source	Penny Darbyshire, *Sitting in Judgment: The Working Lives of Judges* (Hart Publishing 2011)

Exam questions

Essay question 1

'Lay participation in the English legal system is a waste of time. Only qualified lawyers should be arbiters of both fact and law.'

Critically discuss this statement in light of the pros and cons of using laypersons in the legal system of England and Wales.

Essay question 2

'The distinction between the legal professionals of the English legal system is clouded and lacks any real divergence in their respective roles.'

Critically consider this statement.

Online resources

For outline answers to these essay questions, as well as multiple-choice questions, please visit the online resources.

#7
The Criminal Justice System

Key facts

- The criminal justice system (CJS) is built upon procedural, evidential, and substantive foundations. These foundations dictate its direction and progression.
- The criminal procedure is methodical and is largely codified in procedural rules.
- A case will always begin with an investigation by the police or some other investigatory body. An individual may then be charged with an offence where he/she is provided with the option of pleading guilty or not guilty. Trial may follow.
- Where the defendant's case will be tried depends on the type of offence in question and, in some cases, the decision of the defendant.
- The criminal courts have wide-ranging powers of sentencing, which can be adapted to suit the intricacies of the particular offence.
- A convicted person may appeal against either conviction or sentence, for which the defendant will be required to prove why they either should not have been convicted or why their sentence should be reduced.

Chapter overview

The criminal justice system

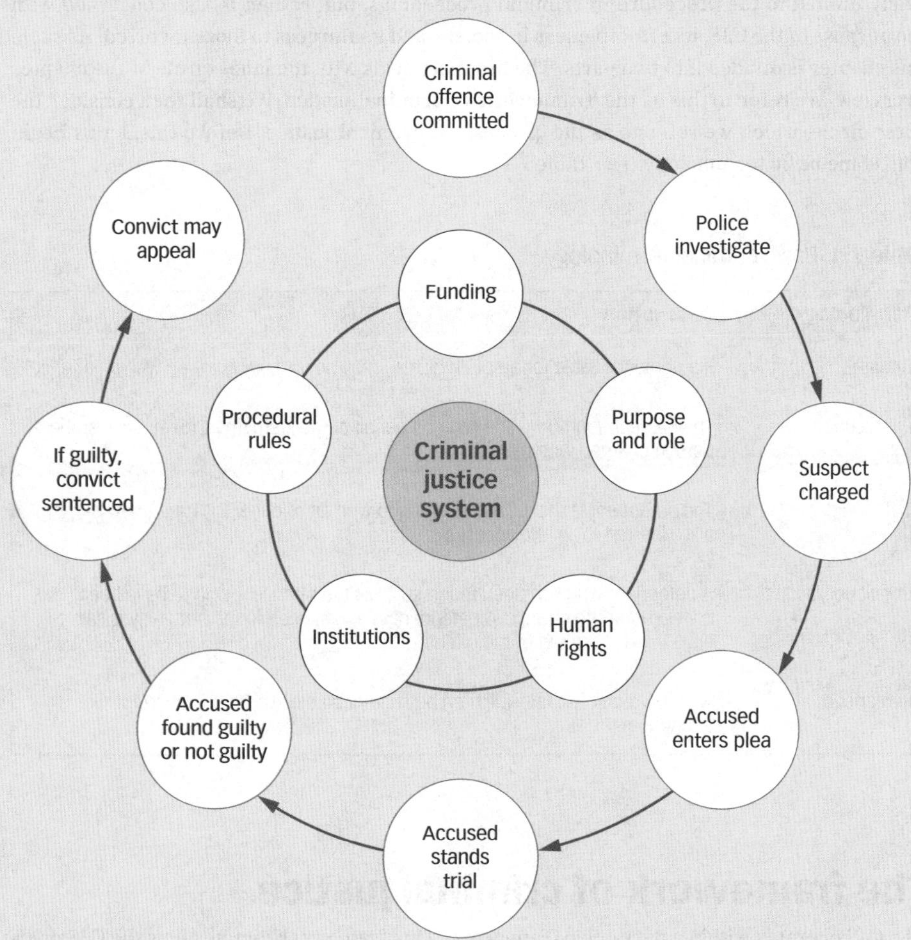

Introduction

The criminal justice system (CJS) is composed of many elements and raises a multitude of procedural, evidential, substantive, philosophical, political, and psychological questions. As with Chapter 1, it is imperative that you understand the dynamism of the CJS in that it is not solely limited to the procedure in criminal proceedings, but, rather, is also concerned with the purpose of the CJS, its effectiveness in society, and its fairness to those involved. As such, this chapter is divided into two parts. The first part deals with the inner circle of the chapter overview. We refer to this as the 'framework' of criminal justice. We shall then consider the outer circle, which we refer to as the 'process' of criminal justice. Before this, let us begin with some basic terminology (see Table 7.1).

Table 7.1 Basic criminal terminology

Terminology	Description
Charge	If a person is liable for an offence, they may be formally *charged* with an offence.
Prosecution	The *prosecution* brings the case on behalf of the state (the Crown) against the person charged with the offence.
Defendant	The *defendant* is the individual charged with an offence. The defendant is often also referred to as 'the accused'.
Conviction/acquittal	A defendant who has been found guilty of the offence is said to have been *convicted* of the offence. A defendant who has been found not guilty is said to have been *acquitted* of the offence.
Sentenced	A convicted defendant will then be *sentenced* (i.e. will be punished for their wrongdoing).

The framework of criminal justice

The CJS operates within a particular framework. This framework dictates how the CJS operates, the manner in which it is to operate, and the reason why the CJS operates in that fashion. The framework of the CJS provides a contextual understanding to our discussion of the process of the CJS.

Please note, we shall not be dealing with 'Funding the CJS' or the effect of human rights on the CJS, as both are dealt with in exclusive chapters of their own (see Chapters 9 and 5, respectively).

Purpose and role

The starting point when considering the operation of any rule, design, or system is to ask 'Why?' The 'purpose' of the CJS is a matter up for debate and, if interested, you can consult Jeremy Horder, *Ashworth's Principles of Criminal Law* (9th edn, Oxford University Press 2019).

We note that there are several key purposes of the criminal law and the justice system, among them being:

- protection of fundamental freedoms and rights;
- enforcement of legal rules and orders;
- punishment of behaviour contrary to legal rules and orders.

The list could go on and on. The point is that the purpose of the CJS and the actual operation of the CJS are two different things. The CJS is based on a principle of fairness between the parties (known as the 'equality of arms'). An element of its purpose is to promote such equality of arms. In practice, however, that equality of arms may be a mere fantasy, with the rules of disclosure, applications of public interest immunity, and the qualifications of legal professionals affecting procedural matters.

The role of the CJS is another matter entirely. The debate at the heart of this subject is whether the criminal law acts in a positive or negative manner:

- **positive**: individuals are prohibited from engaging in certain activities and conduct;
- **negative**: individuals are free to act in any manner, subject to the notion that there may be legal consequences as a result of their actions or activities.

The latter is advocated by the likes of Michael Tonry, 'The Questionable Relevance of Previous Convictions to Punishments for Later Crimes' in Julian Roberts and Andreas von Hirsch (eds), *Previous Convictions at Sentencing: Theoretical and Applied Perspectives* (Hart Publishing 2010), who argues that:

> No citizen is obligated not to offend. Every citizen is a free moral agent and may choose whether or not to offend. The citizen who chooses to offend is vulnerable to prosecution, conviction and punishment. That's it.

That, in basic form, is the purpose and role of the CJS. There are multiple different elements within our framework that may go towards fulfilling this role and purpose.

Revision tip

Remember that the CJS operates for the citizens of the state. Therefore, when considering the purpose of the CJS, ensure you consider what the regular members of society would consider the purpose of the CJS to be. Some may say that the CJS is built for punishment of offenders; others would say it is to protect the public. What do you think?

Institutions

When we speak of the 'institutions' of the CJS, we are referring specifically to the numerous different authorities and services that operate within the CJS. This section does not consider the 'individuals' that work in the CJS; for that, see Chapter 6. This section concerns the two main institutions, namely:

- investigatory bodies;
- prosecuting bodies.

Although certain bodies such as the Prison and Probation Services are outside the remit of this text, it is still useful to know of their existence.

Investigatory bodies

The police are responsible for the majority of all investigations into alleged criminal offences. The police force is divided into 43 regional police forces, each of which is under the direction of a Chief Constable. The police are responsible specifically for:

- the investigation of crime;
- the collection of evidence; and
- the arrest or detention of suspected offenders.

Prosecuting bodies

Established as an independent body by the **Prosecution of Offences Act 1985**, the Crown Prosecution Service (CPS) is the principal prosecuting authority for England and Wales. As a result of the statutory charging procedure introduced by the **Criminal Justice Act (CJA) 2003**, the CPS acts as an independent prosecuting authority in the majority of cases.

The CPS, however, holds no formal power of investigation. Instead, the CPS must work closely with the police and other investigators to obtain all relevant information and consider all possible lines of inquiry. McConville (1991) (see 'Key debates' at the end of the chapter) argues that this reliance on the police force questions the independence of the CPS in its decision making. This is furthered by Ian Brownlee, 'The Statutory Charging Scheme in England and Wales: Towards a Unified Prosecution System' (2004) Crim LR 896, who suggests that the CPS is subject to undue pressure from the police. Upon consulting with the police, the CPS will ultimately decide on the appropriate charge against an individual (they may decide not to charge at all).

The CPS is headed by the Director of Public Prosecutions (DPP) under the superintendence of the Attorney General.

The CPS operates under a structure of 13 areas in England and Wales, which can be seen in Figure 7.1.

There are four key personnel within the CPS. These are listed below with their role in order of seniority:

- **Senior Crown Prosecutor**: legally qualified solicitor or barrister;
- **Crown Prosecutor**: legally qualified solicitor or barrister;
- **Associate Crown Prosecutor**: not legally qualified. May only appear in non-imprisonable summary-only offences;
- **Case officer**: individual who works on the case, establishing what the correct charge is, the evidence that needs to be obtained, and assigning the correct prosecutor to the case.

The CPS clearly plays a pivotal role in the prosecution of criminal offences; however, they are not the only public bodies who prosecute criminal offences. These other bodies specialize in a particular area of the criminal law and a few examples are detailed in Table 7.2, with a brief description of their role.

Procedural rules

The procedural rules of the CJS are detailed in the **Criminal Procedure Rules (Crim PR) 2015**. The Rules, first introduced in 2005, provide a comprehensive criminal procedure code that governs the conduct (including procedural and evidential matters) of all criminal cases. The Rules are regularly updated by the Criminal Procedure Rule Committee and are split into 14 categories to allow ease in accessibility. These categories include such matters as:

- preliminary proceedings;
- custody and bail; and
- evidence.

These categories are then further sub-divided into 50 'parts', for example:

- Part 10: The indictment;
- Part 14: Bail and custody time limits;
- Part 19: Expert evidence.

The full list can be found on the www.justice.gov website.

The Rules are accompanied by 13 **Criminal Practice Directions (Crim PD)** made by the Lord Chief Justice, which go into further detail of those Rules. As with the Rules, the Practice Directions are updated on a regular basis.

Overriding objective

The **Crim PR** begins with a statement as to what the 'overriding objective' of the **Crim PR** is. Essentially, it informs the reader what the purpose of the Rules is. Specifically, **Part 1.1** provides:

> (1) The overriding objective of this procedural code is that criminal cases be dealt with justly.
>
> (2) Dealing with a criminal case justly includes—

Figure 7.1 The thirteen geographic areas of the CPS

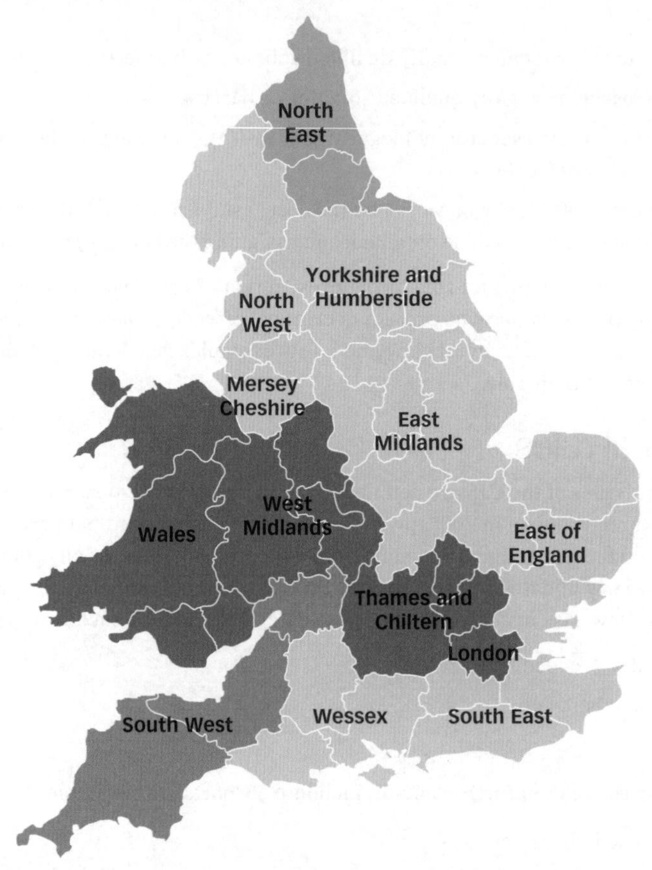

Table 7.2 Other prosecuting authorities

Authority	Role
Serious Fraud Office (SFO)	Investigates and prosecutes serious or complex fraud
Health and Safety Executive (HSE)	Investigates and prosecutes criminal offences arising out of accidents in the workplace
Environment Agency (EA)	Investigates and prosecutes environmental crime

(a) acquitting the innocent and convicting the guilty;
(b) dealing with the prosecution and the defence fairly;
(c) recognising the rights of a defendant, particularly those under Article 6 of the European Convention on Human Rights;
(d) respecting the interest of witnesses, victims and jurors and keeping them informed of the progress of the case;
(e) dealing with the case efficiently and expeditiously;
(f) ensuring that appropriate information is available to the court when bail and sentence are considered; and
(g) dealing with the case in ways that take into account;
  (i) the gravity of the offence alleged,
  (ii) the complexity of what is in issue,
  (iii) the severity of the consequences for the defendant and others affected, and
  (iv) the needs of other cases.

It is not just simply for the courts to fulfil the overriding objective, however. Rather, 'each participant' involved in the criminal justice process must prepare and conduct cases in accordance with the overriding objective (**Crim PR, Part 1.2**). Further to this, the court must engage in an active and robust management of cases. Active case management includes such factors as the early identification of the real issues, monitoring the progress of the case and compliance with directions, and making use of technology. For the full list, see **Part 3.2**.

Looking for extra marks?

Show the examiner that you are up to date on developments in the law. In particular, the case management responsibilities under **Part 3** must be read in conjunction with the principles enshrined in the Stop Delaying Justice (SDJ) initiative. This initiative, in force from January 2012, applies to all cases tried in the magistrates' court.

The initiative's main aim is to ensure:

> All contested trials in the magistrates' court are fully managed from the first hearing and disposed of at the second hearing.

Look at other initiatives such as the Criminal Justice—Simple, Speedy and Summary (CJ-SSS) initiative and the Transforming Summary Justice (TSJ) initiative.

Evidential rules

When you study criminal law at degree level, you will learn the substantive elements of a number of criminal offences. You will learn the general principles of criminal liability, including observing the meaning of terms such as *actus reus* and *mens rea* and how they apply to each offence. However, in practice, a defendant would never be convicted of a criminal offence simply based on the theory of the substantive law. Rather, the substantive law operates alongside the rules of evidence in the CJS.

Our discussion of evidence will only be brief and, if interested, you are advised to consult Maureen Spencer and John Spencer, *Evidence Concentrate* (6th edn, Oxford University Press 2019).

The rules of evidence are predicated on certain core principles that apply to most forms of evidence. These core principles are detailed in Table 7.3.

There are varying forms of evidence that may be admitted in a criminal trial. These include the use of:

- live testimony from a witness who has direct knowledge of the evidence they provide;
- documentary evidence, such as a book or a piece of paper;
- real evidence, such as a knife or a gun;
- opinion evidence, both expert and non-expert; and
- hearsay evidence, meaning any evidence outside of court.

The law of evidence carries with it a number of obligations on the parties, including the requirement of disclosure (see later under 'Pre-trial process') coupled with the role of the court in determining the admissibility of evidence. Importantly, whether the evidence is admissible is a matter for the arbiter-of-law (i.e. the trial judge); whereas the actual application of the evidence to the facts in question is a matter for the arbiters-of-fact (i.e. the jury).

Table 7.3 Core principles of evidence

Core principle	Explanation
Admissibility	The admissibility of evidence is a matter for the judge/magistrate. In ***R v Terry* (1996)**, it was held that evidence will be admissible if it is: (a) relevant; (b) such that a jury, properly warned about any defects it might have, could place some weight on it; and (c) not excluded.
Relevance	Relevance was defined by Lord Simon in ***DPP v Kilbourne* (1973)** as 'Evidence is relevant if it is logically probative or disprobative of some matter which requires proof.'
Weight	Weight, like relevance, is a question of degree. At one end of the spectrum it may be of little probative value, being so weak that it is described as 'insufficient evidence'. At the other end, it may be virtually conclusive of the facts in issue, that it is described as '*prima facie* evidence'.

Looking for extra marks?

One of the most controversial aspects of laypersons sitting as magistrates is that they are both the arbiters of fact and of law. This means that the magistrates will decide whether or not a piece of evidence is admissible, and then from that decision will go on to try the defendant.

Take, for example, the circumstance where the defendant has a previous conviction. Under **s101 CJA 2003**, there is a general presumption that a defendant's 'bad character' should not be admitted. If the prosecutor wishes to have his/her convictions admitted to evidence, he/she will have to go through certain tests detailed in **s101**. Suppose that the magistrates rule that the evidence is 'inadmissible'—do you think they would be able to ignore the information they just heard?

Layout of the criminal courts

The layout of the criminal courts will naturally vary according to the size, age, and accessibility of the building. There are several general principles that apply in all cases though:

- In the Crown Court, defence advocates always sit closest to the jury; whilst prosecuting advocates will always sit closest to the witness box.
- The 'dock' (where the defendant stands) is generally towards the back of a courtroom; however, this can also vary, depending on space. The dock is also generally sealed within a glass frame and locked by the Court Bailiff. The use of the dock in modern times has recently been called into question by the Human Rights Group, Justice, in their Report *In the Dock: Reassessing the Use of the Dock in Criminal Trials* (Justice 2015).
- The magistrates' bench and the judges' bench are on raised platforms above the rest of the courtroom.
- Dependent on the courtroom, the public gallery may be quite small or quite large. Many of the large courtrooms include an upstairs public gallery, where the trial can be viewed from above.
- Magistrates' courts tend to be more traditional in style, with ageing wooden panels (see Figure 7.2); whereas the Crown Court tends now to have a modern approach to layout (see Figure 7.3).

Figure 7.2 Layout of a traditional magistrates' court

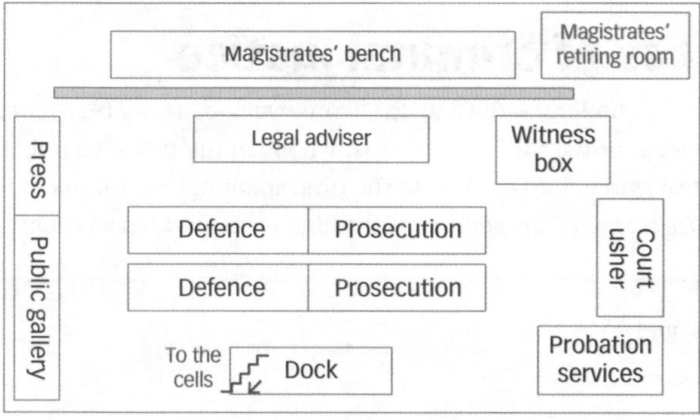

Figure 7.3 Layout of a traditional Crown Court centre

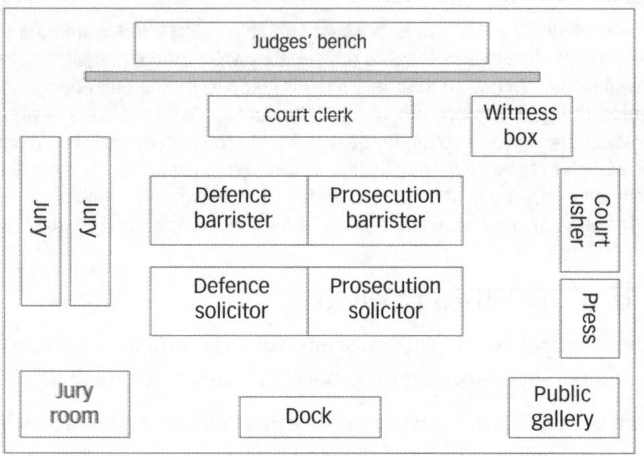

Looking for extra marks?

Seeing the layout of a standard courtroom is useful information and will provide context to your understanding. However, the main reason you need to understand the layout of a courtroom is to assess what sort of effect the layout of the courts has on the individuals who must attend.

For example, in the Crown Court, the judge sits on a raised platform. Naturally, this will be an intimidating state should anyone be before the court charged with an offence.

Also, the defendant is held within a 'dock'. From the perspective of an individual who knows nothing, or relatively little, of the CJS, they may believe that the defendant is dangerous or hostile, thus requiring a separate space just for him/her.

Our point is that you should not settle on the layout of the court. You should be asking, 'Why is it like that? Could it be more accessible? What effects does it have on individuals?'

The process of criminal justice

Now that you have an understanding of the framework of the CJS, it is essential that you appreciate the process of the CJS. By process, we mean the procedure that is adopted from the start of an investigation into a crime to the time spent in imprisonment should the matter reach that stage. As a result, this section of the chapter is divided as such:

- pre-trial process;
- trial process; and
- post-trial process.

It is important to have a broad understanding of the stages that an individual will go through when they come into contact with the criminal law.

Looking for extra marks?

It would be naïve to think of the criminal process as only including the stages that an individual who has allegedly committed the crime must go through. Make clear that certain others persons, mainly the victim (or complainant), will also have to go through a number of stages during the criminal process, many of which may be very difficult for them to do. These include:

- making the complaint;
- being interviewed regarding the complaint;
- undertaking medical tests (in certain cases);
- being examined in court;
- being cross-examined in court.

The CJS can be just as challenging and daunting for an individual who seeks to have another prosecuted. So, bear that in mind in relation to any answers you provide.

Figure 7.4 provides a brief flowchart of the process of criminal justice for an individual charged with an offence.

Pre-trial process

Crime allegedly committed

At the very start of the CJS is the alleged commission of a criminal offence. Without the commission of a criminal offence, the criminal law cannot be involved. For example, suppose Mark and Claire are next-door neighbours. Claire plays loud music late into the night, causing Mark to lose sleep. This is not a criminal offence; it is a tort of 'private nuisance'. Therefore, no criminal offence has been committed. Should Mark attack Claire as a result of her playing loud music, at that point the criminal law would be invoked.

Revision tip

Ensure that when you are considering the process of the CJS that you use the term 'allegedly' in relation to the commission of a criminal offence.

This is the essential element to the CJS and to the framework of criminal justice. The use of allegedly connotes the fundamental principle of 'innocent until proven guilty', as enshrined in the **Human Rights Act 1998**.

Crime recorded by the police

In order for the alleged criminal offence to come before the prosecuting authorities, it first has to be recorded. In the majority of cases, it is the responsibility of the alleged victim/complainant of the criminal offence to report the crime to the relevant authority. Naturally,

Figure 7.4 Process of the criminal justice system

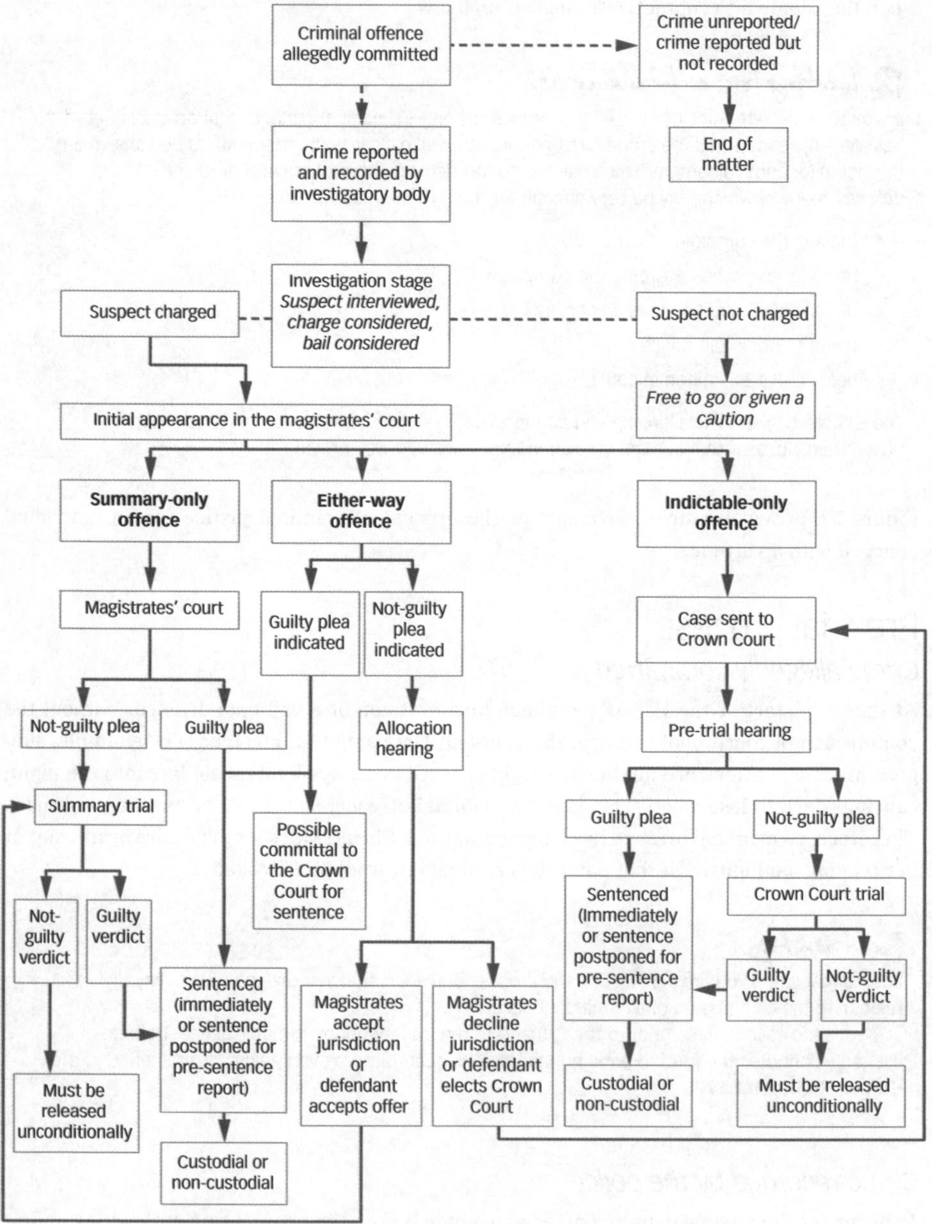

there may be situations where this is not possible, for example in the case of unlawful homicide where the victim is dead. Further to this, in many cases, the victim of a crime may be incapacitated or of a vulnerable age (both young and old), and thus the CJS allows for other persons to raise concerns and report such offences on behalf of the victim. The police will first wish to question the victim/complainant. If the victim is unwilling to assist, the police may be forced to end their investigation early. Without a thorough investigation of the facts by the police, the CPS are unlikely to consider charging the defendant for the alleged offence.

The majority of criminal offences are recorded by the police; however, they are not the only body in the CJS that holds such a role. Other investigatory bodies responsible for the recording of certain offences include, amongst others: the Serious Fraud Office (SFO), the National Crime Agency (NCA), and the Royal Society for the Prevention of Cruelty to Animals (RSPCA).

Looking for extra marks?

In September 2015, the prosecution powers of the RSPCA came under review by government ministers. Neil Parish, chairman of the Environment, Food and Rural Affairs Select Committee, commented that the RSPCA's powers of investigation and prosecution must be reconsidered in light of the cases being brought before the courts. Parish stated that the RSPCA must consider the fine balance between its prosecuting role and its campaigning role. It has been suggested that the RSPCA should only investigate matters, and the decision whether a case should be prosecuted would then be left for the state. The RSPCA has refuted this suggestion, claiming to have saved the government over £5 million in legal fees by private prosecutions.

The Review concluded in 2018 that the RSCPA should continue in their role as a prosecuting body, but were advised to ensure transparency in doing so.

Once a crime has been recorded, the body responsible will then conduct an investigation into the alleged offence.

Looking for extra marks?

Don't misunderstand statistics published by the government or the police regarding crime committed and reported. In recent years, it has been reported that crime is on the 'decrease'. We speak of the 'dark figure' of crime as the crime that goes unreported by a victim or unrecorded by the police. Be wary of saying that the commission of crime is on the decrease; rather, the reporting of crime or recording of crime may be on the decrease, whilst the commission of such may remain the same.

Investigation stage

At this stage, it is the responsibility of a designated officer, or team of officers, to investigate the alleged offence. Such investigation may include the viewing of a crime scene, the taking of forensics, and the questioning of witnesses.

Looking for extra marks?

Importantly, the questioning of witnesses (including the victim or any eyewitnesses) is far different from the questioning of suspects. Ensure that you make this distinction clear. In the former, although interviews must be recorded in accordance with the **Police and Criminal Evidence Act (PACE) 1984** and the respective Codes of Practice, the duties on investigating officers are not as stringent as they are when the officers are questioning a suspect.

You could ask whether, to ensure fairness to the suspect, more stringent means should be adopted for the interviewing of non-suspect witnesses.

If an investigation proves successful, the body in charge of the investigation may feel they have reasonable grounds to arrest an individual suspected of committing the offence in question. The essential words in this section are 'reasonable grounds'. Under **PACE 1984**, a police officer may arrest without a warrant any person whom he/she has reasonable grounds to suspect of having committed a criminal offence (**s24(2)**).

Looking for extra marks?

In any answer you give, consider the meaning of the words 'reasonable grounds' in full. The test is described in **Code A, para 2.2** as an objective one. There must be an objective basis for the suspicion grounded on facts, information, and/or intelligence relevant to finding an article of a certain kind or to the likelihood that a person is a terrorist. The officer must consider all of the circumstances during the matter.

Take your answer even further and state that **Code A, para 2.2** emphasizes that reasonable suspicion can 'never be supported on the basis of personal factors', either alone or in combination with each other or with other factors. A 'reasonable suspicion', therefore, cannot be based on generalizations, stereotypical images, or religion.

During this investigation stage, an officer of the law has a multitude of powers granted to him/her by way of the **PACE 1984 Codes of Practice**. These **Codes** (drawn up by the Home Secretary under **s66(1) PACE 1984**) set out what powers investigating bodies have; but they also set out how they must exercise these powers. These codes are detailed in Table 7.4.

Table 7.4 PACE Codes of Practice

Code	Coverage	Last updated	Behaviour regulated
A	Stop and search	2015	Exercise by police officers of statutory powers to search a person or a vehicle without first making an arrest and the need for a police officer to make a record of a stop or encounter
B	Entry and search of premises	2013	Police powers to search premises and to seize and retain property found on premises and persons

Code	Coverage	Last updated	Behaviour regulated
C	Treatment and questioning at the police station	2019	Requirements for the detention, treatment, and questioning of suspects not related to terrorism in police custody by police officers. Includes the requirement to explain a person's rights while detained
D	Identification procedures	2017	Main methods used by the police to identify people in connection with the investigation of offences and the keeping of accurate and reliable criminal records
E	Tape recordings	2018	Audio recording of interviews with suspects in the police station
F	Video recordings	2018	Visual recording with sound of interviews with suspects—there is no statutory requirement on police officers to visually record interviews, but the contents of this code should be considered if an interviewing officer decides to make a visual recording with sound of an interview with a suspect
G	Guidance for extended police powers of arrest	2012	Powers of arrest under **s24 PACE 1984** as amended by **s110 Serious Organised Crime and Police Act 2005**
H	Detention, treatment, and questioning of suspect terrorists	2019	Requirements for the detention, treatment, and questioning of suspects related to terrorism in police custody by police officers. Includes the requirement to explain a person's rights while detained in connection with terrorism.

Non-observance of the Codes does not of itself give rise to any criminal or civil liability (**s67(10) PACE 1984**); however, there may be two outcomes as a result of any such breach:

- exclusion of evidence, should it be obtained in breach of the Codes (**s78 PACE 1984**);
- disciplinary action taken against the individual who breached the respective Code.

It is unusual for examinations to focus on police powers. If you are interested in furthering your knowledge on police powers, we advise you to read **PACE 1984** in full or certain texts on criminal justice (e.g. Sanders, Young, and Burton, *Criminal Justice* (4th edn, Oxford University Press 2010)).

Suspect charged

The decision to charge a suspect rests, for the most part, with the CPS. In order for a suspect to be charged, the 'Full Code Test' must be satisfied. The Full Code Test is provided under s4 *The Code for Crown Prosecutors* (8th edn, CPS 2018) and is set out in two parts. The Code states that the individual or body considering the charge(s) must be satisfied that:

(i) there is sufficient evidence to provide for a realistic prospect of conviction (*evidential stage*); and

(ii) it is in the public interest to prosecute (*public interest stage*).

The *evidential test* requires the case officer to consider the evidence of the case; whether it is admissible; whether it is reliable; and whether it has sufficient weight to convince a jury. The *public interest test* requires the case officer to consider the seriousness of the offence, the circumstances of the offence, the circumstances of the offender, and the circumstances of the victim.

Revision tip

Although the CPS will discontinue the process should the case fail the evidential test, you should still go on to consider the public interest test, as there may be multiple factors which suggest an arguable case can be made on the seriousness of the public interest.

At present, there are three methods of commencing a prosecution. These are detailed in Table 7.5.

Table 7.5 Commencing a prosecution

Method of prosecution	Description
Laying of information	The procedure is to lay information before a magistrate and, if the information appears correct, the magistrate will then issue a summons requiring the accused to appear before the court and answer any allegations contained within the information.
Arrest and charge	The procedure here is simple: arrest the suspect and charge them with an offence at a police station. The police will either release the suspect on police bail or hold them in custody before they can be taken before the magistrates' court at the earliest possible convenience.
Written charge and requisition	Under this method, all public prosecutions can be commenced by the prosecution issuing a written charge, which charges a person with an offence and a requisition requiring the recipient to appear before the court to answer the charge. As of 2015, this method remains only partially in force; however, at an appointed date, the laying of information will be replaced in full with written charge and requisition.

The CPS are not the only body with the power to charge an individual with an offence. As a result of the statutory charging procedure introduced by the **CJA 2003**, the decision to charge a suspect rests largely with the CPS. However, the police retain the right to charge in a range of offences. The *DPP's Guidance on Charging* (5th edn, CPS 2013) details that the police may continue to charge:

- any summary-only offence; and
- any either-way offence where there is an anticipated guilty plea or sentence that would be suitable for the magistrates' court.

In cases where the police charge the suspect, it is then the job of the CPS to review the files and confirm that the 'Full Code Test' has been satisfied and the suspect has been charged with the correct offence. Other bodies such as the SFO and the RSPCA have jurisdiction to charge individuals with relevant offences also, including cruelty to animals for the latter organization.

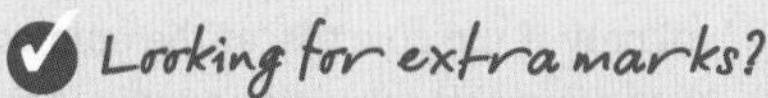

A magistrates' court is not entitled to try a defendant for a summary offence unless the charge has been 'laid' within six months of the alleged commission of the offence (**s127(1) Magistrates' Courts Act (MCA) 1980**). There is no such limit on indictable offences.

Initial appearance in the magistrates' court

Regardless of the offence committed, whether it be a minor motoring offence or a serious offence such as murder, a defendant will always appear first in the magistrates' court. It is at this stage that the defendant will be asked to enter a plea at first instance; matters of bail and whether or not the defendant will be held in custody will be discussed. Depending on the seriousness of the case or the business of the court, in practice, the magistrates will inform the defendant that he/she is to return on a certain date for his/her case to begin properly.

Bail

Bail is the release of the defendant on remand subject to the duty to surrender to the court at a specified time and date. The rules relating to bail are contained within the **Bail Act (BA) 1976** and bail may be granted conditionally (e.g. the wearing of an electronic tag, the surety of money in the court etc.) or unconditionally.

Section 4(1) BA 1976 provides a defendant with a *prima facie* right to bail when charged with a criminal offence. This presumption applies from post-charge up until pre-conviction and even continues to apply post-conviction where the court adjourns for pre-sentence reports (**s4(4)**).

Looking for extra marks?

Although the term 'right' is used, be aware that bail is not a 'human right'. Although **Article 5(1) European Convention on Human Rights (ECHR)** grants a freedom of liberty and security, such liberty is subject to lawful arrest and detention for the purposes of bringing an individual in front of a competent court. As a result, therefore, it is better to speak of the 'right' in **s4** as a 'presumption' in favour of bail, but no more.

There are, of course, certain circumstances where there is no presumption in favour of bail. These include:

- when the accused is being arrested;
- when the accused is being charged with an offence;
- when a warrant for the accused's arrest is issued.

Further to this, there are several circumstances where the presumption in favour of bail is reversed. The most cited of these are cases involving homicide and rape under **s25 Criminal Justice and Public Order Act (CJPOA) 1994**, as amended by **s56 Crime and Disorder Act 1996**.

Section 25 provides that where an accused is charged with or convicted of murder, attempted murder, manslaughter, rape, or attempted rape and has previously been convicted of any of these offences, the accused shall be granted bail only if the court is 'of the opinion' that there are *exceptional circumstances* justifying it. Previously, this provision required the court to deny outright bail to this kind of defendant (the terms used were 'shall not be granted bail'); however, this was amended after ***Caballero v UK* (2000)**, where the European Court of Human Rights (ECtHR) found there to be a breach of **Article 5**.

Further restrictions are also applied in certain cases, such as the offence of murder. In a murder charge, only a judge of the Crown Court may grant bail (**s115(1) Coroners and Justice Act (CorJA) 2009**), and may only do so where the court is of the opinion that there is 'no significant risk' that, if released on bail, the defendant would commit an offence that would be likely to cause physical or mental injury to another person (**s114(1) CorJA 2009**).

In cases where the presumption exists, there are a number of 'grounds' for denying bail listed under **sch 1 BA 1976. Schedule 1** divides the grounds for denying bail into two categories:

- cases where the offence is punishable with *imprisonment* (**sch 1, Part 1**);
- cases where the offence is *not* punishable with *imprisonment* (**sch 1, Part 2**).

In terms of offences punishable by imprisonment, **sch 1(1), para 2** further divides the grounds for denying bail into 'substantial grounds' and 'further grounds'; Table 7.6 explains this distinction.

Table 7.6 Grounds for denying bail

'Substantial grounds'	'Further grounds'
For believing that the defendant would . . . • fail to surrender to custody; or • commit an offence while on bail; or • interfere with witnesses or otherwise obstruct the course of justice, whether in relation to himself/herself or any other person.	• He/she was on bail in criminal proceedings on the date of the offence; or • he/she should be kept in custody for his own protection; or • he/she is already serving a custodial sentence; or • he/she has been arrested for absconding or breaking conditions.

Schedule 1, Part 1, para 9 requires a court to have regard to a number of 'statutory factors' in determining whether the grounds for denying bail are made out.

These statutory factors (non-exhaustive) include:

(i) the nature and seriousness of the offence or default (and the probable sentence);

(ii) the character, antecedents, associations, and community ties of the defendant;

(iii) the defendant's record as respects the fulfilment of his/her obligations under bail in criminal proceedings in the past;

(iv) except in the case of a defendant whose case is adjourned for inquiries or a report, the strength of the evidence of his/her having committed the offence or having defaulted;

(v) if the court is satisfied that there are substantial grounds for believing that the defendant, if released, would commit an offence, the risk that D may do so through conduct which would, or would be likely to, cause injury to another.

The grounds for offences not punishable by imprisonment are similar to those above; however, they are less stringent. In the majority of cases, bail is granted.

Disclosure of evidence

The **Criminal Procedure and Investigations Act (CPIA) 1996** creates a duty of disclosure on both the prosecution and defence. Further to this, an investigating officer is under a duty to retain material obtained in a criminal investigation which may be relevant to that investigation.

In addition to **CPIA 1996**, the sources of law relevant to the disclosure of evidence are as follows:

- **Criminal Procedure and Investigations Act 1996, Code of Practice**;
- CPS Disclosure Manual;
- **PACE 1984** and the Codes of Practice therein; and
- the Attorney General's Guidelines on Disclosure.

The important point to emphasize is that disclosure is a continuing duty from charge to conviction.

Looking for extra marks?

In November 2018, the Attorney General published his report into the *Review of the efficiency and effectiveness of disclosure in the criminal justice system*. The catalyst for this review concerned a number of high-profile prosecutions for sexual offences which were halted due to disclosure failures by the police and the CPS. The Report seeks to rebuild public confidence in the disclosure framework and calls for a culture of zero tolerance in handing over material obtained during investigation. Consider whether this report has made any difference to the problems of disclosure.

Trial process

Once an individual has been charged with an offence, the route their case will then take is entirely dependent on the classification of the offence in question.

> **Revision tip**
>
> When confronted by a problem question requesting you to advise on the procedure that is to be undertaken, always begin by addressing the potential offence for which they may be liable. This will dictate the procedure that is to follow.

As described in Chapter 2, there are three classes of offence in the criminal law and these are detailed in Figure 7.5.

The following sections will discuss the procedure to be adopted when dealing with each of these classifications of offence.

Summary offences

A summary offence is the least serious offence that a defendant can be tried for. A summary offence can be defined as an offence which can only be tried in the magistrates' court with a penalty for summary conviction alone. For example, the offence of common assault, punished under **s39 Criminal Justice Act (CJA) 1988**, is a summary-only offence with a maximum custodial penalty of six months and a level 5 fine (see Chapter 6 for a description of the standard scale of fines). The personnel of the magistrates' court are detailed in Chapter 6 and will not be repeated here.

At the start of the hearing in the magistrates' court, the defendant's plea will be taken, unless taken at the initial appearance (described earlier under 'Initial appearance at the magistrates' court'). **Section 9(1) MCA 1980** provides that, upon taking a plea, the court shall state

Figure 7.5 Types of offences

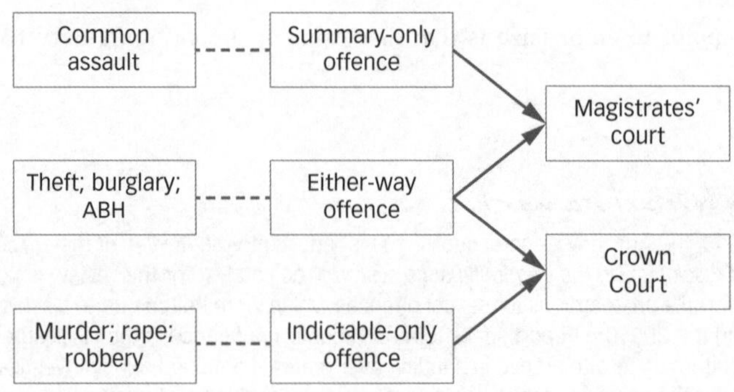

to the defendant the substance of the information and ask him/her whether he/she pleads guilty or not guilty.

The defendant therefore may provide only one of the following answers:

- guilty; or
- not guilty.

The defendant must plead 'unequivocally, clearly and unambiguously' (*ex parte Rubens* **(1970)**). To ensure the defendant's plea is unequivocal, the court clerk must ensure that he/she understands the elements of the offence, especially where there is possibility of a defence (***R v Blandford Justices*** **(1967)**).

Should the defendant not answer, or refuse to enter a plea, the court shall enter a plea of not guilty on his/her behalf and continue to hear the evidence in the case.

Where a defendant pleads 'guilty', **s9(3) MCA 1980** provides that the court may convict him/her without hearing evidence. Procedurally, the prosecutor will outline the facts of the case to the court and then the defendant, through his/her legal representation, will present any circumstances which may mitigate his/her sentence. The magistrates or district judge may decide to sentence immediately, as happens in most summary offences, or adjourn the case for a pre-sentence report.

Where the defendant pleads 'not guilty', the criminal trial will begin. Figure 7.6 details the procedure for trying summary offences in the magistrates' court.

In Figure 7.6, reference is made to the principles in ***Galbraith***. This statement refers to the case of ***R v Galbraith*** **(1981)**, which established two guiding principles to assist the magistrates or judge in determining whether the case against the accused should be ended at this stage (i.e. there is 'no case to answer' for the defendant). The two principles are as follows:

- The submission should succeed if the judge comes to the conclusion that the prosecution evidence, taken at its highest, is such that a jury, properly directed, could not properly convict on it. In this case, the judge should direct the jury to acquit.
- The submission should fail if the strength or weakness of the prosecution case depends on the view to be taken of the reliability of a witness or where there is an actual case to answer. In this case, the case must continue to the defence case and no reference or comment should be given to the jury.

This guidance, although applying specifically to Crown Court trials, is also applicable in the magistrates' court.

Either-way offences

An either-way offence is a middle-ranking offence in terms of seriousness. An either-way offence can be defined as an offence which can be tried in both the magistrates' court and the Crown Court, with a penalty for both summary conviction and conviction on indictment.

Figure 7.6 Summary offence trial procedure

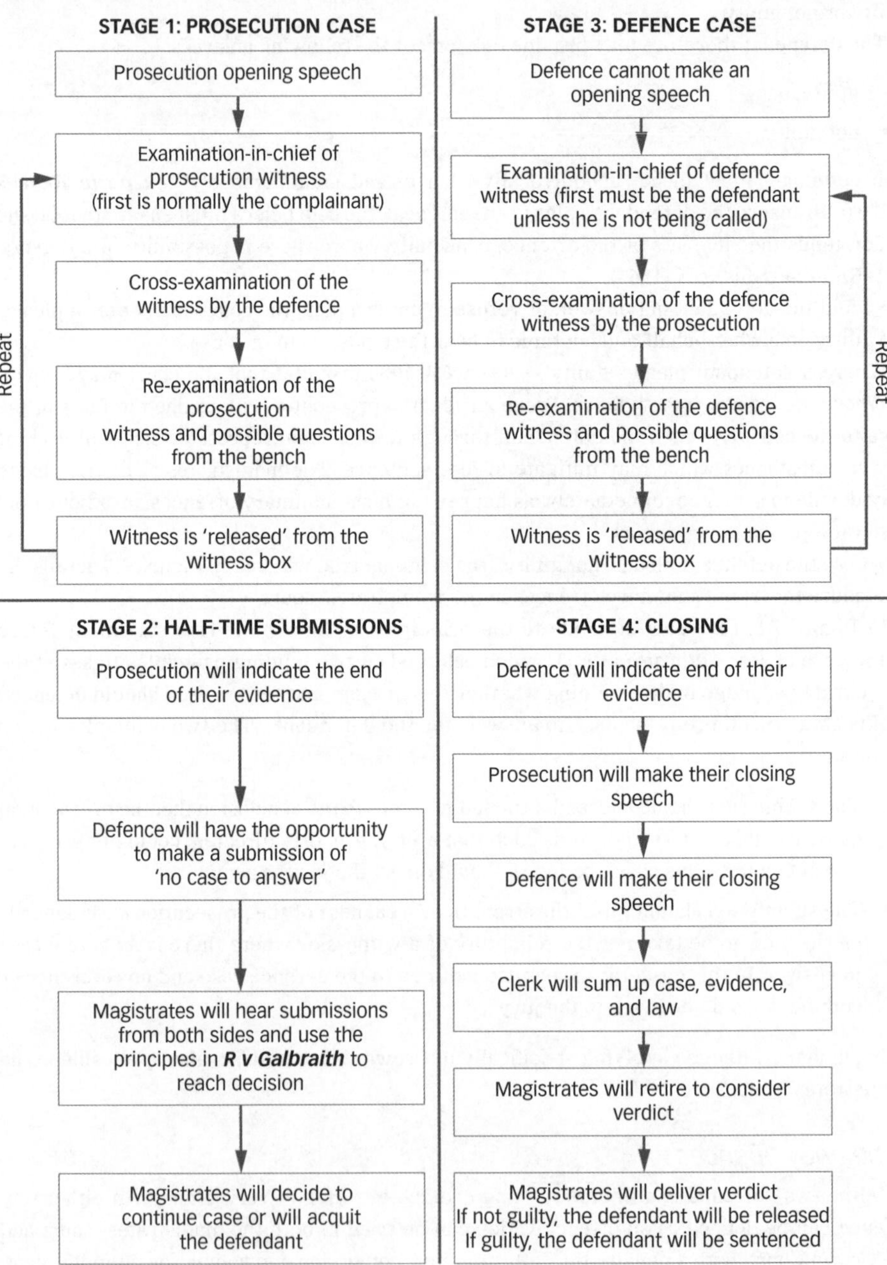

Offences which are triable either-way are listed in **sch 1 MCA 1980**. For example, theft is an either-way offence with a maximum custodial penalty of six months in the magistrates' court but seven years in the Crown Court.

The first element of an either-way offence is known as the plea before venue. This is provided for in **s17A–E MCA 1980**, which requires the court to explain to the accused in 'ordinary language' the procedure that will follow and ask the defendant whether he/she will indicate a plea.

Under **s17E(6)**, where the defendant indicates a plea of 'guilty', the magistrates' court will hear the facts from the prosecutor and shall either sentence immediately, adjourn for a pre-sentence report, or shall commit the defendant to the Crown Court for sentencing where the magistrates believe their own powers to be inadequate.

Where the defendant indicates a plea of 'not guilty', the magistrates' court will then proceed to what is known as an allocation hearing. An allocation hearing is the procedure whereby the magistrates will decide where the either-way offence will be heard (this is also known as 'mode of trial'). There are three alternatives that may arise as a result of an allocation hearing (see Figure 7.7):

1. Where the court feels that the Crown Court would be a more suitable venue, it will direct that the defendant will be tried in the Crown Court and will duly `send' him/her (s51 Crime and Disorder Act (CDA) 1998). The defendant had no say in this scenario.
2. Where the court feels that the magistrates' court is the more suitable option, the court will then offer the magistrates' court as the venue for the defendant's trial, and:
   (i) the defendant may accept the offer and be tried in the magistrates' court; or
   (ii) the defendant may decline the offer and elect trial in the Crown Court.

Figure 7.7 Allocation hearing flowchart (**s51 Crime and Disorder Act (CDA) 1998**): the defendant has no say in this scenario

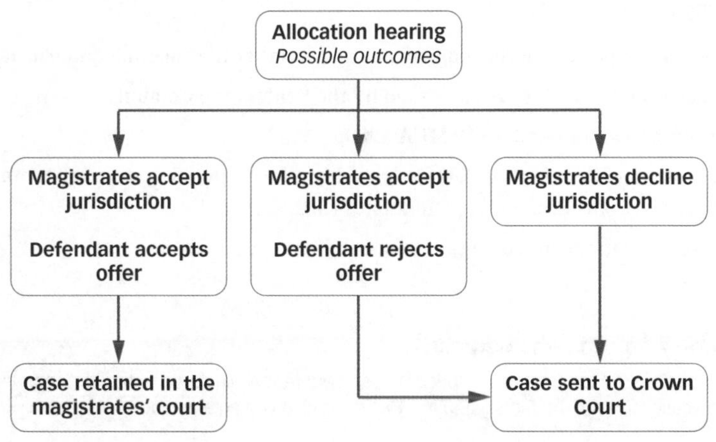

Looking for extra marks?

There have been numerous calls in recent times for the removal of a defendant's right to elect trial by jury. The most notable are as follows:

- Royal Commission Report on the Criminal Justice System (1993)—known as the Runciman Commission;
- Criminal Justice (Mode of Trial) Bill 2000;
- Criminal Justice (Mode of Trial) (No. 2) Bill 2000.

Look at the proposals in Table 7.7 and come up with your own thoughts on the right to elect jury trial.

Table 7.7 Which court should one choose?

Choose the magistrates' court	Elect trial by jury
Sentencing powers of the magistrates are significantly lower than those of a judge in the Crown Court.	Conviction rates are lower in the Crown Court compared with the magistrates' court, with juries more likely to acquit.
Cases in the magistrates' court will often proceed on a much faster basis, taking less time from start to finish.	Magistrates are often 'case hardened' given their length of service; compared with juries, who will often only ever sit as a juror once.
Appeals from decisions of the magistrates' court are easier to come by, given that leave to appeal is not required.	Matters of fact and law are kept separate (the judge dealing with matters of law, and the jury with fact). In the magistrates' court, magistrates are arbiters of both fact and law, despite not being legally qualified.

Before the court will make its decision on the most suitable location for trial, it must consider the following under **s19(2)** and **(3)**:

- the sentencing powers of the magistrates and whether they are 'adequate' in a given case;
- the **Allocation Guideline (2016)** issued by the Sentencing Council;
- the statutory factors under **s19 MCA 1980**;
- any relevant sentencing guidelines issued by the Sentencing Council contained in the Magistrates' Court Sentencing Guidelines (MCSGs); and
- any representations made by the prosecution or the accused.

Looking for extra marks?

There are certain offences, known as 'special cases', where the allocation of trial is dependent on the value of the case, and not the facts listed in **s19**. Let us give you an example. ➜

→ **Section 22 MCA 1980** concerns the allocation of low-value criminal damage. **Section 22** provides that where the amount is:

- £5,000 or less: the court must proceed to summary trial. The defendant has no right to trial on indictment and cannot be committed to the Crown Court for sentence. The maximum sentence available to the magistrates is three months' imprisonment or a £2,500 fine;
- more than £5,000: the offence is triable either way, and the court goes through the usual procedure to determine mode of trial. The maximum sentence is six months' imprisonment or a £5,000 fine.

Find other examples to further develop your answer. As a head-start, go and research **s22A MCA 1980** on low-value theft cases.

Indictable-only offences

An indictable-only offence is the most serious offence that a defendant may be tried with. An indictable-only offence can be defined as an offence which can only be tried before a judge and jury in the Crown Court, with a penalty for conviction on indictment alone. For example, robbery is an indictable-only offence with a maximum custodial penalty of life imprisonment.

The Crown Court deals with only a minority of cases each year. The Court will consist of a jury of 12 laypersons, who will decide a defendant's guilt or innocence, and the trial judge, who may be a recorder (a part-time judge), a circuit judge, or a puisne judge. For a list of other parties within the Crown Court, refer back to Chapter 6.

When a defendant appears before the magistrates for his/her first appearance, should he/she be charged with an indictable offence, he/she will be 'sent' to the Crown Court for trial, under **s51 CDA 1998**.

Revision tip

As from 28 May 2013, committal proceedings (except a committal for sentence) were abolished throughout England and Wales. Since then, defendants charged with an either-way offence are subject to the 'allocation procedure'.

The magistrates no longer 'commit' a defendant to the Crown Court; but rather, now 'send' a defendant to the Crown Court.

Once at the Crown Court, the defendant will be subject to a pre-trial procedure. Prior to January 2016, a defendant would be subject to a plea and case management hearing (PCMH), which was obligatory in all cases tried in the Crown Court. The PCMH would be the opportunity for counsel to make submissions in relation to the case, specifically the admissibility of evidence, the use of special measures for vulnerable witnesses, and many other issues.

However, with effect from January 2016, the pre-trial procedures for cases to be tried on indictment have been reformed. These changes have come about as a result of the Better

Case Management (BCM) initiative and the changes introduced under the Transforming Summary Justice (TSJ) initiative in the magistrates' court.

The main developments as a result of these initiatives are explained in Table 7.8.

Table 7.8 Better case management

New procedure	Description
Digital case system (DCS)	Adoption of paperless trials in the Crown Court. Now, essential documents such as the indictment, witness statements (including the defence statement), and written orders are 'uploaded' onto the DCS. These documents can then be accessed on computers, tablets, and smart phones.
Plea and trial preparation hearing (PTPH)	Preliminary hearings and PCMHs have been abolished and replaced with a PTPH. At the PTPH the defendant will be arraigned. Should the defendant plead guilty, he/she should be sentenced on that day. Should the defendant plead not guilty, the trial judge will set a trial date and provide a timetable of actions that must be taken by counsel pre-trial, such as adhering to the rules of disclosure.

Should the defendant plead not guilty at the PTPH, the case will then progress to the trial proper. Before considering the process of a Crown Court trial, it is first important to identify a number of factors:

- **The indictment**: for a trial to be heard in the Crown Court, there is the requirement for the prosecution to draw up an indictment. The indictment is the written or printed document which formally sets out counts (charges) to be tried in the Crown Court and is signed by the Clerk of the Court. The defendant is required to enter a plea for all counts on the indictment individually. In respect of the content of an indictment, **s3(1) Indictments Act 1915** provides that:

> Every indictment shall contain, and shall be sufficient if it contains, a statement of the specific offence or offences with which the accused person is charged, together with such particulars as may be necessary for giving reasonable information as to the nature of the charge.

An example of a standard indictment is provided below in Figure 7.8.

- **Plea bargaining**: unlike our American counterparts, there is no 'formal' system of plea bargaining in England and Wales. This is to ensure that the defendant has a genuine choice whether to plead guilty or not guilty. However, it is commonplace for the prosecution and the defence to negotiate the charge and the defendant's plea where a lesser alternative offence is available. For example, a defendant charged with causing grievous bodily harm (GBH) with intent contrary to **s18 Offences Against the Person Act 1861 (OAPA)** may agree to plead guilty to the lesser offence of inflicting GBH contrary to **s20 OAPA 1861**. Importantly, the trial judge must have no part in this process (***R v Goodyear*** **(2005)**).

Figure 7.8 Indictment

No. [2020/1234]

INDICTMENT

IN THE CROWN COURT AT [*LOCATION*]

REGINA v. MARK THOMAS

MARK THOMAS is charged as follows:—

Count 1:

STATEMENT OF OFFENCE

THEFT, contrary to section 1(1) of the Theft Act 1968.

PARTICULARS OF OFFENCE

MARK THOMAS on the 1st day of September 2016, stole a bag belonging to Claire McGourlay.

Date [*1 October 2016*]

Crown Court Officer

Trial in the Crown Court will follow a similar pattern to that of trial in the magistrates' court, except that it will be a jury of 12 deciding whether an individual is guilty or not guilty. The jury does not have to provide reasons for its decision and the trial judge must accept whatever decision the jury reaches (***Bushel's Case* (1670)**). See Figure 7.9 below.

The jury is generally expected to reach a unanimous verdict, meaning that all 12 individuals must agree as to whether the defendant is guilty or not guilty. However, **s17(1) Juries Act (JA) 1974** provides the trial judge with the power to accept a majority verdict from the jury. This verdict will ultimately depend on the number of jurors sitting on the particular trial (i.e. should a juror or a number of jurors be dismissed). Table 7.9 details the majority verdicts that may be accepted, dependent on the number of jurors.

By **s17(4) JA 1974**, a trial judge must not accept a majority verdict from a jury unless:

> it appears to the court that the jury have had such period of time for deliberation as the court thinks reasonable having regard to the nature and complexity of the case; and the Crown Court shall in any event not accept such a verdict unless it appears to the court that the jury have had at least two hours for deliberation.

The jury is thus expected to retire for a minimum of two hours. The **Crim PD, Part VI, para 26Q.2** provides that best practice dictates the requirement that the jury be out for a minimum of two hours *and* ten minutes. The addition of ten minutes is to ensure that the jury (taking into account the time from the courtroom to the jury room) has been afforded a full two-hour period.

Figure 7.9 Indictable offence trial procedure

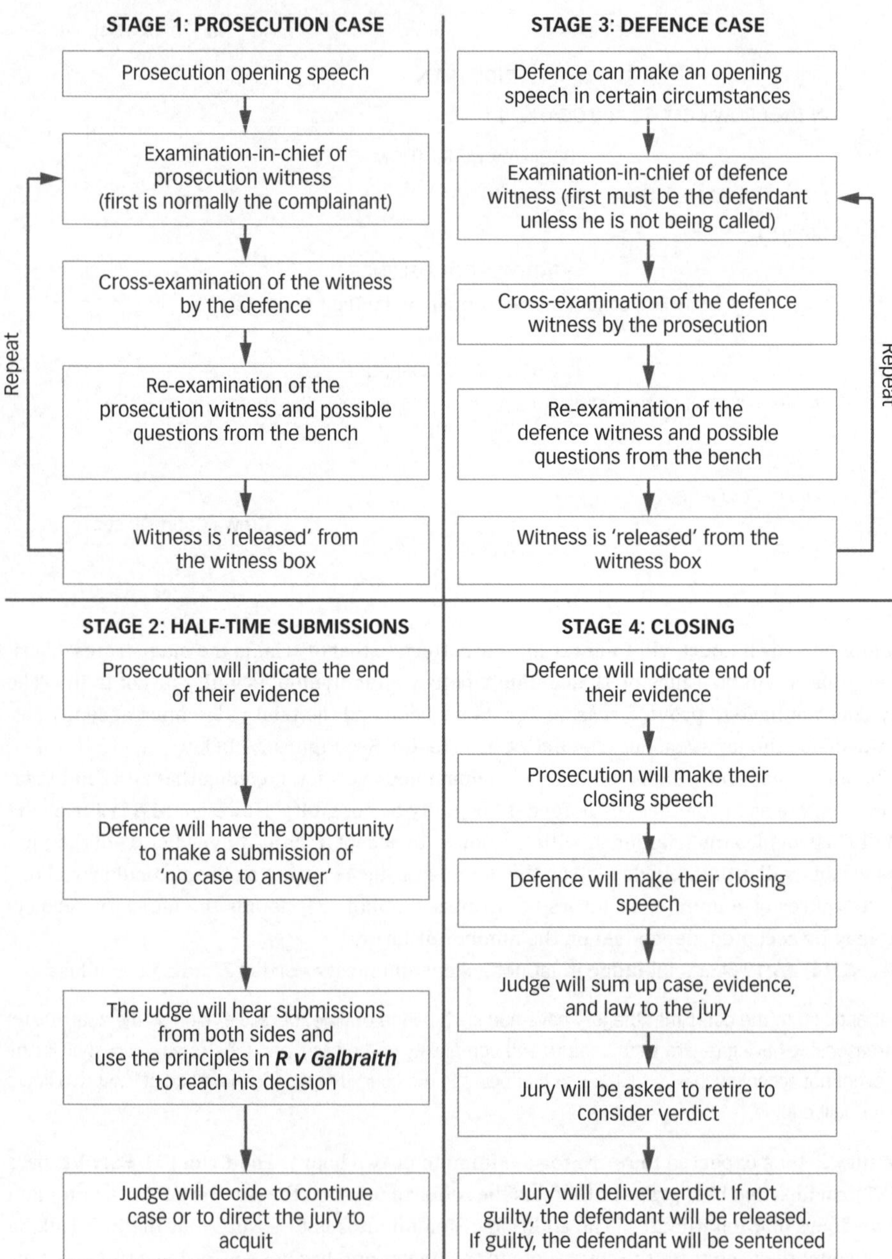

Table 7.9 Majority verdicts

Number of jurors	Acceptable majority
12 jurors	11–1 or 10–2
11 jurors	10–1
10 jurors	9–1
9 jurors	9–0 (must be unanimous)

As above, should the verdict be not guilty, the defendant must be released unconditionally. Should the verdict be guilty, the Crown Court will proceed to sentencing. Should the guilty verdict arise by majority, as opposed to unanimous vote, the foreman of the jury must state in open court the number of jurors who respectively agreed to, and dissented from, the verdict (**s17(3) JA 1974**; see also ***R v Pigg* (1983)**). This restriction only applies to guilty verdicts; no statement as to numbers in and out of the majority is required for not-guilty verdicts.

Looking for extra marks?

There are occasions where a trial can be heard in the Crown Court, without a jury. These are known as judge-only trials, and can only arise in a single circumstance, namely:

- on application by the prosecution where there is a risk of 'jury tampering' (**s44 CJA 2003**)—see ***R v Twomey* (2009)**.

It is useful to note also that a second exception existed, namely on application by the prosecution where the case is a serious and complex fraud (**s43 CJA 2003**). However, this provision was repealed by the **Protection of Freedoms Act 2012**, without ever having been brought into force.

In an answer, you could question the validity of juryless trials and ask whether they favour one side or the other.

Post-trial process

The post-trial criminal process is split into several different categories and stages:

- sentencing; and
- appeals.

Sentencing

A defendant will be sentenced before the Crown Court or magistrates' court upon conviction, either after pleading guilty or having been found guilty after a trial.

Looking for extra marks?

In January 2020, the government introduced the **Crown Court (Recording and Broadcasting) Order 2020**. This Order will allow cameras to broadcast the sentencing remarks of High Court and senior circuit judges. Recordings have been permitted in the Supreme Court since 2010 and the Court of Appeal since 2018. The filming will be restricted to the sentencing remarks of the judge; no recording of the trial is permitted. The recording will only feature the judge; no other party to the proceedings will be recorded. Only senior judges may be recorded, and approval must first be sought. Opinions are divided as to the utility of the scheme: many suggest that such recordings will allow for greater transparency in the legal system and will be informative to the public; others suggest that the government's intentions and motivations as to this development are to open up criticism to the judiciary. Writing in *The Justice Gap* (17 January 2020), Nicholas Reed Langen remarks:

> Of all areas of law likely to incite the ire of the angry and the ignorant, criminal sentencing is the most inflammatory, with viewers unlikely to be sympathetic to the legal constraints that judges operate within. Instead, sentencing may become an exhibition akin to the executions of the Dickensian age, but with the audience directing their opprobrium at the judges for failing to bring the full weight of the law, as they perceive it, upon the convicted.

What are your thoughts on this development?

The 'purpose' or 'objectives' of sentencing are detailed in **s142(1) CJA 2003**, to which the courts are required to have regard when dealing with adult offenders, these being:

(a) the punishment of offenders;

(b) the reduction of crime (including its reduction by deterrence);

(c) the reform and rehabilitation of offenders;

(d) the protection of the public; and

(e) the making of reparation by offenders to persons affected by their offences.

A similar list exists for offenders under the age of 18 (**s142A CJA 2003**). The court is assisted in its sentencing decision by the Definitive Guidelines published by the Sentencing Council for England and Wales (SC) (formerly the 'Sentencing Guidelines Council'). The SC is responsible for the formulation and issuing of Sentencing Guidelines. Importantly, the courts are under a duty to follow these Guidelines unless it would be contrary to the interest of justice to do so (**s125 Coroners and Justice Act (CorJA) 2009**). The majority of Guidelines are offence-specific, such as 'Theft—general' (February 2016) and 'Robbery—dwelling' (April 2016). However, there are also some Guidelines of a more general nature, such as 'Overarching Principles—Sentencing Youths' (November 2009). The Definitive Guidelines follow the same format and allow the participants in the sentencing hearing to understand the structure to be adopted:

- **Step 1—Offence category**: in which the courts assess both culpability and harm according to a set list of factors and characteristics (e.g. an offence would likely be one of 'high culpability' if it involved the use of a weapon to inflict violence).

- **Step 2—Starting point and range**: having determined the offence category, the court will then assess the appropriate starting point for that offence and consider any appropriate range. In determining the sentence range, the court will identify factors increasing seriousness and factors reducing seriousness or reflecting personal mitigation.
- **Step 3—Any other factors indicating reduction**: the court will be able to to take into account any assistance by the offender (see **ss73 and 74 Serious Organised Crime and Police Act 2005**) and 'any other rule of law by virtue of which an offender may receive a discounted sentence in consequence of assistance given (or offered) to the prosecutor or investigator'.
- **Step 4—Reduction for guilty plea**: by **s144 CJA 2003**, a court must take into account any guilty plea supplied by the defendant. In terms of the amount of reduction available to the courts, reference should be made to the *Reduction in Sentence for a Guilty Plea* (June 2017) guidance document. The document works on a sliding scale, according to the stage in the proceedings when the defendant supplied his/her admission of guilt. The sliding scale is indicated in Table 7.10.

Table 7.10 Reduction in sentence

Stage of proceedings	Amount of reduction
Plea indicated at the first stage of the proceedings	One-third reduction should be made where a plea is entered at the first hearing or stage where a plea is sought by the court.
Plea indicated after the first stage of proceedings	After the first stage of proceedings, a maximum of one-quarter may be awarded. The reduction should be decreased from one-quarter to a maximum of one-tenth on the first day of trial. The reduction should normally be decreased further, even to zero, if the guilty plea is entered during the course of the trial.

- **Step 5—Dangerousness**: the court should then consider whether the offence which requires an extended sentence due to its seriousness (e.g. **s225(2) CJA 2003** allows the court to pass a life sentence for the protection of the public for committing a serious violent or sexual offence).
- **Step 6—Totality principle**: the court will need to consider whether the sentence imposed is just and proportionate to the offending behaviour in circumstances where the offender is being sentenced for more than one offence or where the offender was already serving a sentence. Reference is to be made to the *Totality Guidelines* (June 2012).
- **Step 7—Compensation and ancillary orders**: the Court must always consider whether to make a compensation and/or other ancillary orders, for example, a confiscation order.

- **Step 8—Reasons**: all courts are obligated to provide reasons for the sentences imposed and to explain the effect of those sentences (**s174 CJA 2003**).
- **Step 9—Consideration for time spent on bail**: a court needs to finally consider whether or not they will give credit to the offender for time spend on bail (**s240A CJA 2003**). The procedure is largely the same whether the defendant is sentenced in the Crown Court or the magistrates' court. Specifically, sentence may be passed immediately upon conviction (more likely in the magistrates' court than the Crown Court) or sentence may be adjourned to obtain a pre-sentence report. A pre-sentence report is defined in **s158 CJA 2003** as a report prepared by an 'appropriate officer' to assist the court in determining the most suitable method of dealing with an offender. An 'appropriate officer' is normally a probation officer in the case of adults or a social worker in the case of youths. The report will include, amongst other matters:
  - information about the offence;
  - factors in the commission of the offence;
  - the offender's attitude to the offence;
  - background information on the offender;
  - an assessment on the likelihood of re-offending; and
  - considerations as to a community order or proposals for an 'appropriate sentence'.

The procedure for sentencing is detailed in Table 7.11.

Table 7.11 Sentencing procedure

Stage	Procedure on guilty plea
1.	Prosecutor presents the facts of the case. Defence may dispute facts.
2.	The prosecutor will then provide the court with information about the 'character and antecedent' of the offender.
3.	The defence counsel will then proceed to make a plea in mitigation in an attempt to reduce the severity of the sentence.
4.	The judge will consider the submissions made alongside a number of factors, including: • offences taken into consideration (TICs); • the seriousness threshold; • credit for a guilty plea (should there be one); and • victim impact statements (VIS).
5.	Sentence is 'pronounced' and takes effect immediately. The court is obligated to provide reasons for the sentence and the effect that the sentence will have on the individual.

The types of sentences available to a court will depend on how they are 'constrained' in the operation of their powers. A court may be constrained by any of the following:

- a statutory maximum sentence for the offence;
- the court where the sentence is imposed (magistrates' courts' powers are limited);
- age of the defendant (i.e. distinction between sentencing individuals at the age of 21, 18, and younger);
- the defendant's plea in a given case.

Sentencing generally can take one of two forms (or both):

- custodial; and
- non-custodial.

The sentencing powers of both the magistrates' court and the Crown Court are detailed in Table 7.12.

Looking for extra marks?

A rather controversial matter in sentencing law concerns the amount of time an individual actually spends in prison serving their sentence. By **s244(1) CJA 2003**, a prisoner serving a sentence of imprisonment for a term of 12 months or more must be released by the Secretary of State on licence after they have served one-half of their sentence. In the Queen's Speech in January 2020, it was indicated that the government would increase this early release from one-half of their sentence to two-thirds. Offer your opinion on whether you think it is right for prisoners to be released after serving only half of their sentence, or whether the period of time should be increased to one-third or above.

Appeals

In the majority of cases, the defendant will appeal against the 'safety' of the conviction and/or the severity of the sentence. There is also the possibility for the prosecution to appeal against conviction or sentence. The main form of appeals that we are concerned with are indicated in Figure 7.10 and detailed below.

1. **Reopening a case**: this form of appeal may only be brought by the defence. Following conviction by a magistrates' court, a defendant is entitled to ask the magistrates to 're-open the case'. The effect of this is to set aside the conviction or vary/rescind a sentence (i.e. to correct mistakes—***R (Williamson) v City of Westminster Magistrates' Court*** **(2012)**). If the magistrates agree, the conviction is set aside and the case is reheard by a different bench of magistrates. This process may be used once only. Any subsequent appeal must be made either to the High Court or to the Crown Court (**s142(2) MCA 1980**).

Figure 7.10 Criminal appeals

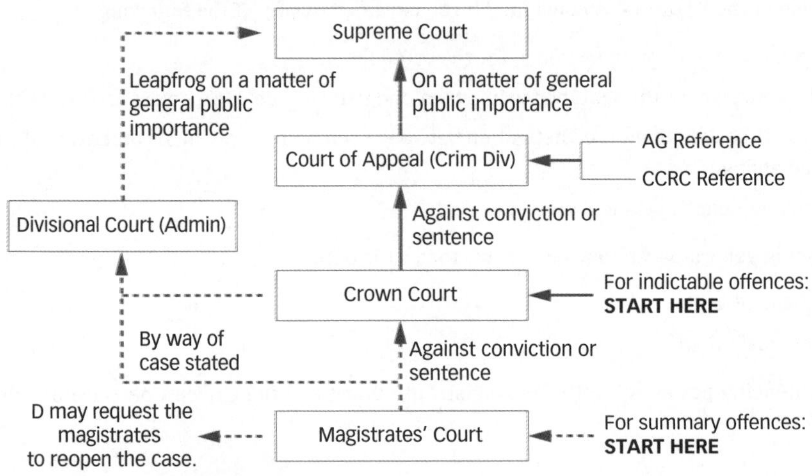

Table 7.12 Sentencing powers

Sentencing power	Magistrates' court	Crown Court
Custodial	• Maximum six months (for a single offence); or • Maximum 12 months (for multiple either-way offences).	No maximum except statutory maximum.
Non-custodial	**Fine**: maximum £5,000	**Fine**: unlimited
	Community order: maximum three years for the order. Includes such things as: • unpaid work; • curfew requirement; and • electronic monitoring requirement. **Discharge**: this is when the court decides that punishment would not be appropriate for this particular defendant. There are two types of discharge: • **absolute discharge**—no further action is taken, although the offender will receive a criminal record; • **conditional discharge**—no further action is taken, although the offender will receive a criminal record. Action may be taken where the individual commits a further offence within a period of time set by the court. **Bind over**: which simply means that the convicted person must agree to refrain from certain activity for a set period; must be of good behaviour; and must comply with any orders made. The standard bind over adopted is that under the **Justices of the Peace Act 1361**, which gives courts the power to bind over offenders to 'keep the peace'.	

2. **Appeal from the magistrates' court to the Crown Court**: this form of appeal may only be brought by the defence. A defendant convicted in the magistrates' court may appeal against conviction and/or sentence to the Crown Court. The appeal in the Crown Court is a complete rehearing of the case, meaning that new evidence may be produced if it has come to light in the intervening period. Appeals from the magistrates' court to the Crown Court will not be heard by a jury; instead, the case will be tried before a judge sitting with two lay magistrates (**s108 MCA 1980**). The powers of the Crown Court on appeal from the magistrates' court are contained in **s48 Senior Courts Act 1981**.
3. **Appeal 'by way of case stated' (from the magistrates' court to the Divisional Court)**: this form of appeal may be brought by any person who was a party to any proceeding before a magistrates' court or is aggrieved by the conviction, order, determination, or other proceeding of the court (**s111 MCA 1980**). Any party to the proceedings may appeal to the Divisional Court by way of case stated. The appeal cannot be on a matter of fact (for that, they should appeal to the Crown Court). The grounds for making an appeal are either that the procedure is:
   - wrong in law; or
   - in excess of its jurisdiction.

   The appeal is heard by the Divisional Court, specifically the Administrative Court, before a bench of three judges. As this is an appeal on the law, no evidence is to be admitted at this hearing.

   The Divisional Court has the power to reverse, amend, or affirm the magistrates' decision (**s111 MCA 1980**).
4. **Appeal from the Crown Court to the Divisional Court**: following the re-trial in the Crown Court from a decision of the magistrates' court (see 2. above), a defendant may seek a further appeal from the Crown Court to the Divisional Court, specifically the Administrative Court (**s28 Senior Courts Act 1981**). This appeal is by way of case stated and is concerned with a point of law. Importantly, this appeal route is only open to defendants whose case began in the magistrates' court. Should the defendant be charged on indictment from the outset (i.e. in the Crown Court), there is no appeal route to the Divisional Court. Instead, the appeal route would be to the Court of Appeal.
5. **Appeals from the Divisional Court to the Supreme Court**: parties in the Divisional Court can appeal to the Supreme Court (known as a Leapfrog Appeal) but only in circumstances where the case involves a point of law of general public importance and it appears to the Divisional Court or the Supreme Court (as the case may be) that the point is one which ought to be considered by the Supreme Court (**s12(1) Administration of Justice Act 1960**). This leapfrog option exists because by **s18 Senior Courts Act 1981**, no appeal shall lie to the Court of Appeal from any judgment of the High Court 'in any criminal cause or matter'.
6. **Appeal from the Crown Court to the Court of Appeal**: this form of appeal may be brought by both the prosecution and defence. Leave (permission) to appeal against conviction and/or sentence to the Court of Appeal is always required.

Leave may be given by:

- the trial judge granting a certificate that the case is fit for appeal, or
- the Court of Appeal.

The Court of Appeal may only allow an appeal against conviction if it thinks that the conviction is 'unsafe' (**s2(1)(a) Criminal Appeal Act (CAA) 1968**).

The appeal will take the form of a hearing on the legal issues in the case; however, by **s23 CAA 1968**, the Court of Appeal can hear 'fresh evidence' in exceptional circumstances.

7. **Appeal from the Court of Appeal to the Supreme Court**: this form of appeal may be brought by both the prosecution and defence. Both parties in the Court of Appeal can appeal to the Supreme Court, but only in circumstances where the case involves a point of law of general public importance (**s33(2) Criminal Appeal Act 1968**).
8. **Attorney General's reference**: the Attorney General has the ability to intervene on two separate occasions, the first against sentence and the second on a point of law. First, the Attorney General may, with leave of the Court of Appeal, refer any sentence imposed by the Crown Court where he/she considers the sentence was 'unduly lenient' (**s36 CJA 1988**). The Court can quash the original sentence and impose a harsher one (**s36(1) CJA 1988**). Second, the Attorney General may refer a point of law to the Court of Appeal for review following an acquittal (**s36 CJA 1972**). The Court of Appeal will review the point of law and provide an opinion, or may refer the point of law to the Supreme Court. Whatever opinion is reached, the acquittal is not affected (**s36(7) CJA 1972**).
9. **Criminal Cases Review Commission (CCRC)**: by **s9 CAA 1995**, the Commission may refer to the Court of Appeal:
   - a conviction for an offence on indictment;
   - a sentence imposed for an offence on indictment; or
   - a finding of not guilty by insanity.

They will only do so, however, where appeal has been decided or leave to appeal has been refused, and the CCRC considers that there is a 'real possibility' that the verdict or sentence would not be upheld if the reference was made (**s13 CAA 1995**).

Looking for extra marks?

The CCRC was established in 1997, under the **Criminal Appeal Act 1995**, as an independent body responsible for referring cases back to the Court of Appeal where there is an arguable 'miscarriage of justice'. Prior to this, such responsibility lay with the Home Secretary. A miscarriage of justice is defined in the Oxford Dictionary as:

> A failure of a court or judicial system to attain the ends of justice, especially one which results in the conviction of an innocent person.

→

➔ Ensure, however, that you make the point clear that until an appellate court has quashed the conviction of an individual, there is no 'formal' miscarriage of justice; rather, there is only an 'alleged' miscarriage of justice.

Look at some of the most famous miscarriages of justice, including:

- the Birmingham Six; and
- Sally Clark.

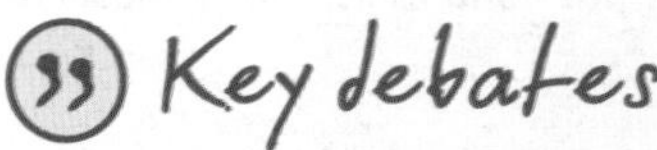

Topic	**Adversarial nature of the CJS**
Academic	Michael Mansfield QC
Viewpoint	Argues that the CJS should replace the 'accusatorial system', up to the time of trial, with an inquisitorial system. He argues that this would ensure that a trial judge properly supervises the investigation of crime by the police. This would result in the investigation seeking out the truth, as opposed to allowing the prosecution merely to secure a conviction.
Source	Michael Mansfield, *Presumed Guilty: British Legal System Exposed* (Mandarin Publishing 1994)

Topic	**Relationship between CPS and police**
Academic	Mike McConville
Viewpoint	Argues that in order to make any of its decisions, the CPS rely on the police and the file they prepare, which contains information about the offence and the information the police provide. McConville specifically argues that the CPS relies heavily upon evidence collated by the police that is 'not objective but of a particular version of events'. He argues that this limits the ability of the CPS to make independent decisions.
Source	Mike McConville, *The Case for the Prosecution* (Routledge 1991)

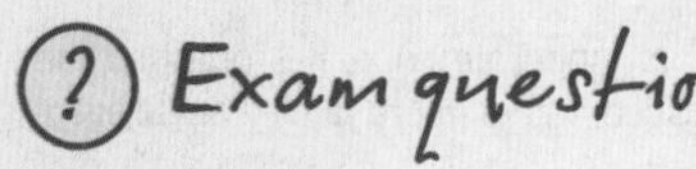

Essay question

'The criminal justice system is a maze that even the smartest defendant cannot escape from. Rights are curtailed; freedom is restricted; and the process is one-sided.'

Critically discuss this statement in light of the functions of the criminal justice system and the process in which the criminal justice system operates.

Problem question

You have been asked to provide advice to an individual at your **pro bono** clinic. The individual requires advice on the following matter:

'I need your help.

The police are thinking about prosecuting me for a rape I didn't commit. I didn't do it. I'm panicking that I will be put in prison and need your advice. Could you please advise me on:

- the powers of the police in relation to this process;
- the trial process and in which court my case will be heard in;
- the evidence that may be submitted against me; and
- whether I can appeal if I am found guilty.

Please help me.

Mark McGourlay'

For outline answers to these exam questions, as well as multiple-choice questions, please visit the online resources.

#8 The Civil Justice System

Key facts

- Civil justice is focused on achieving a system that is accessible, fair, and efficient.
- Civil justice is concerned with the private dispute between individuals in the absence of the state (though see Chapter 3 under 'Judicial review').
- Civil justice seeks to solve disputes before they have had a chance to enter the legal structure, through the use of alternative dispute resolution (ADR).
- Civil justice follows a similar pattern to its criminal counterpart; however, some of the procedural rules (specifically those relating to evidence) appear to be much more relaxed than in the criminal justice system.

Chapter overview

The civil justice system

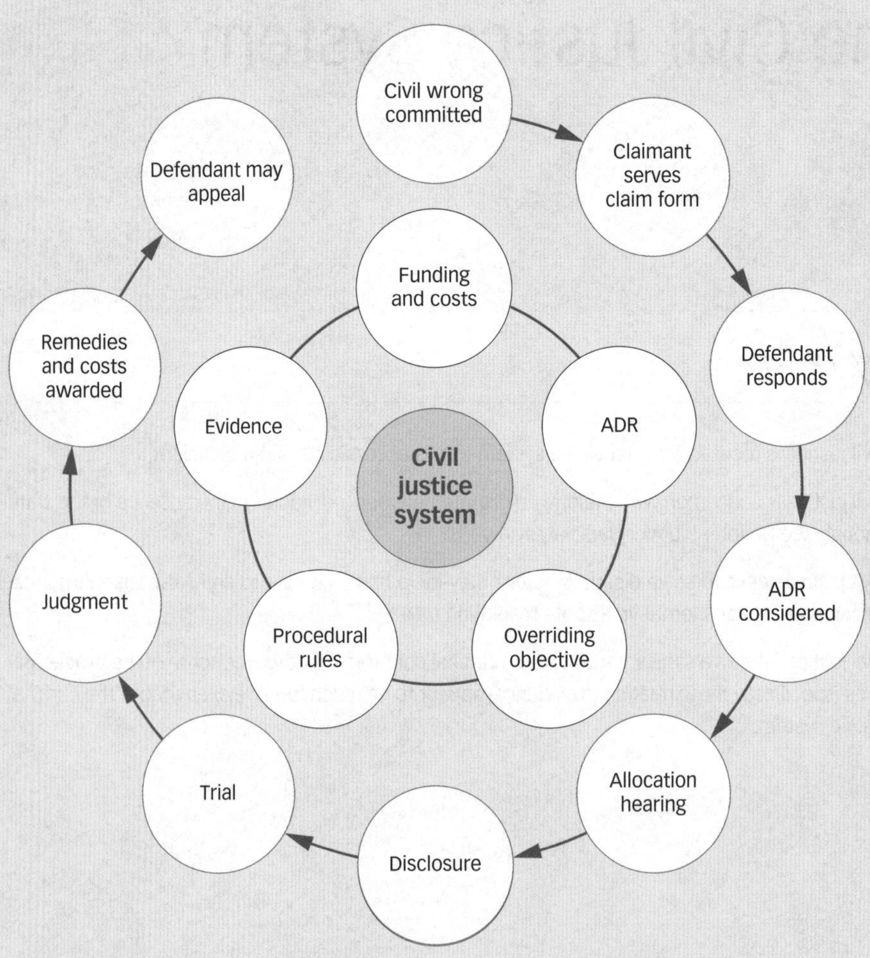

Introduction

In Chapter 7 we considered the criminal justice system (CJS). This system is predicated on the commission of a criminal offence. The offence may be committed by a single individual, or multiple individuals, against another person, against property, or against public order. In each scenario, the criminal law operates with the involvement of the state. It is a public law matter. The civil justice system (CivJS), on the other hand, is purely a matter of private law. With a few exceptions, the CivJS is concerned with the commission of a 'civil wrong' by one individual against another and does not concern the involvement of the state. As with the CJS, the CivJS is also composed of a 'framework' and 'process' that ensures the system fulfils its role and purpose. We shall first consider the framework of the CivJS before then considering the process of the CivJS.

Before this, let us begin with some basic terminology (see Table 8.1).

Table 8.1 Basic civil terminology

Terminology	Description
Suit	Civil proceedings involve the commission of a civil wrong resulting in one individual suing another (or better yet, they 'bring an action' against another individual).
Claimant	The *claimant* is the party that brings the action against another. Prior to 1999, they were known as the 'plaintiff'.
Defendant	The *defendant* is the party against whom proceedings have been brought. They are defending the claim.
Judgment	As opposed to criminal law, which involves 'convictions' and 'acquittals', civil law involves findings or judgments in favour of one party or another. Defendants are not found 'guilty' of a civil wrong; instead, the issue is whether the case has been made and to whose favour judgment is made.
Remedy	A *remedy* is an award given to the winning party in civil proceedings. Remedies may involve, for example, 'damages' (monetary compensation) and 'injunctions' (orders prohibiting certain conduct).

The framework of civil justice

The framework of the CivJS largely mirrors that of the CJS, as both operate to deal with cases efficiently and effectively. As such, we wish to avoid repetition where possible.

Private law matters

In general, proceedings in the CivJS will involve a private matter between individuals. Indeed, Stephen Bailey, Nick Taylor, and Jane Ching, *Smith, Bailey, and Gunn on the Modern English System* (5th edn, Sweet & Maxwell 2007) characterize the CivJS as concerned with contractual and tortious matters, and a few examples of actions within the civil law can be listed as including:

- breach of contract between Party A and Party B (contract);
- act of negligence by Party A to Party B where there was a duty of care (tort); and
- order for divorce by Party A from Party B (family).

Indeed, these cases cover the broad nature of civil work and will be determined in a private context to the exclusion of the state. However, civil law may also deal with certain public law matters (see Chapter 2). For example:

- judicial review of the acts of public officials is considered to be both a matter of civil law and public law, given that the ruling of the court may affect more individuals than the one before the court in question;
- family matters involving adoption and fostering are matters of public law as they involve the state in the conclusion as to what is the most appropriate action to take in the best interests of the child (**s1 Children Act 1989**).

This chapter is concerned with the civil litigation of purely private matters between individuals to the exclusion of the state. However, it is essential that you remain comfortable with the understanding that the civil law can encompass both public and private law matters, and that the procedure to be adopted for each matter, although roughly the same, does vary on such matters as commencement and disclosure.

Civil Procedure Rules 1998

The **Civil Procedure Rules (CPR) 1998** embodies the entire civil legal system in one place. Now in its 113th update, the **CPR 1998** is comprised of 89 parts, supplemented by 84 Practice Directions and accompanied by 13 Pre-Action Protocols. The **CPR 1998** provides a detailed, comprehensive, methodical code for the operation of civil litigation in England and Wales.

Development of the Rules

Prior to 1998, civil litigation was in a constant state of flux. Characterized by its delays, unreasonable costs, and extreme complexity, the CivJS was hardly accessible to the everyday man. This resulted in what can best be described as a complete overhaul of civil procedure as it was known in 1998. Lord Woolf undertook a complex inquiry into the operation of civil litigation in 1994. In 1996, Lord Woolf produced his report (*Access to Justice: Final Report to the Lord Chancellor on the Civil Justice System in England and Wales*), known as the *Woolf Report*. This Report detailed over 300 recommendations for reforming the CivJS, which Lord Woolf characterized as a 'new landscape' of civil litigation.

The recommendations led to the introduction of the **Civil Procedure Act 1997**, which set out to implement the reforms spoken of by Lord Woolf in his Report. Specifically, **s1(1)** provided, quite simply, that:

> There are to be rules of court (to be called 'Civil Procedure Rules') governing the practice and procedure to be followed in the Court of Appeal (civil division); the High Court; and the county courts [now the County Court].

According to **s1(3)**, these Rules are 'to be exercised with a view to securing that the civil justice system is *accessible, fair and efficient*' (emphasis added).

The **1997 Act** also had the effect of creating two institutional bodies responsible for the creation and maintenance of the CPR. These bodies are:

- Civil Procedure Rules Committee—responsible for creating the **CPR (s2)**; and
- Civil Justice Council—responsible for reviewing the CivJS to ensure it remains 'accessible, fair and efficient' and to propose changes necessary to achieve that aim (**s6**).

Jacqueline Martin, *The English Legal System* (8th edn, Hodder 2016) comments that the Woolf reforms remain a 'qualified success' in that cases are being dealt with faster within the courts and more cases are being dealt with outside of the courts. The Rules continue to develop as time passes, with one of the most recent overhauls of the system occurring in 2013 with Lord Justice Jackson's review of costs (see under 'Funding and costs' below). This review, however, was not the last, this being Lord Justice Briggs' Civil Courts Structure Review in 2016, which was discussed in Chapter 2.

The overriding objective

As a result of the introduction of the **CPR 1998**, civil litigation became founded on a single principle, known as the 'overriding objective'. This objective is stated in **r1.1(1) CPR** as 'enabling the court to deal with cases *justly and at proportionate cost*' (emphasis added).

How the court does so is listed in **r1.1(2) CPR** and includes:

> (a) ensuring that the parties are on an equal footing;
> (b) saving expense;
> (c) dealing with the case in ways which are proportionate—
> (i) to the amount of money involved;
> (ii) to the importance of the case;
> (iii) to the complexity of the issues; and
> (iv) to the financial position of each party;
> (d) ensuring that it is dealt with expeditiously and fairly;
> (e) allotting to it an appropriate share of the court's resources, while taking into account the need to allot resources to other cases; and
> (f) enforcing compliance with rules, practice directions and orders.

The parties to a civil case are required by **r1.3 CPR** to 'help the court to further the overriding objective' and the court remains under a continuous duty to 'actively' manage cases in order to further the overriding objective (**r1.4(1) CPR**). Lightman (2003) (see 'Key debates' at the end of the chapter) argues that 'The law and the legal system should be a protection, a safeguard, a source of peace of mind, to which recourse should be available by all at an affordable cost.' You may question whether this statement is merely an ideal or whether it occurs in practice.

Funding and costs

Although funding is dealt with specifically in Chapter 9, the issue of costs in civil proceedings is a matter of grave importance. Between 2008 and 2009, Lord Justice Jackson undertook a full review of costs in civil litigation, publishing his final report, *Review of Civil Litigation Costs: Final Report*, in December 2010. As a result of the **Legal Aid, Sentencing and Punishment of Offenders Act (LASPO) 2012**, the law relating to costs under **Part 43** was overhauled and replaced by the new and improved **Part 44**. Table 8.2 provides a summary of costs.

Table 8.2 Costs in civil litigation

Term	Description
Costs	Covers 'profit costs' and 'disbursements'. • Profit costs are the amount of time that a legal representative spends on a matter. • Disbursements are such things as counsel's fees, court fees, expenses, and many other items.
Starting point	A client has a contractual obligation to pay for all costs incurred in bringing or defending a claim.
Recovery of costs	A client may be able to recover costs from his/her opponent. He/she may do so either: • by agreement; or • by an order of the court.
General principle on recovery	There are two general principles in relation to the recovery of costs, namely that: • the payment of costs by one party to another is at the discretion of the court; and • the loser should pay the winner's costs.
Further principles	When deciding how much the winning party is entitled to recover, the court will consider: • the indemnity principle, which provides that the winning party cannot recover costs of a greater amount than he/she has paid to his legal representative; and • the bases of assessment, which provides for a standard and indemnity basis for the court's consideration.

Term	Description
Awards available	By **r44.2(6) CPR**, the court is to make the following orders of costs recovery: **(a)** a proportion of another party's costs; **(b)** a stated amount in respect of another party's costs; **(c)** costs from or until a certain date only; **(d)** costs incurred before proceedings have begun; **(e)** costs relating to particular steps taken in the proceedings; **(f)** costs relating only to a distinct part of proceedings; and **(g)** interest on costs from or until a certain date, including a date before judgment.
Fixed costs	Not all costs will be assessed by the court. In certain cases, costs will be 'fixed'. Fixed costs are provided for in **Part 45 CPR 1998**, the most notable being fixed costs on the fast track.
Wasted costs orders	Wasted costs orders are governed by **s51(6) Senior Courts Act 1981**, which provides the courts with the power to make an adverse award of costs against a party where the conduct of their legal representative has been shown to have been improper, unreasonable, or negligent. In this case, the legal representative will be ordered to either: • pay his own client's costs (following the indemnity principle); or • pay the costs of his opponent.

Stuart Sime, *A Practical Approach to Civil Procedure* (23rd edn, Oxford University Press 2020) argues that adverse costs may be awarded where there is a breach to the overriding objective (e.g. the duty to co-operate).

Looking for extra marks?

As of April 2013, a new principle was introduced to costs proceedings, namely qualified one-way costs shifting (QOCS). At a very basic level, QOCS operate in personal injury cases and provide that a claimant will not be required to pay the defendant's costs if the claim fails. However, the defendant will have to pay the claimant's costs if the claim succeeds.

This new provision has been ripe for debate and it may provide you with some useful ammunition when dealing with an essay on costs.

Alternative dispute resolution

This chapter is focused on the study of what is commonly known as 'civil litigation'. According to Susan Cunningham-Hill and Karen Elder, *Civil Litigation 2019–2020* (12th edn, Oxford University Press 2019), however, the term is 'somewhat misleading'. The pair argue that a 'more accurate description would be "dispute resolution", as there is now an emphatic move away from resolving disputes through the court system'. Indeed, the pair are correct in that the CPR is designed on the idea that the parties consider alternative means of resolving their dispute before resorting to legal proceedings. Where a party does resort to alternative means, this is known as alternative dispute resolution (ADR).

Encouragement of ADR

As part of the overriding objective, the court must deal with cases at proportionate costs with an element of saving expense. In order to actively manage a case, the court is required to:

- encourage the parties to co-operate with each other in the conduct of proceedings (**r1.4(2)(a) CPR**); and
- encourage the parties to use an ADR procedure if the court considers that appropriate, and facilitate the use of such procedure (**r1.4(2)(e) CPR**).

There is a clear expectation that parties are to consider ADR prior to the issuing of proceedings.

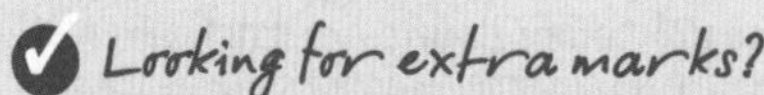

Make clear that although the courts can 'encourage' the parties to consider ADR, they are not entitled to 'compel' the parties to undertake ADR. To do so would be a breach of **Article 6 European Convention on Human Rights (ECHR)**.

Despite the court's inability to compel parties involved in a civil dispute from undertaking ADR, it does have the power to sanction a party for unreasonable refusal to attempt ADR. This sanction often takes the form of an adverse costs order made against the party unreasonably dismissing ADR.

Forms of ADR

There is no single definition of ADR. As a starting point, ADR is defined in the Glossary of the **CPR 1998** as a 'collective description of methods of resolving disputes otherwise than through the normal trial process'. Given that there is no overarching definition of ADR, it is better to see what ADR covers. The best understanding of ADR is taken from Julie Browne, Stuart Sime, and Susan Blake, *The Jackson ADR Handbook* (2nd edn, Oxford University Press 2016), which provides that ADR covers:

> any option where: there is a dispute between two (or more) parties; that dispute relates to civil legal rights and/or duties; and the dispute could potentially go to court for resolution.

It is this description which has led to many regulators, such as the Bar Standards Board, to argue that a better term for ADR is 'ReDOC—resolution of disputes out of court'. This is the term adopted on the current version of the Bar Professional Training Course (BPTC).

The main forms, or options, of ADR are numerous and are detailed in Table 8.3 alongside their benefits and downfalls and their use in common practice.

For a more detailed account of ADR, see Browne, Sime, and Blake (2016).

Table 8.3 Forms of ADR and their benefits

Type of ADR process	Description	Pros	Cons
Negotiation	It is relatively informal, involving the discussion of some or all of the issues in a case with the aim of resolving said issues. There is no set procedure and the process may involve simple exchanges between the parties or more complex structured settlement meetings.	• Very flexible and can be conducted by parties/and or lawyers. • Relatively cost effective, with limited preparation required. • Clients retain complete control of the outcome through giving instructions and approval to agreements.	• Negotiation can lead to a relatively weak outcome for a client if the strengths of a case are not properly exploited. • The informality can lead to confusion as to process. • Negotiations may fail where the parties' expectations are unrealistic.
Mediation	A non-adjudicative dispute resolution process under which the parties agree to try to reach a settlement of their dispute with the assistance of an independent third party using a process agreed by the parties.	• Neutral third party can assist in making the case clearer (both the strengths and weaknesses). • A robust mediator can help find a way forward in even the most difficult cases. • Confidential. • Avoids emotional stress generated by court proceedings. • Appropriate where the parties wish to preserve their relationship.	• Success depends partly on the abilities of the mediator. • Mediation can increase costs. • Mediation may not work where the parties are antagonistic. • Mediation can be difficult where neither party is represented.
Conciliation	This normally involves a neutral third party who facilitates a negotiation between the parties, or the conciliator may propose a decision if the parties cannot reach one (though not binding).	• Conducted on a confidential, without prejudice basis. • Cost effective. • Assists parties to see the other side of the story. • Useful where relations are still good between the parties.	• If the process fails, costs will escalate in using an additional procedure.

Type of ADR process	Description	Pros	Cons
Arbitration	An adjudicative dispute resolution process under which the parties agree to submit their dispute to an impartial tribunal appointed by a process agreed by the parties. The process is binding on the parties. (**Arbitration Act 1996**).	• The parties can select an arbitrator with appropriate expertise and experience in a relevant field. • The process is private and confidential, unlike a trial in open court, which is in the public domain. • Many aspects of the process can be tailored to the needs of a specific dispute. • The process can be relatively structured. • The process can be simple and cost effective if the dispute is decided on the basis of written submissions. • It can be tailored to a particular venue.	• Not necessarily a cost-saving option if a process similar to trial is used. • The parties leave the final decision to a third party, and will be bound by it. • The process cannot deal easily with a party who fails to co-operate, as an arbitrator will not have the wide powers of a judge. • The arbitrator needs to be selected with care as regards expertise, experience, etc.
Adjudication	This involves a neutral third party with appropriate specialist knowledge acting under an agreed process (usually a surveyor, architect, engineer, solicitor, or barrister). The process may be binding, but only where the adjudication agreement provides so.	• The process can be carefully adjusted to meet specific commercial or other needs. • The process tends to be more flexible and cost effective than arbitration.	• Adjudication is not necessarily low cost if experts are in dispute. • If the adjudication agreement does not provide that the adjudicator's decision will be final and binding on both parties, either litigation or arbitration may still be necessary (which itself will raise the costs).

The process of civil justice

Now that you have an understanding of the framework of the CivJS, it is essential that you appreciate the process of the CivJS. This section of the chapter is divided as such:

- pre-litigation process;
- commencing litigation;
- pre-trial process;
- trial process; and
- post-trial process.

It is important to note that during this process, a number of issues may arise which bring the procedure to an end, and to appreciate that these issues are constantly featured in the background of civil litigation. These issues include:

- ADR—the parties may decide to settle the case at any point;
- default judgment—judgment may be entered against a defendant at any point in the proceedings;
- offers to settle—known as a 'Part 36 Offer', this is where an individual makes an offer to another without prejudice.

Figure 8.1 provides a brief flowchart of the process of civil justice.

Revision tip

Ensure that you are comfortable with the terminology used in civil litigation. As a result of the **CPR 1998**, terminology changed for reasons of simplicity and clarity. You may encounter many phrases in your studies of the ELS, so be aware of the following:

- plaintiff (pre-1998)→ claimant (post-1998);
- writ (pre-1998)→ claim form (post-1998);
- pleadings (pre-1998)→ statements of case (post-1998).

Pre-litigation process

Civil wrong allegedly committed

At the very start of the CivJS is the alleged commission of a civil wrong. A civil wrong may take many forms and may hold a number of bases in civil law. For example, the civil wrong may be:

- an alleged breach of contract;
- an alleged tortious act committed against another; and
- an alleged interference with intellectual property (IP) rights.

Figure 8.1 Process of civil justice system

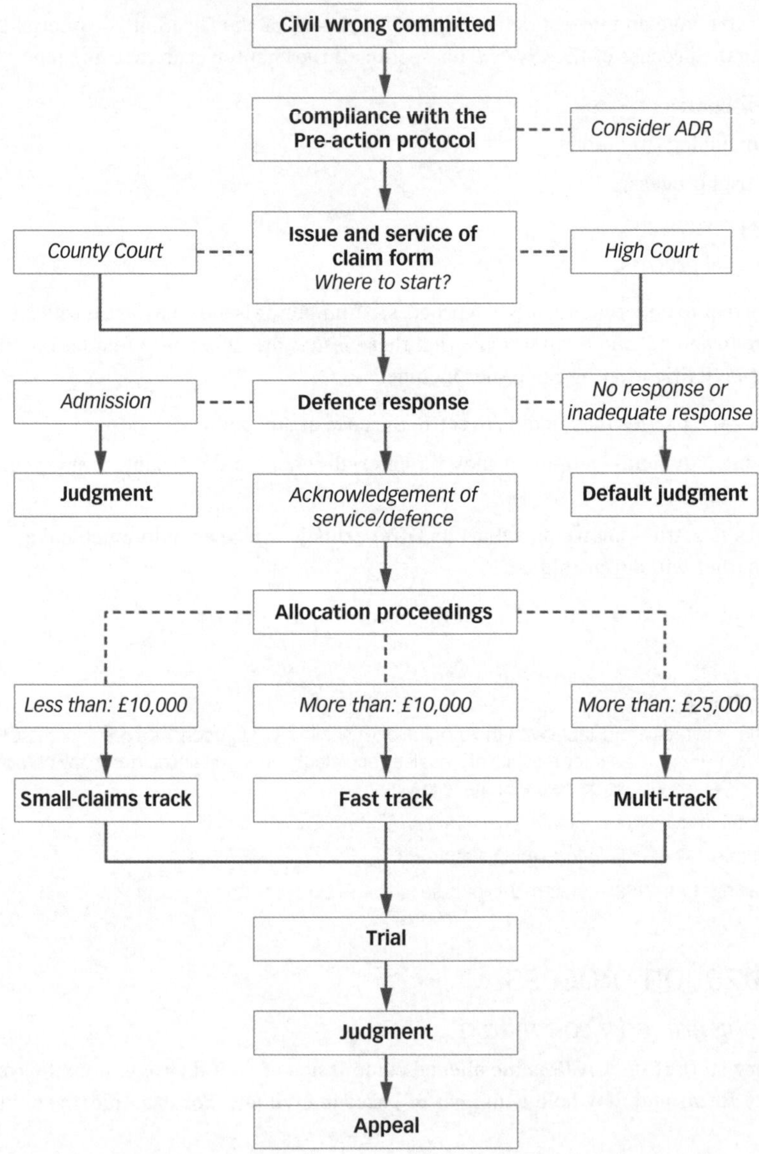

Revision tip

Ensure that you make the distinction between civil and criminal law clear.

- In criminal law, we are concerned with alleged criminal OFFENCES.
- In civil law, we are concerned with alleged civil WRONGS.

It is thus inappropriate to speak of a civil offence.

Pre-action protocol

Adjoined to the **CPR 1998** are a number of **Pre-Action Protocols** which contain specific guidance on the conduct of the parties before they consider issuing legal proceedings. At present, there are 13 **Pre-Action Protocols** and a **Practice Direction on Pre-Action Conduct and Protocols (PDPACP)**. It is important to note that there is not a specific Protocol for every type of case that may come before the courts.

The **PDPACP** came into effect in April 2015 and makes the expectations of the parties clear before they consider litigation in all types of cases. In particular, **para 3 PDPACP** provides that:

> Before commencing proceedings, the court will expect the parties to have exchanged sufficient information to—
> (a) understand each other's position;
> (b) make decisions about how to proceed;
> (c) try to settle the issues without proceedings;
> (d) consider a form of Alternative Dispute Resolution (ADR) to assist with settlement;
> (e) support the efficient management of those proceedings; and
> (f) reduce the costs of resolving the dispute.

Paragraph 6 details the procedure to be adopted during the pre-litigation process. These steps are listed below:

- **Identify protocol**: where there is a relevant pre-action protocol, the parties should comply with that protocol before commencing proceedings.
- **Use PDPACP**: where there is no relevant pre-action protocol, the parties should treat the PDPACP as if that were the protocol.
- **Exchange information**: the parties should exchange correspondence and information.

By **para 6**, the necessary steps include:

- a letter of claim by the claimant, providing concise details of the claim;
- acknowledgement from the defendant;
- letter of response from the defendant, to be provided within a reasonable time (14 days in a straightforward case and no more than three months in a very complex one);
- disclosing key documents relevant to the issues in dispute;
- taking steps to obtain relevant and necessary expert evidence; and
- seeking to agree a form of ADR process and embarking on the process.

Commencing litigation

The process of commencing litigation is complex and detailed. For a full account of the civil litigation process, see Stuart Sime and Derek French (eds), *Blackstone's Civil Practice* (20th edn, Oxford University Press 2020).

Commencement

Although the majority of cases are commenced using the **Part 7** procedure in the **CPR 1998**, there are certain 'special cases' that are to be commenced by alternative means in **Part 8 CPR 1998**. Such **Part 8** claims include:

- proceedings in which there are no substantial factual disputes; or
- where a Practice Direction directs the use of a Part 8 claim form (e.g. in actions seeking a company director's disqualification).

For our purposes, we shall only be concerned with **Part 7**, as this is the most common source for commencing proceedings.

Proceedings are officially started 'when a court issues a claim form at the request of the claimant' (**r7.2(1)CPR**). The claim form (known as the 'N1 Form') is a simple but essential document setting out the general nature of the claim made by the claimant against the defendant. The claim form will, according to **r16.2(1) CPR**:

(a) contain a concise statement of the nature of the claim (i.e. is it in tort, contract etc.) otherwise it can be struck out;
(b) specify the remedy the claimant seeks;
(c) where the claimant is making a claim for money, contain a statement of value;
(cc) where the claimant's only claim is for a specified sum, contain a statement of the interest accrued on that sum; and
(d) contain such other matters as may be set out in a practice direction.

Further to this, the claim form must be verified by a 'statement of truth' under **Part 22 CPR**. A statement of truth is simply a sentence in the claim form stating that the person signing the claim form believes the facts contained in the form to be true.

To 'issue' a claim form, simply means the process whereby the court seals the claim form with its official seal (**r2.6 CPR**).

Service

By **r7.5(1) CPR**, a claim form must be served within four months of the date of issue. This means that a claim form is valid for four months and a day—e.g. 9 May–9 September. 'Service' simply involves the formal notification to the defendant of the action against them. Under **Part 6**, the following documents are required to be served:

- a sealed claim form (N1 Form);
- the particulars of claim (see below); and
- a response pack (N9 Form).

A particulars of claim (PofC) is simply a form of 'statement of case'. In accordance with **r16.4(1) CPR**, a PofC must include:

(a) concise statement of the facts on which the claimant relies;
(b) if the claimant is seeking interest, a statement to that effect and the details set out in paragraph (2);
(c) if the claimant is seeking exemplary or aggravated damages, a statement to that effect and his grounds for claiming them;
(d) if the claimant is seeking provisional damages, a statement to that effect and his grounds for claiming them;
(e) such other matters as may be set out in a practice direction.

The PofC must either be contained or served in the claim form or must be served on the defendant within 14 days after service of the claim form (**r7.4(1) CPR**).

Effecting service is possible through various different methods. These methods are set out in **r6.3 CPR** and are divided into the 'method' of service and the 'step required' to effect that service. These methods and required steps are detailed in Table 8.4.

Choosing a court

It is essential to understand what court a case may be heard in. The choices available to an individual are the High Court and the County Court. In general, by **Practice Direction 7A CPR**,

Table 8.4 Methods of service

Method of service	Step required
Personal service (**r6.3(1)(a) CPR**)	Leaving it with that individual (**r6.5(3) CPR**)
First-class post, document exchange, or other service that provides for delivery on the next business day (**r6.3(1)(b) CPR**)	Posting, leaving with, delivering to, or collection by the relevant service provider (**r6.2(b) CPR**)
Delivery of the document to, or leaving it at, the *relevant place* (**r6.3(1)(c) CPR**)	Relevant place may be to leave it: • with the defendant's solicitors (**r6.7 CPR**); • at an address provided for the purpose of being served with the proceedings (**r6.8 CPR**)
Fax or other electronic method (**r6.3(1)(d)CPR**)	Completing the transmission of the fax, or sending an email or other electronic transmission (*though there must be an indication that the other party is willing to accept service by fax or email*) (**PD6A.4.1**)
Any method authorized by the courts (**r6.3(1)(e) CPR**)	Posting it to an address of a person who knows the other party Sending an SMS text message or leaving a voicemail message at a particular telephone number (**PD6A.9.3**)

a party has an ability to issue his claim in either court. However, there are two key terms you must be aware of that will affect the claimant's ability to choose a court.

These terms are where the court has:

- exclusive jurisdiction; and
- concurrent jurisdiction.

To begin with, **r7.1 CPR** states that there are certain restrictions on where proceedings can be started. These restrictions concern the exclusive jurisdiction of the courts and are provided for in **PD7A**. They have been detailed in Table 8.5.

Where the High Court and County Court appear to have concurrent jurisdiction, the general rule under the **CPR** and **High Court and County Court Jurisdiction Order 1991** is that the claimant has the choice as to where proceedings are commenced.

Although the High Court and County Court do share concurrent jurisdiction, and the claimant has a choice as to where to start, there are several exceptions and provisos to this general rule. These are detailed in Table 8.6.

Further to this, **PD7A.2.4** provides that proceedings should not be commenced in the County Court if the claimant believes that the claim should be tried by a High Court judge by reason of:

(1) the financial value of the claim and the amount in dispute; and/or

(2) the complexity of the facts, legal issues, remedies, or procedures involved; and/or

(3) the importance of the outcome of the claim to the public in general.

Defence response

A defendant who intends to contest proceedings must respond to the claim by filing an acknowledgement of service or by filing a defence. By **r9.1(2) CPR**, the defendant need not respond to the claim until the particulars of claim have been served on him/her. Upon the particulars of claim being served on him/her, the defendant has a number of

Table 8.5 Exclusive jurisdiction

ONLY in the High Court examples	ONLY in the County Court examples
Claims in respect of libel or slander (**PD7A.2.9(1)**)	Claims to enforce regulated agreements and linked transactions under the **Consumer Credit Act 1974** where the upper credit limit is £25,000 (**s141 CCA 1974**)
Claims in which the title to any toll, fair, market, or franchise is in question (**PD7A.2.9(2)**)	Claims to redress unlawful discrimination (**Equality Act 2010**)
Applications for a writ of *habeas corpus* (**PD7A.2.6**)	
Claims for damages under the HRA 1998 in respect of judicial acts (**PD7A.2.10(2)**)	

Table 8.6 Exceptions to concurrent jurisdiction

Type of claim	Jurisdiction
Non-personal injury proceedings (**PD7A.2.1**)	Non-personal injury proceedings (whether for damages or for a specified sum) may not be started in the High Court unless the value of the claim is more than £100,000.
Personal injury proceedings (**PD7A.2.2**)	A claim for damages in respect of personal injuries must not be started in the High Court unless the value of the claim is £50,000 or more. *(A claim can be started in either County Court or High Court if over £50,000.)*
Required by an enactment (**PD7A.2.3**)	A claim must be issued in the High Court or County Court if an enactment so requires.
A money claim issued in the High Court (Royal Courts of Justice)	A claim may be commenced in the High Court, but the claim will usually be transferred to the County Court if the claim is worth less than £100,000, unless one of the exceptions stated in **PD29.2.2** applies.

options or actions that he/she may take. These are detailed in **r9.2 CPR** and are provided in Table 8.7.

Of course, a defendant may decide to ignore the claim form. If a defendant fails to make any response to a claim, the usual result is that a default judgment will be entered against him/her within a relatively short period after service. Default judgment is explained in further detail under 'Pre-trial process' later in this chapter.

Allocation

Once the defendant has responded to the claim with a defence, the court shall then decide the appropriate track on which the case will be heard. **Rule 26.1(2) CPR** sets out that there are three tracks, which are:

- small-claims track;
- fast-track;
- multi-track.

The respective scope of each track is detailed in **r26.6 CPR** and is provided for in Table 8.8.

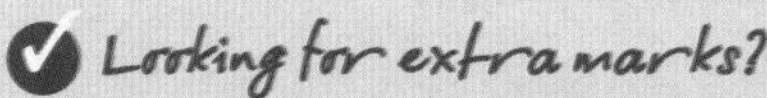

Be aware of new updates to the law. In November 2015, the government announced its intention to increase the limit for pain, suffering, and loss of amenity (PSLA) in the small-claims track from £1,000 to £5,000. Following consultation, however, the government announced in March 2017 that the limit shall increase to £2,000 in all cases except for road traffic accidents, for which the limit shall be increased to £5,000. It is intended that these plans will come into force in October 2020.

Table 8.7 Options by the defendant

Actions that may be taken	Description
File or serve an admission (**Part 14 CPR**)	At any time, a party may admit the truth of the whole or any part of another party's case.
	However, he/she must do so by giving notice in writing. If an admission is not in writing, it may still be admissible in evidence, but it is not a formal admission for the purposes of **Part 14**. Where the defendant files an admission, judgment may be entered against him/her.
File a defence (and potentially a counterclaim) (**Parts 15 and 16 CPR**)	In his/her defence, the defendant must state: • which of the allegations from the particulars he/she denies; • which allegations he/she is unable to admit or deny, but which he/she requires the claimant to prove; and • which allegations he/she admits. Where a defendant denies an allegation: • he/she must state his/her reasons for doing so; and • if he/she intends to put forward a different version of events, he/she must state his/her own version.
File an acknowledgement of service (**Part 10 CPR**)	An acknowledgement of service is simply a document which states that the defendant has received the claim form, or particulars of claim, should it be served later.

Table 8.8 Civil claim tracks

Type of claim	Qualifications
Small-claims track	**Personal injury cases:** • less than £10,000; AND • claims for pain, suffering, and loss of amenity (PSLA) are not more than £1,000 (*more than £1,000 goes to the fast-track*). **Non-personal injury cases**: • any claim which has a value of not more than £10,000.
Fast-track	**Any case**: • between £10,000 and £25,000; AND • which lasts no longer than one day; AND • which does not require more than one expert per party.
Multi-track	**Any case**: • over £25,000; OR • under £25,000, BUT requires longer than one day or more than one expert per party.

The court will take into account a number of matters relevant to allocation. These factors are listed in **r26.8(1) CPR** and include:

(a) the financial value, if any, of the claim;
(b) the nature of the remedy sought;
(c) the likely complexity of the facts, law, or evidence;
(d) the number of parties or likely parties;
(e) the value of any counterclaim or other Part 20 claim and the complexity of any matters relating to it;
(f) the amount of oral evidence which may be required;
(g) the importance of the claim to persons who are not parties to the proceedings;
(h) the views expressed by the parties; and
(i) the circumstances of the parties.

In relation to the 'views expressed by the parties', the judge will be assisted in his decision by reference to the directions questionnaires sent out to all parties. Each track has a number of identifiable features which makes each track a distinct and unique part of the CivJS.

The main features of each track are listed in Table 8.9.

Pre-trial process

Disclosure

The disclosure of evidence in civil proceedings is similar to that of their criminal counterparts in that a party has a general right to inspect the evidence before trial. In criminal proceedings, disclosure means the exchange of documents and evidence between the parties.

Table 8.9 Features of the tracks

Type of claim	Features
Small-claims track	• Hearings will be informal, heard before a district judge. • The strict rules of evidence do not apply. • The court may limit cross-examination. • The court must give reasons for its decision. • Parties may represent themselves, instruct a solicitor or barrister, or even use a lay representative. • Costs are restricted.
Fast-track	• A strict timetable is to be followed. • Costs are restricted to fixed costs. • There is a restriction in the use of expert evidence and promotion of joint experts.
Multi-track	• Case management conferences (CMCs) are used to identify issues as early as possible and to try specific issues before the main trial. • Expert evidence is actively controlled and managed by the trial judge.

In civil proceedings, however, disclosure simply means stating that the document exists or has existed. Disclosure may then be followed by inspection, where the parties are entitled to request copies of the documents for their consideration (**Part 31 CPR**).

The key to understanding this rule is to consider it in the following way:

- Stage 1: Disclosure—this is where parties will send each other lists of documents.
- Stage 2: Inspection—this is where parties will request copies of documents appearing on the list of documents.

In terms of inspection, there is a general right under **r31.3(1) CPR** to inspect the documents. However, two major exceptions apply to this rule. These are:

(a) the document is no longer in the control of the party who disclosed it; and
(b) the party disclosing the document has a right or a duty to withhold inspection of it.

The rules of disclosure and inspection in a given case will depend on the track where the case is being heard. Table 8.10 details this.

Table 8.10 Disclosure and the tracks

Track	Rule
Small-claims track	**Part 31 CPR** does not apply
Fast-track	Standard disclosure unless dispensed with by courts or parties
Multi-track	Detailed list detailing evidence that should be disclosed

Evidence

The general principles of evidence are broadly the same for both criminal and civil law. However, it is apparent from the rules of civil litigation that the admission of evidence is by far the easier task than doing so in criminal proceedings.

In civil proceedings, the power of the court to control evidence is provided in **Part 32 CPR 1998**. In particular, **r32.1(1) CPR** provides that the court may control the evidence by giving directions as to:

(a) the issues on which it requires evidence;
(b) the nature of the evidence which it requires to decide those issues; and
(c) the way in which the evidence is to be placed before the court.

Further to this, the court holds the power to exclude any evidence even where that evidence would otherwise be admissible (**r32.1(2) CPR**).The general rule in relation to evidence is provided for in **r32.2(1) CPR**, which states that any fact which needs to be proved by the evidence of witnesses is to be proved:

(a) at trial, by their oral evidence given in public; and
(b) at any other hearing, by their evidence in writing.

By **r32.5(2) CPR**, where a witness is called to give oral evidence his witness statement shall stand as his evidence in chief unless the court orders otherwise. This means that counsel for that witness shall merely call the witness to present them to the opposition for cross-examination.

We advise that you refer back to Chapter 7 to observe the sorts of evidence that may be admitted at trial.

Interim applications

An interim application is any application made to the court, between a case being issued and the final trial, that requires a judicial decision to be made. An interim application is often necessary in order to:

- enable an action to progress to trial in a speedier fashion;
- preserve evidence; or
- exert pressure on an opponent.

Interim applications may take the form of:

- applications for minor procedural matters, such as an extension of time for performing a necessary act;
- applications for the court to exercise their case management powers, such as requiring further disclosure or inspection; and
- applications for specific remedies, most importantly interim injunctions and interim payments.

An interim application may be made with or without notice (the latter formerly known as *ex parte* applications). The general rule under **r23.3(1) CPR** is that all applications should be made with full notice to the opposing party. Notice may be dispensed with, however, if the court considers there to be an exceptional urgency to the application or where the overriding objective is best furthered by doing so.

The most significant interim applications made under **Part 23** are interim injunctions. An interim injunction is a court order prohibiting a person from doing something (Prohibitory Order) or requiring a person to do something (Mandatory Order). In general, the court will only grant an interim injunction where it appears to the court to be *just and convenient to do so* (**s37(1) Senior Courts Act 1981**). The party seeking the injunction must satisfy the test in ***American Cyanamid Co. v Ethicon* (1975)**.

Part 36 offers

Also known as a 'without-prejudice' offer, a **Part 36** offer to settle is a formal offer made by one party to the other to settle the dispute out of court. This offer may be made at any time in the proceedings, including before the commencement of proceedings. **Part 36** offers differ from regular offers to settle in that the court may take such offers into account when awarding costs. In particular, the court will consider whether there was an unreasonable refusal of a reasonable offer.

In order for a **Part 36** offer to be valid, it must (according to **r.36.5(1) CPR**):

(a) be in writing (it may be by letter or by using Form N242A);
(b) state on its face that it is intended to have the consequences of a Part 36 offer;
(c) specify a period of not less than 21 days within which the defendant will be liable for the claimant's costs if the offer is accepted;
(d) state whether it relates to the whole of the claim or to part of it or to an issue that arises in it and if so to which part or issue; and
(e) state whether it takes into account any counterclaim.

A **Part 36** offer is made 'without prejudice' under **r36.16 CPR**. This means that the trial judge must not be informed of the offer until the case has been decided. Without-prejudice orders are quite complex and will not be discussed in any great detail.

Figure 8.2 provides an overview of how a **Part 36** offer works in practice.

Default and summary judgment

Under **Part 12 CPR 1998**, default judgment simply means 'judgment without trial'. By **r12.1 CPR**, this may occur in two circumstances:

(a) where the defendant has failed to file an acknowledgement of service; or
(b) where the defendant has failed to file a defence.

Default judgment is not an automatic right provided for by the courts; rather, the claimant must apply to the courts for default judgment. Default judgment is available in the majority of cases but a number of exceptions are listed in **r12.2 CPR** and include:

(a) on a claim for delivery of goods subject to an agreement regulated by the **Consumer Credit Act 1974** (amounts up to £25,000);
(b) where he/she uses the procedure set out in **Part 8** (alternative procedure for claims); or
(c) in any other case where a Practice Direction provides that the claimant may not obtain default judgment.

Alternatively, by **Part 24 CPR 1998**, the court may give summary judgment against a claimant or defendant on the whole of a claim, or on a particular issue, if it considers that:

1. the claimant has no *real* prospect of succeeding on the claim or issue; or that the defendant has no *real* prospect of successfully defending the claim or issue; and
2. there is no other compelling reason why the case or issue should be disposed of at a trial [emphasis added].

The inclusion of the word 'real' in **r24.2 CPR** means that the defendant has to have a case which is better than merely arguable (***E D & F Man Liquid Products Ltd v Patel* (2003)**).

Figure 8.2 Part 36 offers

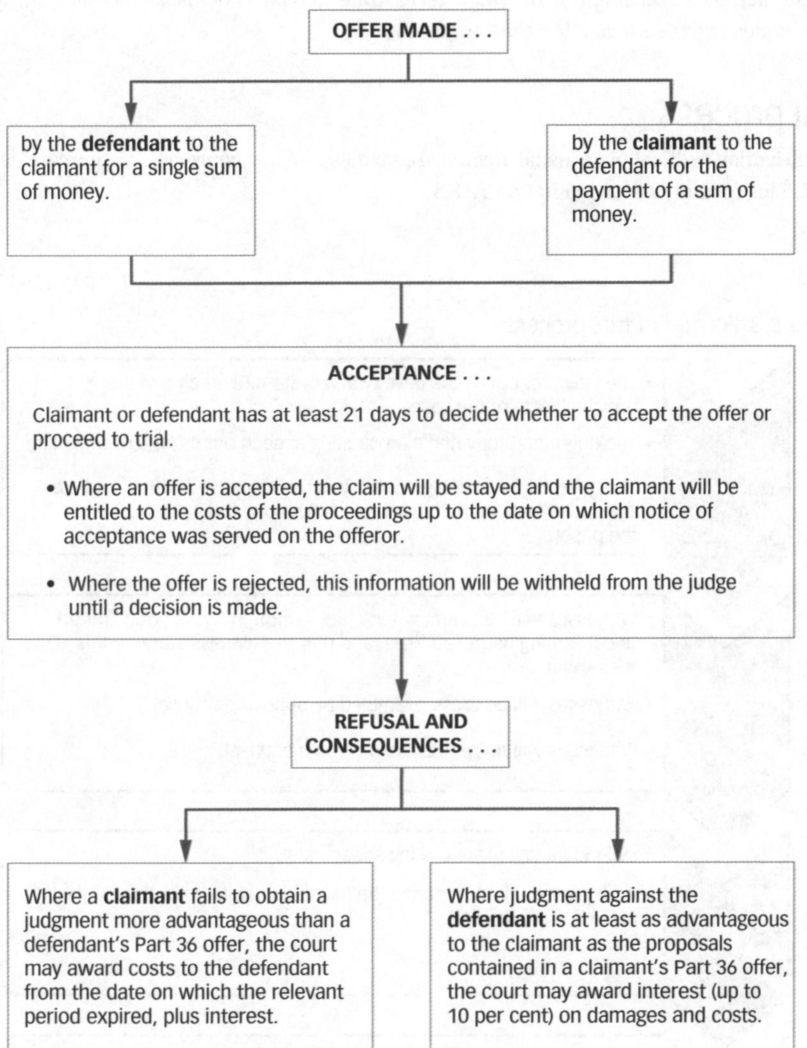

Summary judgment may be awarded against the claimant in all cases (**r24.3(1) CPR**), and may be issued against a defendant in all cases except for proceedings relating to the possession of residential premises (**r24.3(2) CPR**).

An application for summary judgment is not appropriate to resolve a complex question of law and fact, the determination of which necessitates a trial of the issue having regard to all of the evidence (***Apvodedo NV v Collins*** **(2008)**).

Trial process

Civil litigation will follow a usual format, regardless of the court where the case is to be heard. This format is detailed in Figure 8.3.

Figure 8.3 Format of trial process

Opening speeches
- The claimant opens the case with a systematic recital of the principal facts of the case.
- The defendant may make an opening speech but it remains unusual.
- The need for an opening speech is often dispensed with in fast-track and sometimes in multi-track cases because the judge has read the papers.

Questioning of witnesses
- Witnesses will be examined-in-chief (although this is often limited to confirming name, address, and that the witness statement is their own).
- Witnesses will be cross-examined by opposing counsel.
- Witnesses will be re-examined by own counsel.

Closing speeches
- Defendant will make closing speech first.
- Both parties will summarize their case and state what they wish to achieve from the court.

Judgment
- The judge will provide his/her judgment either immediately or after an adjournment.
- Judgment will be divided into the decision of 'who wins' followed by the statement of remedies and costs.
- The judge will give reasons for his/her decision.

Post-trial process

The post-trial process is concerned with the potential routes for appeal against decisions of the trial judge. The procedure for appeal is laid out in **Part 52 CPR 1998**.

The routes of appeal are set out in the **Access to Justice 1999 (Destination of Appeals) Order 2000**. Under that Order, two factors are pertinent in deciding where an appeal will be heard:

1. the seniority of the judge presiding over the original case; and
2. the court in which he/she sat when reaching his/her decision that is being appealed.

Table 8.11 details the general rule on destination according to these factors.

Table 8.11 Destination of civil appeals

Seniority of trial judge and court	Destination of appeal
District judge (County Court)	Circuit judge (County Court)
Circuit judge (County Court)	High Court judge (High Court)
Master (High Court)	High Court judge (High Court)
High Court judge (High Court)	Lord Justice of Appeal (Court of Appeal)
Lord Justice of Appeal (Court of Appeal)	Justice of Supreme Court (Supreme Court)

In her research, Darbyshire (2011) found that circuit judges do not like sitting on the appeals of district judges, especially those who sit in the same building as they do. Darbyshire raised the question of actual and apparent bias in that the appeal judge may uphold the ruling of his colleague for a 'quiet life'. For a fuller account of this research see Penny Darbyshire, *Sitting in Judgment: The Working Lives of Judges* (Hart Publishing 2011).

Need for permission

By **r52.3(1) CPR**, an individual who wishes to appeal from the decision of a judge in the County Court or the High Court requires permission to appeal. The test for permission varies according to whether the appeal is a 'first appeal' or a 'second appeal'.

Permission for a first appeal may be obtained from the lower court which the party wishes to appeal from or to the respective appellate court in an appeal notice. Permission for a first appeal may only be granted under **r52.6(1)** where:

(a) the court considers that the appeal would have a *real prospect of success*; or

(b) there is *some other compelling reason* why the appeal should be heard [emphasis added].

Permission for a second appeal (i.e. appeals to the Court of Appeal following a first appeal) may only be obtained from the Court of Appeal itself (**r52.7(1) CPR**). The test for granting permission is provided in **s55(1) Access to Justice Act 1999** and in **r52.7(2) CPR**:

The Court of Appeal will not give permission unless it considers that—

(a) the appeal would—
   (i) have a real prospect of success; and
   (ii) raise an important point of principle or practice; or

(b) there is some other compelling reason for the Court of Appeal to hear it.

Real prospect of success has been described in ***Swain v Hillman* (1999)** as 'realistic and not merely fanciful'. This was furthered by Jackson LJ in ***R (a child)* (2019)**, in which it was explained that '[t]here is no requirement that success should be probable, or more likely than not'.

The appeal

By **r52.21(1)**, every appeal will be limited to a review of the decision of the lower court. This means that the appeal hearing will be on the law and shall not be based on facts. There are two exceptions to this rule, namely:

(a) a practice direction makes different provision for a particular category of appeal; or

(b) the court considers that in the circumstances of an individual appeal it would be in the *interests of justice* to hold a rehearing [emphasis added].

Further to this, under **r52.21(2)**, the Appeal Court will not hear oral evidence, or evidence which was not before the lower court.

Test for allowing the appeal

Under **r.52.21(3)**, the Appeal Court will only allow an appeal where the decision of the lower court was:

(a) wrong; or

(b) unjust because of a serious procedural or other irregularity in the proceedings in the lower court.

Wrong has been understood to mean that the lower court:

- erred in law;
- erred in fact; or
- erred in the exercise of its discretion.

Outcome of the appeal

By **r52.20(1) CPR**, the Appeal Court has all the powers of the lower court. Under **r52.20(2) CPR**, the powers of the appeal courts are as follows:

(a) affirm, set aside, or vary any order or judgment made or given by the lower court;

(b) refer any claim or issue for determination by the lower court;

(c) order a new trial or hearing;

(d) make orders for the payment of interest;

(e) make a costs order.

Alternative to civil courts

There are a number of non-judicial remedies (i.e. outside of the civil courts) that are available to individuals who feel aggrieved by the actions of the state. We have already considered the use of ADR; however, there are further non-legal remedies available to individuals. These include:

- tribunals;
- inquiries; and
- the Ombudsman.

Tribunals

Tribunals were discussed at length in Chapter 2.

Inquiries

In very broad terms, inquiries can be divided into two types:

- land inquiries; and
- inquiries into national events/scandals.

Land inquiries

When a local authority refuses to grant planning permission, an individual may seek to challenge such a decision by way of appeal to the Planning Inspectorate. The determination of this appeal can be processed in three different ways (each including an inspector from the Planning Inspectorate):

- the written representations procedure;
- the hearing procedure; and
- the local inquiry procedure.

The last is the most formal of all the appeals and considers the most complicated or largest appeals, whilst the first two are less formal and deal with less complex matters.

Inquiries into national events/scandals

The second type of inquiry investigates and makes recommendations in respect of a national event or public scandal. There are two categories of these types of inquiry:

- a statutory inquiry; and
- a non-statutory inquiry.

Importantly, these inquiries are not courts and their findings have no legal effect (**Inquiries Act 2005**). Inquiries do, however sit in public and have the power to call witnesses and order the production of documents or other relevant evidence.

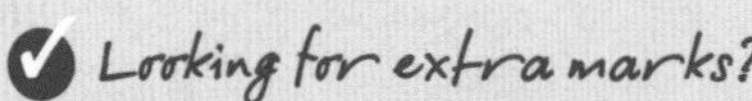

Show your knowledge by detailing some of the most notable statutory and non-statutory inquiries.

Statutory:

- The Macpherson Inquiry (1998) into the death of Stephen Lawrence, under **s49 Police Act 1996.**
- The ICL Inquiry (2007) into an explosion at a Glasgow factory, under the **Inquiries Act 2005.**

Non-statutory:

- The Scott Inquiry (1996) into the export of equipment to Iraq.
- The Shipman Inquiry (2004) into the deaths caused by Dr Harold Shipman.
- The Grenfell Tower Inquiry (2017) into the Grenfell tower fire, which killed 72 people and destroyed the Grenfell Tower.

Ombudsman

In 1967, Parliament established the Parliamentary Commissioner for Administration, also known as the Ombudsman, under the **Parliamentary Commissioner Act 1967**. The current role of the Parliamentary and Health Service Ombudsman, held by Rob Behrens since April 2017, combines two former statutory roles of Parliamentary Commissioner for Administration (the Parliamentary Ombudsman) and Health Service Commissioner for England (Health Service Ombudsman).

Maladministration

The role of the Ombudsman is to hold public bodies to account and expose maladministration where it has occurred. The Ombudsman, therefore, may only investigate matters of 'maladministration'.

Maladministration is not expressly defined in the Act, therefore the courts have relied on the use of the famous Crossman Catalogue to indicate the type of behaviour that maladministration covers. It includes:

> Bias, neglect, inattention, delay, incompetence, inaptitude, perversity, turpitude, arbitrariness and so on. It would be a long and interesting list.
>
> (*Hansard HC* Vol. 734, col. 51)

The Ombudsman's website illustrates that maladministration also embraces, *inter alia*:

- faulty procedure;
- rudeness;
- avoidable delay;
- refusal to answer reasonable questions;
- failure to indicate a right of appeal.

Investigation process

The Ombudsman follows a set process for investigating claims of maladministration. This is detailed in Table 8.12.

Table 8.12 Investigation process of the Ombudsman

Stage	Description
Filter stage	The aggrieved must write to an MP (whether their own or another), whereby the MP should refer the claim to the Ombudsman. The complaint must be made within 12 months of the alleged grievance; however, the Ombudsman has the discretion to allow a complaint out of time.
Investigation stage	Relevant powers of the Ombudsman are listed below: • The Ombudsman has discretion whether or not to carry out investigation (**s5**). • The Ombudsman has discretion as to how to carry out investigation (**s7**). • The Ombudsman has the 'same power as the court' in respect to witnesses and evidence (**s8(2)**).
Report stage	The Ombudsman must publish a full report and send it to the aggrieved, the referring MP, and anyone else concerned (**s10**). The Ombudsman's recommendations are not legally binding; however, they are generally accepted due to their persuasive nature. If conducting an investigation and the Ombudsman believes the aggrieved will not be remedied, a special report can be issued which will bring it to the attention of Parliament and the public (**s10(3)**).

Should an individual still feel aggrieved by this process, their complaint may still find itself in the civil courts after all.

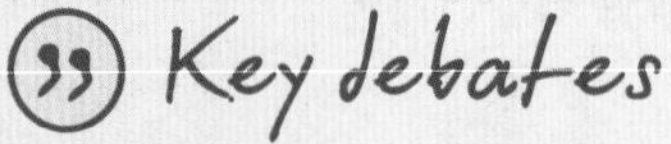

Topic	ADR and costs
Academic	Geoffrey Davies
Viewpoint	Argues that although one of the main purposes of ADR is the desire to reduce costs, yet the use of ADR can result in the increase of costs. Davies argues that this is because if ADR is likely to fail, this will result in further delays and expense in then commencing legal proceedings.
Source	Geoffrey Davies, 'Civil Justice Reform: Why We Need to Question some Basic Assumptions' (2006) 25 Civil Justice Quarterly 32

Topic	Disappearance of civil litigation
Academic	Hazel Genn
Viewpoint	Argues that placing too much weight on ADR may result in ignoring certain key aspects of civil justice. Genn argues that civil justice has an important social function; in particular, judges are 'publicly stating the law, reinforcing norms of social and economic behaviour, identifying the limits of executive power and publicising the values of the society'.
Source	Hazel Genn, *Judging Civil Justice* (Cambridge University Press 2010)

Topic	Woolf reforms
Academic	Gavin Lightman
Viewpoint	Argues that the Woolf reforms have 'not altered the general position that delays and costs remain problematic' in civil litigation.
Source	Gavin Lightman, 'The Civil Justice System and Legal Profession' (2003) 22 Civil Justice Quarterly 235

Essay question

'Civil justice remains a complex and inaccessible framework for litigants. The reforms issued by Lord Woolf are ineffective and the reforms issued by Lord Justice Jackson are too complex, even for the professional to understand.'

Critically discuss this statement in light of the operation of the CivJS.

Problem question

You have been asked to provide advice to an individual at your pro bono clinic. The individual requires advice on the following matter:

'I bought a watch from a guy on the street who told me it was a genuine Rolex watch. I paid £200 for it and it turns out to be fake. I went back to him but he says it isn't his fault and he refuses to give me a refund. What can I do?'

Your supervisor has asked you to advise this individual on the following:

(a) the potential action they may have against the vendor;

(b) how he is to commence litigation and the formalities for doing so;

(c) what the options for settling the dispute out of court are;

(d) where the case will be held; and

(e) whether he has to pay for his costs if he wins or loses.

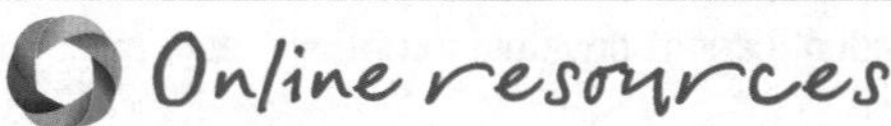

For outline answers to these exam questions, as well as multiple-choice questions, please visit the online resources.

#9 Funding Access to the English Legal System

Key facts

- Funding legal services may be provided publicly (i.e. by the state) or privately (i.e. by the individual).
- **Legal aid**, meaning state-funded assistance in legal matters, is available in both criminal and civil cases, but is restricted to narrow circumstances and types of cases.
- Where legal aid is not available and the individual cannot privately fund their case, pro bono institutions may be available to provide advice.
- The availability of legal aid depends on several tests set by the government.

Chapter overview

Legal funding in England and Wales

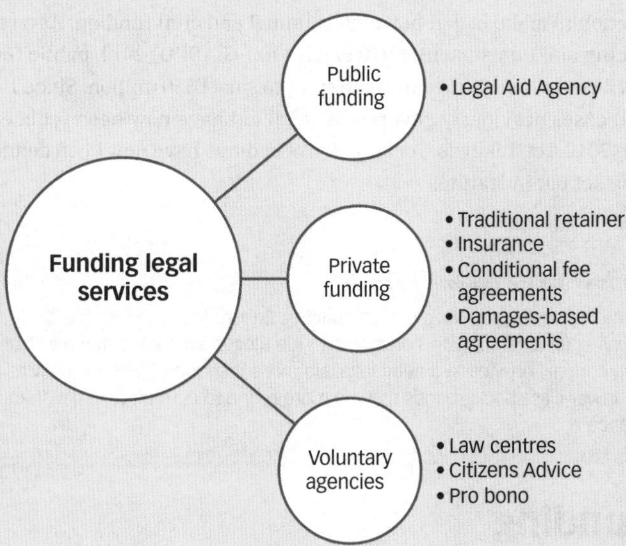

Introduction to funding

Funding the services one requires in the English legal system is not cheap. Many individuals and families are often stricken with debt as a result of seeking legal advice or representation. Darling J is reported as having said, 'The law, like the tavern, is open to all.' In recent times, however, it may be more correct to follow the words of nineteenth-century Irish judge, Mathew LJ, who commented that, 'In England justice is open to all, like the Ritz.'

Certain individuals may benefit from certain types of funding, both private and public. This funding may ease the burden on the individual to fund the legal services personally. In recent times, a number of voluntary agencies designed to offer free and impartial legal advice, and occasionally legal representation, have arisen.

Public vs private funding

The first major distinction to be made is between that of public and private funding. Public funding relates to funding available from the state, whereas private funding specifically refers to the assets and monetary resources available to that specific individual. Only certain individuals are entitled to benefit from public funding, whilst all persons can, in theory, privately fund legal services, though the reality of that is far different.

Criminal vs civil funding

The next distinction to make is that between criminal and civil funding. As a result of the **Legal Aid, Sentencing and Punishment of Offenders Act (LASPO) 2012**, public funding for both criminal and civil cases was slashed in an attempt to save £350 million. Since 1 April 2013, the majority of civil cases previously covered by legal aid have now been reduced to a detailed list set out in the 2012 Act. Likewise, criminal proceedings have now been defined and the test for legal funding set out in statute.

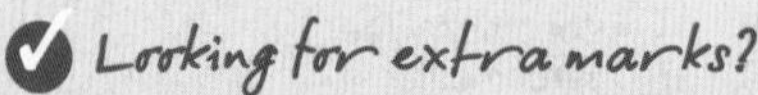

Be practical in any discussion you have of legal funding. Ensure you consider the 'likely' individuals who may be applying for legal funding. For example, Joe Bloggs, who earns the minimum wage and is charged with a criminal offence, will need legal aid more than John Smith, who earns a high salary. Individuals from lower-class backgrounds may be more prone to commit criminal offences, thus requiring assistance.

Public funding

Legal Aid Agency

As a result of **LASPO 2012**, which came into force on 1 April 2013, the Legal Aid Agency (LAA) was created and replaced the former independent body of the Legal Services Commission (LSC). The LAA is an executive agency of the Ministry of Justice (MOJ) and is responsible for the provision of both criminal and civil legal aid in England and Wales.

Governance

The governance of the LAA is compiled into the LAA Framework Document. The Document concerns arrangements as to governance, accountability, staffing, and finances. Figure 9.1 details the hierarchy of the LAA with appropriate descriptions of the roles of the individuals.

Purpose and objectives

According to the LAA Business Plan 2014–2015, the purpose of the LAA was: 'Delivering legal aid efficiently and effectively as part of the justice system'.

The LAA aims to meet its purpose by satisfying three 'strategic objectives'. These objectives are detailed in Table 9.1 alongside their intention as to the manner of meeting these objectives.

Figure 9.1 Governance of the Legal Aid Agency

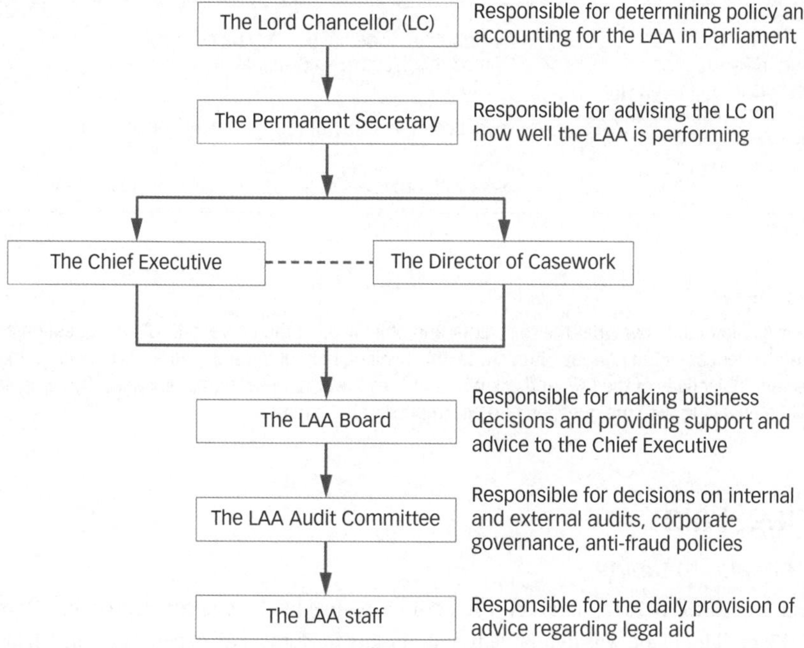

Table 9.1 Objectives of the Legal Aid Agency

Strategic objective	Manner of meeting objective
1. Improve casework to reduce cost, enhance control, and give better customer service.	Deliver efficient and excellent customer service.
	Improve our processes for paying bills and processing applications.
	Deliver value for money.
2. Improve organizational capability to meet the challenges ahead, including developing and engaging our people.	Develop our staff and improve levels of engagement.
	Improve performance management and learning and development.
	Develop capability within the organization, ensuring we are ready for Digital by Default.

Strategic objective	Manner of meeting objective
3. Build and maintain strong partnerships to secure quality provision and contribute fully to wider justice and government aims.	Contribute to wider justice system aims contained in the Transforming Justice Programme.
	Work positively with other government departments.
	Work with providers to ensure provision of quality service.

Revision tip

It is always helpful to know what the role, aims, and objectives of the LAA are. If asked a question as to the effectiveness of the LAA (as often crops up), it will be helpful to refer your answer back to the purpose and objectives of the LAA and ask whether they have met these goals in reality. By doing so, you will be engaging with the question and will impress the examiner.

Civil legal aid

Overview and meaning

As a result of **LASPO 2012**, legal aid for civil cases has been severely restricted. Before 1 April 2013, civil legal aid was available to individuals for almost all aspects of English law. Of course, there were exceptions to this presumption; however, such exceptions were narrow.

Section 8(1) LASPO 2012 details the meaning of civil legal aid as including:

(a) providing advice as to how the law operates;

(b) providing advice and assistance in legal proceedings;

(c) providing other advice and assistance to the prevention of disputes about legal rights or duties or the settlement or other resolution of disputes; and

(d) providing advice and assistance in relation to the enforcement of decisions in legal proceedings or other decisions by which legal disputes are settled.

As you can see, the definition is quite broad. Whether an individual actually qualifies for such assistance, however, is a different matter.

Revision tip

Bear this point in mind when considering the availability of legal aid. It is often said that legal aid is available with an open hand but, upon application, the hand is closed. What we mean by this is that legal aid is available in a vast number of cases, but only a minimum number of people will be eligible to acquire legal aid.

Eligibility

When considering the eligibility of an individual for legal aid, three factors must be considered:

(i) scope—whether the case is one for which legal aid is available;

(ii) merits—the likelihood of success; and

(iii) means—financial eligibility.

We shall briefly consider each in turn in Table 9.2.

Table 9.2 Eligibility for civil legal aid

<table>
<tr><th>Test for eligibility</th><th colspan="2">Explanation</th></tr>
<tr><td rowspan="2">Scope</td><td colspan="2">Since 1 April 2013, LASPO 2012 has reversed the position, resulting in civil legal aid now being available only in prescribed cases listed in Part 1 sch 1 LASPO 2012. These prescribed cases are known as 'general cases' and 'exceptional cases' and generally cover matters involving children or the liberty of individuals.</td></tr>
<tr><td>Examples of cases covered by LASPO
• habeas corpus cases;
• human rights cases;
• immigration cases (involving detention);
• protection from harassment;
• care and supervision orders of children.</td><td>Examples of cases excluded by LASPO
• employment cases;
• general contract cases;
• tortious cases;
• land cases;
• private family cases.</td></tr>
<tr><td>Merits</td><td colspan="2">Before an application is made, the individual must consider the merits of their case and the likelihood of success. A detailed account of the merits criteria is covered in the Civil Legal Aid (Merits Criteria) Regulations 2013. According to Regulation 5, merits are determined on a percentage basis with accompanying terms from 'very good' and 'good' to 'borderline' and 'unclear'. The public interest also plays a part under this heading.</td></tr>
<tr><td>Means</td><td colspan="2">Finally, the financial eligibility of the applicant must also be considered. A detailed account of the means criteria is covered in the Civil Legal Aid (Financial Resources and Payment for Services) Regulations 2013. Under the Regulations, an individual's disposable capital (owned assets—including the equitable value of the home above £100,000) and disposable income (after essential living expenses) are calculated.</td></tr>
</table>

Should an applicant pass all elements of these criteria, they may be eligible for legal aid. However, the aid may only pay for part of their fees, requiring the individual to supplement or contribute to the fees. Quite often, the LAA will impose a 'statutory charge' on any of the 'winnings' from the court case. This charge is similar to that of a mortgage whereby a monthly repayment is necessary to maintain possession of that property or asset. Such a charge has led some academics, such as Jacqueline Martin, *The English Legal System* (8th edn, Hodder 2016), to describe it as a 'clawback of costs from damages', resulting in a claimant having 'very little left from their damages even though they won the case'.

Criminal legal aid

Overview and meaning

Formerly the responsibility of the Criminal Defence Service (CDS), criminal legal aid is now administered by the LAA. Individuals in the criminal justice system may require assistance during multiple stages of the process.

Section 14 LASPO 2012 defines criminal proceedings broadly and includes such matters as criminal trials, sentencing hearings, and appeals. Legal aid may also be available for advice and assistance pre-trial, for example at the police station, bail hearings etc.

Eligibility

Briefly, the test for legal aid for funded representation in court is divided into two distinct sections.

1. interests of justice test; and
2. means test.

Unlike its civil counterpart, there is no merits test for criminal legal aid. Alisdair Gillespie and Siobhan Weare, *The English Legal System* (7th edn, Oxford University Press 2019) note that the reason for this is that to do so would be 'contrary to the presumption of innocence'.

Section 17(2) LASPO 2012 provides a list of factors that must be taken into account when considering the interests of justice test. These factors include the likelihood of loss of liberty, whether there is a substantial question of law to be tried, whether it be in the interests of justice to provide representation, and many others.

The means test considers the person's financial position, for example household income, capital, and outgoings. This test determines whether the client will be liable for any of their defence costs.

A legal right to legal aid?

Article 6(3)(c) European Convention on Human Rights (ECHR) provides that 'Everyone charged with a criminal offence has the right to defend himself in person or through legal assistance of his own choosing or, if he has not sufficient means to pay for legal assistance, to be given it free when the interests of justice so require.' See ***Steel and Morris v UK* (2005)** in 'Key cases' at the end of the chapter.

Technically, therefore, a defendant does have a legal/human right to legal aid; however, such a right is qualified in two ways:

- the necessity for there to be a lack of 'means' to pay for the services; and
- the necessity for the interests of justice to require assistance.

Given that the calculation of 'means' is a mathematical calculation determined by the Director of the LAA, in accordance with his/her working remit and allowance according to the Budget, this supposed human right is now rarely available to those in need.

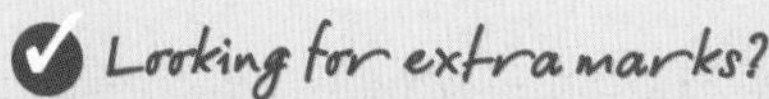

Ensure that you consider the nature of legal aid and the effect a lack of assistance may have on an individual. Technically, every person has a human right to legal assistance funded by the state; however, such can be restricted to a small minority, as dictated by the Director. Can that truly be said to be a human right?

Access to justice denied

In 2016, writing in *The Guardian*, Lord Thomas CJ stated that 'our justice system has become unaffordable to most'. With the closure of courts and advice centres, the increase of costs and court fees, and the substantial removal of legal aid, access to justice has arguably become a mere fanciful dream. Legal advice for everyday matters that may affect each one of us has now become unaffordable and unavailable. Lord Falconer, a Labour Peer and former Lord Chancellor, in 2016 stated that an inability to access justice not only affects the individual, but also affects society as a whole. Furthering this, a research report carried out by Citizens Advice found that only 39 per cent of the population surveyed believe that the justice system 'works well for citizens' and only 17 per cent of those surveyed believe that 'it's easy for people on low incomes to access justice'. These figures are staggering and show a distinct lack of trust placed in the English legal system (ELS). Lord Falconer, writing in *The Guardian*, notes that when society loses faith or trust in the justice system, 'the fundamental principle of the Rule of Law becomes eroded'.

In 2015, Lord Bach, the former Labour Justice Minister, was asked by the Leader of the Opposition (Jeremy Corbyn) to conduct a review into the legal aid system in England and Wales. On 25 November 2016, Lord Bach produced his Interim Report on the matter, finding that 'a great many people who previously relied on legal aid are now being denied access to justice because they cannot afford to pay for it'. In February 2019, the Lord Chancellor and Justice Secretary produced a report, *Legal Support: The Way Ahead* (2019), in which the government committed to expanding legal aid provision for the most 'vulnerable' members of society and to reviewing the means test thresholds. The review also placed great emphasis on 'early intervention' in order to prevent cases from reaching court.

Private funding

In both criminal and civil cases, there may be individuals who are not 'eligible' for assistance from the state. As a result, in both criminal and civil cases, systems have been organized in an attempt to ease the manner and method of paying for legal services. The main sources of funding are:

- traditional retainer;
- insurance funding;
- conditional fee agreements (CFAs); and
- damage-based agreements (DBAs).

With the exception of the traditional retainer, all of these manners of funding are exclusive to civil cases. We shall consider each form of funding in detail.

Traditional retainer

A traditional retainer refers to the situation where a client funds his or her own case from their own resources without support from the state or other providers. As you can imagine, the majority of individuals who are confronted with a legal challenge are unlikely to be able to afford this option, often requiring them to deal with the matter personally. For these individuals, crowdfunding may be an option. For example, in the UK, CrowdJustice was launched in May 2015 by a former Linklaters associate and lawyer for the UN. It invites the public to make donations towards 'public interest cases'. Crowdfunding is still a relatively untested option, and there are several potential legal issues and grey areas, including whether the crowdfunding platform or the individual donors might be held liable for the other side's costs if the funded party loses. As such, there have been calls to regulate crowdfunding for litigation claims.

Solicitors are responsible for drawing up an agreement (known as a 'client care letter') setting out their costs and how they are to be calculated. The agreement forms a contract between the solicitor and client. The fees are calculated on a time basis (in the majority of cases a client is charged for every six minutes/hour) and on charges for certain activities, such as drafting letters and making/receiving phone calls.

Insurance funding

Some clients have the benefit of legal expenses insurance. There are two forms of insurance available to individuals:

- before the event insurance (BTE); and
- after the event insurance (ATE).

Table 9.3 deals with both types of insurance.

Table 9.3 Insurance

Type of insurance	Explanation
BTE	The client's costs will be met by insurers, e.g. motor and home insurance policies. Insurers may require advice on the merits in order to justify continued funding.
ATE	A client concerned about the risks for proposed litigation can take out ATE insurance to cover the risk. The risk is that the unsuccessful party is ordered to pay the other party's costs. ATE insurance is often taken out with another form of funding to cover the client's own legal costs, such as a CFA, DBA, or third-party funding. Premiums tend to be high and get higher the worse the prospects of success. Qualified one-way costs shifting (QOCS) has been introduced for a number of cases as an alternative to ATE.

Conditional fee agreements (CFAs)

More commonly known as a 'no win, no fee' agreement, CFAs are agreements (generally in personal injury cases) between a client and his/her solicitor whereby if the case is lost the client will not have to pay his/her solicitor's and or barrister's fees. If the case is won, the client pays the normal fees and then the solicitor and/or barrister can charge an agreed 'uplift' on their fees, known as a 'success fee'. These agreements were introduced by the **Courts and Legal Services Act 1990** and were extended by operation of the **Access to Justice Act 1999**.

Generally, as discussed in Chapter 6, barristers must accord with the 'cab rank rule' and cannot refuse work. CFA work, however, is an exception to this rule.

A CFA must be documented in writing and must relate to a type of case where CFAs are permitted (i.e. not in criminal or family proceedings). The Law Society has produced a model CFA and guidance, which can be accessed through their website.

Damages-based agreements (DBAs)

Like CFAs, DBAs are also a form of 'no win, no fee' agreements. Under a DBA, lawyers are not paid if they lose a case. If they win the case, however, they may take a percentage of the damages recovered by their client (in this regard, DBAs are also known as 'contingency fee agreements'). Like CFAs, a DBA must be in writing and must relate to proceedings where such funding is permitted. (Following the Jackson Reforms, since 1 April 2013, DBAs can be used in almost all contentious business, except criminal and family proceedings.) Prior to that date, DBAs could only be used in 'non-contentious work'.

Successful claimants using a DBA will recover their solicitor's costs from defendants in the usual way, but the claimants will be responsible for paying from their damages any shortfall in respect of disbursements. DBAs are capped 25 per cent of damages in PI cases and 50 per cent in all other cases (with the exception of employment cases, where the cap is 35 per cent).

Voluntary agencies

In light of the changes brought about by **LASPO 2012**, the number of voluntary agencies now offering legal advice and representation is steadily on the increase.

Law centres

Law centres are independent of the government and of the legal professionals. These centres are charitable-sector bodies and whilst they are funded by local and central government and charitable bodies, they often struggle to find the funds necessary to continue their work. As of January 2020, there were 41 Law Centres in England and Wales listed on the Law Centres Network website. The majority of work undertaken by law centres involves advice alone; however, representation is often provided for matters at tribunal level, such as employment cases (see the Free Representation Unit (FRU) supported by the Bar Council).

Citizens Advice

Citizens Advice (formerly known as the Citizens Advice Bureau (CAB)) is a national network of 316 independent charities. The aims of Citizens Advice are 'to provide the advice people need for the problems they face' and 'to improve the policies and principles that affect people's lives'. Most commonly, Citizens Advice deal with matters such as employment, consumer advice, and contractual matters.

Pro bono

Pro bono, shortened from the Latin term 'pro bono publico', simply means 'for the public good'. In the legal context, pro bono is concerned with the offering of advice, services, and representation on a voluntary basis. Such pro bono services are thriving in England and Wales and are seen by many in the legal profession as a form of 'social responsibility' (Gillespie and Weare 2019). The majority of pro bono clinics can now be found in law schools in universities, most notably the Law School Office operated by Northumbria University and the Legal Advice Centre at Nottingham Trent University, notable for being the first teaching law firm. Other examples of pro bono activities include the work of trade unions providing free advice to their members, most notably for employment matters.

Revision tip

Consider the effectiveness of such units in an essay question. Are these units actually assisting individuals with their troubles or are they simply adding lines to the CV of a hopeful law student?

Case	Facts	Principles
***Steel and Morris v UK* (2005) 41 EHRR 22 (ECtHR)**	McDonald's restaurant sued the defendants for libel. The defendants, two environmental campaigners, handed out leaflets regarding the nutritional value of McDonald's burgers and the way the company was operated. Steel and Morris could not afford a legal team, unlike McDonald's, and thus were disadvantaged at trial.	The European Court of Human Rights (ECtHR) ruled that **Article 6(1) ECHR** demands a right to 'equality of arms' (i.e. both parties should be roughly in the same position in terms of access to the law). Because legal aid was not permitted, there was an inequality of arms, thus there was a breach of **Article 6** on the part of the state.

Key debates

Topic	**The justification for legal aid**
Academic	Michael Zander
Viewpoint	Argues that the denial of legal aid is a 'significant denial of justice' for the poorest in society who are trying to access the law.
Source	Michael Zander, *Cases and Materials on the English Legal System* (10th edn, Cambridge University Press 2007) 144

Topic	**Effect of lack of legal aid in criminal cases and effect on quality of advocacy**
Academic	Anthony Edwards
Viewpoint	Argues that the lack of legal aid in criminal cases 'will represent the end of the proud boast of early legal aid lawyers that they would offer the same quality of service to publicly financed clients as they offer to private services'.
Source	Anthony Edwards, 'Legal Aid, Sentencing and Punishment of Offenders Act 2012—The Financial Procedural and Practical Implications' (2012) Crim LR 584

Exam question

****

 Exam question

Essay question

'Justice is a luxury and not a right.'

Critically discuss this statement in light of the funding available in England and Wales.

 Online resources

For an outline answer to this essay question, as well as multiple-choice questions and interactive key cases, please visit the online resources.

Glossary

Italicized words are defined elsewhere in the glossary. A fuller version of the glossary is available at the Online resources.

Act of Parliament Statutory law created by Parliament. In order to become legislation, an Act must pass through several stages in both Houses of Parliament. An Act of Parliament is an example of *primary legislation*.

Alternative dispute resolution (ADR) A process whereby aggrieved individuals can resolve legal matters outside of court. Includes methods such as arbitration, mediation, conciliation, and negotiation.

Appeal A request to a senior court, from an inferior court, to review the decision of the inferior court.

Appellate court Any court that hears appeals from a lower court. In England and Wales, the highest appellate court is the *Supreme Court*, formerly the *House of Lords*.

Attorney General The government's chief legal adviser who also supervises the work of the *Treasury Solicitor* and the *Director of Public Prosecutions (DPP)*. The Attorney General can refer cases to the *Court of Appeal* where an acquittal is questionable on a point of law or where a sentence has been passed which is considered 'unduly lenient'. He is assisted by the *Solicitor General*.

Barrister One of the two main branches of the legal profession, alongside a *solicitor*. Often referred to as counsel, their role is focused primarily on advocacy, both written and oral. Regulated by the Bar Standards Board. Must be a member of one of the four *Inns of Court*.

Bill A draft piece of primary legislation as it goes through the stages of becoming an *Act of Parliament*. See also *White Paper* and *Green Paper*.

Binding precedent Law established by judges in the senior courts which is binding on all lower courts (see *case law*). Binding precedent may be avoided by *distinguishing* the authority. See also *ratio decidendi* and *stare decisis*.

Brexit The popular term used to describe the UK's withdrawal from the *European Union (EU)*.

Case law Law created by judges through their judgments in cases. Decisions which result in a *binding precedent* are the most important types of case law.

Chambers Offices shared and used by barristers (compare with 'firm' in relation to solicitors). Chambers may also relate to the private room or courtroom of a judge who may hear matters, or conduct certain hearings, in exclusion of the public (i.e. the hearing is not held in *open court*).

Civil law The body of law dealing with non-criminal matters. Often concerned with disputes between individuals without involvement of the state, although there are exceptions, for example judicial review. Civil law may also refer to a civil legal system, i.e. a body of rules contained in a written code. Such systems are used widely in Europe.

Civil Procedure Rules (CPR) Rules introduced by the 'Woolf Reforms' concerning the procedure to be used in the civil courts.

Common law The body of law which has evolved from *binding precedent*, rather than deriving from *Acts of Parliament*.

Counsel Another expression to describe a *barrister*.

County Court The lowest court in the civil court hierarchy, hearing relatively simple matters such as repayment of debts and personal injury.

Court of Appeal One of the superior courts hearing appeals from lower courts. It contains both a criminal and civil division and is second only to the *Supreme Court*. It sits in the Royal Courts of Justice in London.

Court of first instance A court that hears a case for the first time. First instance courts include, *inter alia,* the *magistrates' court, Crown Court, County Court,* and *High Court.*

Court of Justice of the European Union (CJEU) Formerly known as the European Court of Justice (ECJ), the CJEU is the judicial branch of the *European Union (EU).* The court hears actions brought by the European Commission against Member States for breaches of *EU law* and hears Article 234 references from Member State courts to clarify questions of EU law. The CJEU sits at Luxembourg.

Criminal law The body of law dealing with the commission of criminal offences. Criminal law is deemed to be a matter of *public law.*

Crown Court The Crown Court deals with serious criminal cases, known as indictable offences, such as murder. It sits as a first instance court and appellate court for cases appealed from the *magistrates' courts.* Trials at the Crown Court are heard by a *judge* and a *jury.*

Crown Prosecution Service (CPS) An independent prosecuting agency. It is responsible for deciding whether to charge an individual with an offence and for reviewing the charging by the police. The CPS is headed by the *Director of Public Prosecutions (DPP).*

Defendant The party to proceedings who is alleged to have committed the criminal offence or civil wrong. In criminal cases, the defendant is said to be charged with a criminal offence; in civil cases, the defendant is said to be sued for a civil wrong.

Delegated legislation A form of subordinate legislation not passed by an *Act of Parliament* itself but through powers conferred on a body through a parent Act.

Direct effect An EU principle which refers to the ability of individuals to rely on the EU law in domestic courts. Direct effect may either be vertical or horizontal.

Directly applicable EU law is said to be directly applicable where it applies automatically in domestic law. Treaties and Regulations are both directly applicable.

Director of Public Prosecutions (DPP) The government's most senior prosecutor. The DPP is head of the *Crown Prosecution Service (CPS),* and is supervised by the *Attorney General.*

Distinguishing Although bound by the doctrine of *judicial precedent,* judges may distinguish a case on the facts, meaning that they can avoid its binding nature.

Ejusdem generis Meaning of the 'same kind', this phrase is a rule of language that is used in *statutory interpretation.* Where a statute contains a list, an item not specified within that list will only be included if it is the same kind as those listed.

Equity Separate to the *common law,* equity is a body of law that developed originally through the Courts of Chancery in order to combat the harshness of the common law. Its main prominence lies in the law of trusts.

EU law The body of law that has emerged from the *European Union (EU).* Formerly known as EC law.

European Convention on Human Rights (ECHR) An international charter setting out certain fundamental human rights, such as the right to life and right to respect for private and family law. Incorporated into English law by the Human Rights Act 1998. It is not a matter of *EU law.*

European Court of Human Rights (ECtHR) The legal institution of the Council of Europe responsible for interpreting and enforcing the *European Convention on Human Rights (ECHR).* The ECtHR sits at Strasbourg. It is not an EU court.

European Court of Justice (ECJ) Former name for the *Court of Justice of the European Union (CJEU).*

European Union (EU) The EU is comprised of 28 Member States and is responsible for *EU law.* It is composed of several institutions and is built on three pillars.

Executive Refers to one organ of the state and is composed of the Prime Minister and his/her Cabinet of senior ministers. The Executive runs the country and introduces law to the *legislature.*

Expressio unius est exclusio alterius Meaning 'to express one thing is to exclude others', this phrase is a rule of language that is used in *statutory interpretation*. To list a number of specific things within a specified class may be interpreted as impliedly excluding others of the same class.

Fast-track One of the three civil tracks that determine the manner in which claims are to be dealt with by the court. The fast claims track refers to claims which have a value of over £10,000 but less than £25,000, and the trial is likely to last no longer than a day.

Golden rule A rule of *statutory interpretation*. It is used in circumstances where the *literal rule* would produce an absurd result.

Green Paper Consultation documents produced by the government in order to allow people to give feedback on its policy or legislative proposals. See also *Bill* and *White Paper*.

High Court of Justice Often referred to simply as the High Court, it is a civil court, divided into three main divisions, namely the Chancery Division, the Family Division, and the Queen's Bench Division. It acts as both a *court of first instance* and an *appellate court*. The High Court sits at the Royal Courts of Justice in London and has several district registries around the country.

House of Commons The lower chamber of *Parliament*. A branch of the legislative and executive branch of government responsible for the introduction of *Acts of Parliament*.

House of Lords Formerly the most senior court in the land, until replaced by the *Supreme Court* in 2009. Now it sits solely as the Upper House in Parliament and is involved in the introduction of *Acts of Parliament*.

Inns of Court Organizations where membership is required in order to practise as a barrister. There are four Inns of Court: Middle Temple, Inner Temple, Lincoln's Inn, and Gray's Inn.

Judge An individual whose role is to preside over cases and to ensure that the proper pro-cedure is followed and the evidence is properly admitted. A judge is ordinarily the arbiter of law, but may also be the arbiter of fact.

Judgment The decision of a judge in the case concerned. The judgment may include statements that are binding (*ratio decidendi*) and non-binding (*obiter dicta*).

Judicial independence The principle that, in accordance with *natural justice*, the judiciary should be independent of other branches of government and free from a conflict of interest.

Judicial precedent See *binding precedent* and *persuasive authority*.

Judiciary The collective term for the judges. Forms one of the organs of the state. Headed by the *Lord Chief Justice*.

Jury A selection of laypersons who have been randomly selected to act as the arbiters of fact in a case before them. Generally, juries sit in panels of 12 and can feature in both criminal and civil cases.

Jury vetting Investigations carried out by the police on jurors in order to establish whether they are suitable to sit on a *jury*.

Justice of the Peace (JP) Another term for a *magistrate*. They are lay volunteers who hear cases in the *magistrates' court*.

Justice's clerk A qualified lawyer who assists *magistrates* in respect of the law, practice, and procedure.

Justices of the Supreme Court These are the *judges* of the *Supreme Court*. Formerly known as Lords of Appeal in Ordinary (Law Lords) when they sat in the *House of Lords*. There are 12 justices of the *Supreme Court*.

Lawyer An umbrella term used to describe someone who practises law, such as a *solicitor* or a *barrister*.

Legal aid Free legal assistance given by the state to those who qualify for it. Legal aid is heavily restricted and is only available by satisfying a number of tests, focused on the finances of the individual and the merits of their legal case.

Legal executive A member or fellow of the Chartered Institute of Legal Executives (CI-

LEx). An Executive carries out much of the same work as a *solicitor* without the need to obtain a training contract.

Legislation A form of written law distinct from the *common law*. Includes *primary legislation* and *secondary legislation*.

Legislature Law-making body of government. In England and Wales, the legislature is *Parliament*.

Literal rule A rule of *statutory interpretation*. If the wording in a statute is clear, it may be applied literally, which means that it must be given its ordinary meaning.

Lord Chief Justice Head of the *judiciary* in England and Wales.

Magistrate More common name for a *Justice of the Peace*. Layperson who sits in the *magistrates' court*.

Magistrates' court The lowest court in the court hierarchy. It is presided over by lay magistrates or district judges. Most of a magistrates' court's business relates to criminal matters, though magistrates may also deal with some civil matters and family matters.

Master of the Rolls Senior judge who is Head of the Court of Appeal (Civil Division).

Mischief rule One of the rules of *statutory interpretation*. It requires the judge to take into account the 'mischief' or problem that the Act was aimed to resolve.

Monarch Represents the sovereign of the country, whether it be a king or queen. Where a queen is on the throne, the Monarch is known as 'Regina'. When a king is on the throne, the Monarch is known as 'Rex'.

Multi-track One of the three civil tracks that determine the manner in which claims are to be dealt with by the court. The multi-track applies to all claims not falling within the financial limits of the small-claims or fast tracks and/or complex cases.

Natural justice Rules of fairness and justice that dictate how proceedings should run. Natural justice requires the procedure to be free from bias and conflict of interest.

Noscitur a sociis Meaning 'a word is known by the company it keeps', this phrase is a rule of language that is used in *statutory interpretation*. This means that a word in a statute should be interpreted looking at the context of the statute.

Obiter dicta Statements made by judges in judgments that do not form part of the *ratio decidendi* of the case. They are statements of other things said, or things said in passing. Although not binding, they may be persuasive.

Open court The majority of hearings are held in open court; meaning that they are available for members of the public to attend. Some hearings will be held in *chambers* (traditionally referred to as being held 'in camera').

Overruling A case is overruled when a judge departs from a previous decision and overturns its legal basis. Overruling in this context means that the case is no longer good law.

Paralegal General term for individuals working in a clerical and support capacity in a legal firm.

Parliament Makers of *primary legislation* in the English legal system. Parliament consists of the *House of Commons*, the *House of Lords*, and the *Monarch*.

Parliamentary sovereignty *Parliament* is the supreme law-making body. *Parliament* can make or repeal any laws; *Parliament* cannot bind itself or future *Parliaments* and *Parliament* cannot be challenged.

Persuasive authority Decisions of courts that are not binding on other courts. The decisions of lower courts will only ever be persuasive, but decisions of more senior courts, such as the Privy Council, will also only be persuasive.

Primary legislation Another name for an *Act of Parliament*. This is a piece of statute created by *Parliament* and must be contrasted with *secondary legislation*.

Private law Law relating to the relationships between private individuals, rather than an individual and the state. Most *civil law* matters are private, though note the exception of judical review or public family law matters, for example, contract law, the law of torts, property law, and family law. Contrast with *public law*.

Pro bono Meaning 'for good', this term simply refers to legal work carried out that is unpaid.

Public law Law relating to the functions of the state, and the relationship between an individual and the state, rather than between private individuals. Contrast with *private law*.

Pupillage A period of apprenticeship for pupil barristers; it is their final stage of training before becoming a barrister. Pupillage generally takes 12 months to complete; this being broken down into a first six and second six. Compare with *training contract* for solicitors.

Purposive approach A rule of language used by the European courts in interpreting EU law. This approach is wider than the mischief rule and looks to interpret the legislation in line with the purpose of the Act, not just the gap that the legislation wished to fill. This approach has found some favour in the domestic courts also.

Queen's Counsel (QC) An experienced barrister who is deemed to have excelled in advocacy. Also referred to as a 'silk' due to the silk robes they wear.

Ratio decidendi The legal reasoning for the decision in a case. Forms the binding nature of *judicial precedent* in cases.

Reversing A case is reversed when a judge overturns the decision of a previous judge in the same case. For example, the Supreme Court reverses the decision on the Court of Appeal. In doing so, the court will also *overrule* the previous judgment.

Royal assent The final stage required for a *Bill* to become an *Act of Parliament*. The *Monarch* gives approval by convention.

Rule of Law The ideal characteristics of a civilized society, such characteristics include that no person is above the law and that the law shall apply equally to all. The Rule of Law is enshrined in the legal system.

Secondary legislation Legislation passed under delegated powers by *Parliament*, rather than by *Parliament* itself.

Small-claims track One of the three civil tracks that determine the manner in which claims are to be dealt with by the court. The small-claims track refers to claims worth £10,000 or less (£1,000 for personal injury).

Solicitor One of the two main branches of the legal profession, alongside a *barrister*. Governed by the Solicitors Regulation Authority (SRA), solicitors' work is mainly client-focused, with little advocacy (unless they wish to become a *solicitor-advocate*).

Solicitor advocate A solicitor who has undertaken additional training in order to gain full rights of audience in court.

Solicitor General A government legal officer who acts as a deputy to the *Attorney General*.

Solicitors' Qualifying Examination (SQE) A new qualifying examination for any individual who wishes to become a solicitor. Individuals will no longer require a law degree; so long as they have any undergraduate degree, have completed the SQE, and undertake qualifying work experience, the individual will become a solicitor.

Stare decisis Meaning 'let the decision stand', this term is used in the context of *binding precedent*. Lower courts are required to follow this doctrine unless the authority can be avoided for some reason. Occasionally *stare decisis* works to bind courts on the same level also.

Statute Another term for an *Act of Parliament*.

Statutory instrument A form of *secondary legislation*. Used to enact a piece of *delegated legislation*.

Statutory interpretation The task of interpretation of *Acts of Parliament* by the courts. In interpreting the relevant *statute*, the courts will use a number of rules and aids.

Glossary

Summary offences Criminal offences that are tried in the magistrates' court. Often very minor in nature.

Supreme Court The highest court in the court system of England and Wales. It replaced the *House of Lords* in 2009. It is composed of 12 Justices.

Training contract A period of training required to be undertaken by those wishing to become a solicitor. Training contracts are generally two years in length.

Triable either-way offence Serious offences which can be tried either in a magistrate's court or at the Crown Court, for example theft.

Tribunal Akin to a court but falls outside of the court structure. Tribunals deal with a variety of different matters, such as pensions, asylum issues, and employment matters.

White Paper Policy documents produced by the government that set out their proposals for future legislation. A white paper may also include a draft *Bill* proposal. See also *Green Paper*.

Index

Note: Line in the Index as figures and tables are referred in the Index

Index